DATE DUE

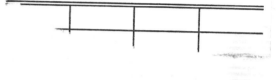

Designing for Diversity

Kathryn H. Anthony

Designing for Diversity

GENDER, RACE, AND

ETHNICITY IN THE

ARCHITECTURAL

PROFESSION

UNIVERSITY OF ILLINOIS PRESS

URBANA AND CHICAGO

7/09

Drawings on pp. vi, xii–xiii, 214, and 258 courtesy of

Kathryn H. Anthony, Jami Becker, Tracey Jo Hoekstra,

and Melissa Worden

Library of Congress

Cataloging-in-Publication Data

Anthony, Kathryn H.

Designing for diversity : gender, race, and ethnicity in

the architectural profession / Kathryn H. Anthony.

p.   cm.

Includes bibliographical references and index.

ISBN 0-252-02641-1 (alk. paper)

1. Women architects—United States—Surveys.

2. Women in the professions—United States—Surveys.

I. Title.

NA1997.A56   2001

720'.8—dc21   00-011854

In memory of my husband, Barry, an inspiration to all

To my parents, Harry and Anne, and my sister, Mary Anne

To my many friends and extended family

To architects of the past, present, and future

Contents

Acknowledgments

I am indebted to many individuals who helped this book to fruition. Bradford C. Grant's invitation to participate in the African-American Task Force meeting at the 1991 Association of Collegiate Schools of Architecture (ACSA) Conference sparked my initial curiosity about designing for diversity. Our subsequent collaboration on the September 1993 issue of the *Journal of Architectural Education,* dedicated to the topic "Gender and Multiculturalism in Architectural Education," was an outgrowth of that meeting. Linda Groat's invitation to co-organize a session called "Confronting the Glass Ceiling" at the Women's Task Force Panel Discussion at the 1992 ACSA conference was also pivotal in launching my interest in this topic. Marcel Quimbey and Joyce Lilie provided valuable input at our panel discussion. Early on, Sharon Sutton and Jack Travis offered their perspectives as African-American architects and encouraged me to pursue this avenue of research. I am especially grateful to the late Walter Blackburn, who hosted my students and me in his Indianapolis office on many occasions. Numerous architects listed in the appendix to this book granted interviews to students in my courses on gender and race in architecture over the past decade. Their experiences, too, underscored the need for this book.

Sherry Ahrentzen, Jean Barber, Denise Scott Brown, Linda Groat, Susan Maxman, and Jack Travis wrote letters on my behalf that helped secure funding for this project. The Campus Research Board of the University of Illinois at Urbana-Champaign as well as the Graham Foundation for Advanced Studies in the Fine Arts provided early financial support for my research–without which this project would never have gotten off the ground. With the assistance of Jean Barber, the American Institute of Architects (AIA) supplied a mailing list for the random survey of AIA members and underwrote the mailing costs for the survey of those attending the 1994 AIA National Diversity Conference.

James R. Anderson, Jean Barber, Sheila Cahnman, Annouk de Wolff Ellis, Pam Hutter, Susan Leverenz Stearn, Allison Maxwell, Diane O'Rourke, Mary Ellen O'Shaughnessey, Elizabeth Scanlan, Robert I. Selby, Jack Travis, and Jeanne Zagrodnik critiqued early drafts of my survey and interview research instruments. Anne S. Anthony, Harry A. Anthony, Bradford C. Grant, Susan Maxman, Amita Sinha, Richard Martin, Linda Puig, Susan Van der Muellen, and Leslie Kanes Weisman all provided valuable criticism on numerous manuscript drafts. Colleen Casey supplied useful information about diversity in the legal profession. Sharon Irish alerted me to numerous sources that I would not have found on my own.

Several alumni of the School of Architecture at the University of Illinois worked on this project as students. Jami Becker, Jill Eyres, Anne McDermott, Ripal Patel, Stella Sze, and Melissa Jo Worden all served as top-notch research assistants. I could not have asked for better help. Cattyann Campbell, Joan Piazza Coote, Jacqueline Tomczak Dearborn, Lawrence Doyle, Tracey Jo Hoekstra, Vicki Kouros, Vanessa Reese, Jim Sopp, Melissa Tekulve, and Yan Xu also assisted in various phases of this research.

A number of University of Illinois staff provided critical assistance. Jane Cook, Tracy Tieman, and Sheri Worden transcribed the interviews. James McKay came to my rescue with computer support on numerous occasions. Kimberly Jenkins formatted the final manuscript and Selah Peterson prepared the graphic materials for publication. Christopher Quinn, Nicholas Watkins, and Dorfredia Williams answered scores of library reference questions. Sue Chapman, Carole Couch, and Barbara Prahl also offered valuable staff support.

At the University of Illinois Press, my editors, Karen Hewitt, Richard Martin, and Carol Bolton Betts, ushered this project through the review and editing process.

Over four hundred architects participated anonymously in surveys and interviews, candidly sharing their personal and professional experiences, their tragedies and their triumphs. Without their participation, this book would not have been possible. Ann Beha, Sheila Cahnman, Carol Crandall, Katherine Diamond, David Fukui, Mui Ho, Johnpaul Jones, Kay Janis, Diane Legge Kemp, David Lee, Sally Levine, and Beverly Willis all provided illustrations of their design work.

Two women, now deceased, inspired me in writing this book. The first was Katina Boretos Skoufis, my maternal grandmother. While a young girl in her native Greece, she was forbidden by her father to attend school. Knowing that she would never be allowed inside, she sat out on the front steps and sobbed as her friends entered the schoolhouse. Although she never learned to read or write, her wisdom surpassed that of many. The afghans she wove and the recipes she cooked remind me that she is always with us. The second was my paternal grandmother, Maria Ftoulis Antoniades, who raised five children on her own on a remote Greek island. As was the custom in that part of the world, she mourned the loss of her husband by wearing only black for nearly half her life. Were my grandmothers alive today, they could only marvel at the diverse paths now available to women.

My parents, Harry A. Anthony and Anne S. Anthony, provided critical support throughout the decade that this book was underway. They served as unpaid research assistants and critics, offering valuable input. While I was on Family and Medical Leave, their dining room table often served as my office. Our regular exercise workouts offered a healthy alternative to my sedentary writing sessions. And their financial assistance made it possible for me to complete this book when I had no other income.

I turn finally to Barry D. Riccio: historian, teacher, scholar, critic, author, playwright, and chef. For two decades he was my husband, hero, and best friend. Plagued by a rare form of cancer for over seven years, Barry passed away at age forty-six shortly before this book was published. His perseverance, resilience, and optimism in the face of adversity served as a constant inspiration to hundreds of friends and family around the world–and especially to me. My long journey to see this book to publication pales by comparison.

Designing for Diversity

Introduction

WHAT IF . . . ?

WHAT IF FRANK LLOYD WRIGHT had been a woman? Would Frances Lloyd Wright have become the most famous architect in American history? Would she become a model for generations of architects? Would her works be listed in the National Register of Historic Places? Would they become popular international tourist attractions? Would her fans be buying Wright-inspired ties, tee shirts, note cards, and calendars?

What if Frank Lloyd Wright had been African American? Would he have been allowed even to study architecture? Would Louis Sullivan have hired him? Would Wright have had the chance to develop a wealthy clientele or been in a position to run off with his client's wife? Would he have had the means to develop his own school and studio? Would he have had the opportunity to leave such an impressive imprint on the American landscape? Would he have been granted commissions to design the Guggenheim Museum or the Marin County Civic Center?

Even today, over a century after Wright was born, women and persons of color still struggle to succeed in the architectural profession. Their voices must be heard. Among the shocking findings from my surveys and interviews of over four hundred architects nationwide:

- Most of the architects who have encountered a glass ceiling in their jobs are women.
- Significant gender and racial differences exist in the perceptions of glass-ceiling barriers in the architectural profession.
- Sharp salary differences for full-time architectural employees occur along gender lines. Women architects employed full-time earn *significantly less* than their male counterparts, regardless of their years of experience on the job.
- Over two-thirds (68%) of the respondents have seen or heard about gender discrimination in an architectural office, and four out of ten (44%) have personally experienced it.

- Four out of ten (42%) have seen or heard about racial discrimination in an architectural office.
- A quarter (27%) have quit their architectural jobs because of unfair treatment.
- Many had horrendous experiences in architectural offices. For instance, many well-qualified women architects watched their male subordinates become their superiors almost overnight.

But there is good news: scores of architects from groups that are underrepresented in the profession—that is, women and nonwhite males—have overcome formidable obstacles and enjoyed tremendous success in their professional lives. Photographs of their work appear in the pages of this book. Years ago, who could have foreseen that major structures such as the U.S. Embassy in Tokyo, the building that houses the San Francisco Ballet, or the Air Traffic Control Tower and Administration Building at Los Angeles International Airport (fig. 1) would all be designed by women? And who would have imagined that one of the most high-profile architectural commissions in America—the replacement for the Alfred P. Murrah Federal Building in Oklahoma City, destroyed by a terrorist

The Air Traffic Control Tower and Administration Building at the Los Angeles International Airport was designed by Katherine Diamond, FAIA, of Siegel Diamond Architecture as consultants to Holmes & Narver, Inc., Architect/Engineer of Record. It was completed in 1995 and publicized in *US News and World Report* and elsewhere as one of the major architectural commissions to be designed by a female architect. Photograph courtesy Siegel Diamond Architecture.

bomb in 1995–would be won by a woman-owned firm?[1] The works of such prolific contemporary architects as Carol Ross Barney, Ann Beha, Denise Scott Brown, Sheila Cahnman, Katherine Diamond, Diane Legge Kemp, and Beverly Willis shatter stereotypes about what women can and cannot do. Similarly, the awe-inspiring designs of Walter Blackburn, David Fukui, Ronald Garner, Mui Ho, Sylvia Kwan, Johnpaul Jones, David Lee, Patricia Saldana Natke, Norma Sklarek, and Donald Stull provide compelling evidence that persons of color have much to offer the architectural profession.

ABOUT THIS BOOK

Most coverage of underrepresented architects in professional journals has featured profiles of successful designers and their work, with their names and photographs prominently displayed. In such a public forum, most architects highlight only their positive experiences; they do not mention the firms that may have mistreated them early in their careers, the pain that may have caused them, or how they rebounded. While such "showcase" publicity is valuable to the profession, its focus is on individual mobility rather than on structural forces. Its scope is limited, and it presents an overly rosy picture of the profession. A structural approach requires a broader perspective, allowing one to examine the context in which individual advances within the field can occur. As the sociologist Natalie Sokoloff argues in her book comparing black women and white women in various professions, "The United States may be a more open society than some, but the myth that hard work will be rewarded regardless of a person's racial/ethnic, gender, or class background is just that–a myth. Only a structural approach allows us to see why people from various groups are more or less likely to succeed in entering and rising in a given profession."[2]

The focus on individual achievement has meant that some potentially powerful information has been overlooked. What about those who have not yet achieved success? Or those who are still struggling in unpleasant, unfair working conditions? Or those who have hit the infamous glass ceiling? This book addresses that gap.

Designing for Diversity focuses on the experiences of underrepresented architects, especially women and persons of color, and how they compare to those of their white male counterparts. To a lesser extent, it also examines the experiences of architects who are gay or lesbian. This book gives voice to those who have long remained silent about the abuses of architectural practice and allows readers to step into the shoes of those who have been marginalized. Based on a substantial body of empirical research, *Designing for Diversity* suggests strategies to reform and further diversify the architectural profession. My goal is to inspire architects to create a more humane work environment that will benefit the profession and ultimately society at large.

This work is an outgrowth of my first book, *Design Juries on Trial*.[3] In fact, the philosophical stances as well as the methodological approaches are similar in both books. The earlier work was among the first to challenge one of the field's "sacred cows," the design jury system, which is the primary mode of critiquing architectural work. My goal was to persuade architectural educators and students to create a more humane academic environment that would ultimately benefit the profession. My research, which drew upon interviews with and surveys of over nine hundred faculty, students, and award-winning designers, documented disturbing gender differences about how students perceived design juries, design studios, and architectural education. It led me to wonder whether the patterns found in school might be present in architectural practice.

Designing for Diversity chronicles the turmoil and triumph that underrepresented architects have experienced in their profession. Many of their frustrations parallel those encountered by mainstream architects. To a certain extent, all architects struggle to survive in a profession where the educational preparation is long, the registration process is rigorous, the hours are grueling, and the pay is incredibly low. Yet many underrepresented architects face additional hardships, such as isolation, marginalization, stereotyping, and discrimination. Still, for many architects–whether they be in the majority or minority–the intense satisfaction of seeing one's project develop from the ground up far outweighs the agony. Admirably, they display an incredible passion for this field. Several respondents to my survey expressed their continued attraction to the practice of architecture, even though they have confronted professional hardships. (In the following comments, respondents are identified by numbers, to preserve their anonymity; see full explanation of numbers below.)

> Architecture is not a career or a profession. It is a way of living. I love it and I always have. I love the ever-changing nature of it. I love the intellectual exchanges. I love the beautiful work it creates. I love the complicated process of conception, design and construction; I love how it keeps me aware of my environment and the impact I can have on it. I have been an architect ever since I can remember. I will never be anything else. (#152, African-American female, age 38)

I've been in it too long to quit. . . . I still get a rush when I sketch a house plan. (#190, African-American male, age 43)

You can look and see the fruits of your labor. . . . Maybe it will be here long after you're not here and maybe [it] will inspire somebody else. (I-#13, African-American male, age 60)

I can't imagine being out of it unless I was so disabled that I couldn't draw or speak or see. (I-#8, Latina female, age 40)

This book is aimed at those who will lead the architectural profession into a new era. It targets several audiences: practicing architects, educators, scholars and students in architecture and related disciplines, along with those in gender, racial, and ethnic studies. It can serve as a text for professional practice, management, and diversity courses in schools of architecture. It is directed toward those individuals who are victims of discrimination—as well as toward their victimizers. In all fairness, it must be said that the majority of architects fall into neither camp, yet these architects will also benefit from my research. They can play an especially critical role in rectifying some of the wrongs. By opening their eyes to what their colleagues face every day, and by viewing their field through a new lens, white male architects in the mainstream of the profession can become powerful voices for change.

While working on this research, I have often been asked the question, Do men and women, African Americans, Latinos and Latinas, or Asian Americans design differently? When interviewing underrepresented architects, many journalists insist on asking just that. My preference here, however, is to avoid gender or racial stereotypes and to let individual voices be heard. I hope to paint a dramatic portrait of all the actors on the architectural stage. While the press has occasionally spotlighted the stars, my light will shine on those waiting in the wings.

Throughout this book are examples of racism and sexism in the architectural workplace, compelling evidence that many architects remain largely unaware of or insensitive to diversity issues. Some instances are obvious, while others are subtle. Most speak for themselves. To a certain extent, the phenomenon of ageism is revealed as well. While some individuals have routinely referred to architecture as a "gentleman's profession," an "old boy's profession," others view it as an "older person's profession." In fact, several architects have told me that excelling in this field before age fifty was next to impossible, and that they were not taken seriously until they had some gray hair to show for their efforts.

Less visible are examples of heterosexism and homophobia in the architectural workplace. This reflects the questions asked in my surveys and interviews; sexual orientation was not my primary focus. Nevertheless, where relevant I have included the perspectives of gays and lesbians. Issues concerning architects with physical disabilities are beyond the scope of this book. A vast literature on universal design focusing on consumers with disabilities already exists. Much more information must be gathered about designers with disabilities, and this topic merits a book of its own.

Designing for Diversity does not simply address what's wrong in the profession. On the positive side, it points to the unique contributions that underrepresented groups have made to the architectural profession, as well as ways they can further reach their potential in the field.

THE GLASS CEILING IN ARCHITECTURE RESEARCH

Funds from the Campus Research Board of the University of Illinois and from the Graham Foundation enabled me to conduct one of the first nationwide studies of gender and racial issues in architectural practice. The goal of this research was to identify and examine those aspects of architectural practice that hinder or support the full participation of women and persons of color–and ultimately to produce information that can be used to improve the professional climate for underrepresented architects. Its objectives were: (1) to compare the situation in architecture with that in other fields, including those in the business world; (2) to compare the professional experiences of white women, women of color, white men, and men of color in architecture; (3) to identify and analyze obstacles and opportunities for professional advancement in architecture, with a special focus on those for underrepresented architects; (4) to analyze some ways in which underrepresented architects have succeeded in shattering the glass ceiling; and (5) to analyze successful strategies for diversifying the architectural profession.

The "glass ceiling" is a major issue explored through my research. The phrase has been used frequently in the last few decades to refer to obstacles that prevent certain people from obtaining high levels of responsibility, prestige, and power in their careers. These barriers are at first invisible but no less real. Once women and people of color have entered the architectural profession, how well do they fare? What *obstacles* do they face? What kinds of professional opportunities are they offered–or denied? How difficult is it for them to be hired, promoted, or named a principal in an architectural firm? Which kinds of clients are they able–or unable–to attract? How do their experiences compare with those of their white male counterparts? How widespread are sexual discrimination and racial harassment?

My research on designing for diversity has spanned a decade and it continues. It has included an extensive review of literature in architecture and other disciplines. This examination was essential in providing a historical, political, and social context for my analysis. Throughout this period, I have received anecdotal information from scores of underrepresented architects who recounted their experiences in letters, e-mail, and phone calls.

My research in this area has paralleled my teaching. Since 1991 I have taught a course on gender and race in architecture at the University of Illinois. My course has included an annual field trip to Chicago where my students and I interviewed underrepresented architects and toured their offices. Hearing their stories provided an impetus to pursue this research in book form.

An overview of my methodological approach is shown in table 1; for a more detailed description consult appendix A. I used multiple methods to compare the experiences of underrepresented architects with those of their white male

TABLE 1. Designing for Diversity Research Methods

Phase	Sample	Survey	Interviews	Archives
1	Underrepresented architects ($n = 58$) women architects architects of color		X	X
2	Professional organizations architects ($n = 23$) non-architects ($n = 17$)			X
3	Underrepresented architects ($n = 30$) women of color ($n = 13$) white men ($n = 11$) men of color ($n = 6$) (possible duplicates for phases 4–6)		X	
4	Sample 1[a] ($n = 94$) volunteers solicited via newsletters and AIA events ($n = 128$)	X		
5	Sample 2[a] ($n = 257$) randomly selected AIA members ($n = 800$) white men ($n = 200$) white women ($n = 200$) men of color ($n = 200$) women of color ($n = 200$) (usable surveys = 783)	X		
6	Sample 3[a] ($n = 58$) volunteers solicited via 1994 AIA National Diversity Conference ($n = 220$; possible duplicates from samples 1 and 2; response rate is inconclusive)	X		

a. Total of samples 1–3 = 409

counterparts. I relied primarily upon archives, surveys, and interviews. Surveys produced largely quantitative data, while interviews and archives yielded qualitative information.

For phase 1, *interviews* with 58 women architects and architects of color were conducted by students in my course on gender and race in contemporary architecture. The students conducted the interviews as part of an assignment to produce exhibit boards featuring profiles of underrepresented architects. Students also collected *archival data,* including resumes, published completed projects, drawings from their architects, and brochures from firms. This material was collected over a ten-year period, beginning in 1991. In phase 2, *archival data,* such as brochures, reports, and surveys, were collected from organizations of underrepresented architects around the country and from professional organizations of underrepresented employees in other fields. The information obtained was used to identify key issues, research studies, and survey questions that could be incorporated into my own research. Phase 3 involved in-depth *interviews* conducted with 30 women architects and architects of color. For phases 4–6, individuals in three research samples were sent a written *survey* containing approximately 400 questions, a combination of "open" and "closed" items, that is, questions that were open-ended and those that were multiple choice. A total of 409 practicing architects from across the United States responded. These included white men, white women, men of color, and women of color. Appendix A describes each sample in detail.

Respondents represent a broad cross section of ages, races, ethnic groups, geographic areas, and levels of professional experience. Several are well-known, highly accomplished figures in the field. For a detailed demographic description of the sample, consult appendixes A and B.

With the exception of those architects interviewed in phase 1, all participants in the surveys and interviews remain anonymous. My intention was to allow individuals to speak freely about their professional experiences, without their photographs or names attached. Discovering what architects have to say under the cloak of anonymity is an essential feature of my study. Note that throughout this book, where responses to the open-ended questions are quoted, each respondent is identified by a number. These are included so that readers can compare responses for the same individuals across different questions when available. In addition, individuals who participated in this research can try to locate themselves if they wish. A survey respondent is identified by number ("#") only, while an interview respondent is identified by "I-#."

Whenever possible, each respondent is also identified by age. Age is an especially important demographic trait, as it indicates how recently the reported events occurred. For example, one might expect that a sixty-five-year-old woman would report an unpleasant incident during her interview for her first architectural job. However, when a thirty-five-year-old woman recounts the same problem, this reveals that the dilemmas of forty years ago persist today.

Although I collected additional identifying information about each participant, such as the geographic region where they worked and their specific involvement in architectural practice, I included none of this data here, in order to protect confidentiality. The community of underrepresented architects is small, especially for women of color. Providing any more detailed information would jeopardize respondents' anonymity.

Preliminary results from my research were presented at two American Institute of Architects (AIA) National Diversity Conferences and published in the proceedings.[4] Several conference participants volunteered to be interviewed or surveyed. In response to their requests, I expanded my survey sample. Early findings were also published in *Progressive Architecture* and mentioned in *Architectural Record*.[5] To date, this coverage represents the greatest exposure my research has received.

Later, my research assistants and I collaborated on an exhibit entitled "Shattering the Glass Ceiling: The Role of Gender and Race in the Architectural Profession," a series of black-and-white collages that illustrated major findings and compelling quotes from the surveys and interviews. Jami Becker, Tracey Jo Hoekstra, Melissa Worden, and I collaborated on the design of the collages, and Melissa Worden and I coproduced the exhibit. In 1996 it was displayed at the Urbana-Champaign campus of the University of Illinois, Harvard University's Graduate School of Design, the AIA National Diversity Conference, and the AIA National Conference in Minneapolis.

A few words of caution: my research is limited by the nature of my research sample. As practicing architects, the respondents were willing participants in the profession. I did not include people who wanted to study architecture but were discouraged from enrolling, those who enrolled but never graduated, and those who received their architectural degrees but never practiced. Only through second-hand reports was I able to gain some understanding of those who did practice but later dropped out of the field. While such individuals would have much to say, tracking them down is a challenge that I will leave to others.

This introduction and chapter 1 make the case for designing for diversity. Chapters 2 and 3 analyze how gender, sexual orientation, race, and ethnicity have interacted with the built environment. They examine how the collective forces of sexism, racism, and the star system in architecture have long silenced the voices of diverse designers, and how these voices eventually began to be heard. These chapters explore several key questions: What roles have diverse designers played as clients, consumers, creators, and critics of the built environment? What spaces and places have they created? How have architectural partnerships between husbands and wives affected women architects? Where can one find buildings that celebrate diversity?

Chapter 4 examines the political and social context by describing how groups of diverse designers banded together in organizations that had a collective impact on the architectural profession. Affinity groups sponsored a myriad of conferences, lectures, publications, and exhibits that served as powerful forces of change.

Although they are sprinkled throughout the book, key themes raised by my empirical research are the primary focus of chapters 5–7. These chapters take on question such as: How are women architects and architects of color faring compared to their white male counterparts? How do their experiences with the internship process, professional registration, and promotions compare? What are their levels of job satisfaction? How do they perceive architectural practice? How do their salaries compare with those of mainstream architects? How do they balance personal and professional lives or deal with layoffs?

Finally, chapter 8 charts a multifaceted plan to restructure and diversify the architectural profession, presenting new strategies for architectural education, individual architects, architectural firms, the American Institute of Architects, and public outreach.

The twentieth century opened the doors of the architectural profession to those who were previously shut out. Architects of the twenty-first century must now transform their profession into one that truly provides equal opportunities for all.

Chapter 1

DIVERSITY IN DESIGN

> Thirty years after the dawn of the civil rights era, architecture remains among the less successful professions in diversifying its ranks—trailing, for example, such formerly male-dominated fields as business, computer science, accounting, law, pharmacology and medicine.
>
> —Ernest Boyer and Lee Mitgang

ERNEST BOYER AND LEE MITGANG, in their seminal work, *Building Community*, raised a deep concern about the practice and study of architecture: "We worry about . . . the paucity of women and minorities in both the professional and academic ranks." They based their findings on extensive research with architectural practitioners, students, faculty, and administrators.[1] In a follow-up piece in *Architectural Record*, Mitgang called for an end to "apartheid in architecture schools" and argued that "the race record of architecture education is a continuing disgrace, and if anything, things seem to be worsening."[2]

While over half the users of the built environment are female and large numbers are people of color, population figures in early 2000 revealed that only 16% of architects in the United States were women, 4% of architects were of Hispanic origin, and 2% were African American.[3] But these figures simply reflect individuals' self-reports. Some individuals may call themselves architects but may not really be licensed in the profession. Others may not yet have passed the licensing exam, making them ineligible to assume legal responsibility for the design of a building.

How have the numbers of women in architecture compared with those in other fields? The U.S. Census data includes all persons who list themselves as architects, regardless of whether or not they are professionally licensed to practice. According to the census, women comprised 4% of architects in 1970, 8% in 1980, and 15% in 1990. While these figures show some increase, the representation of women in architecture is by far the lowest among many arts professions, including photography, music performance, and music composition. In fact, the rate of women's entry into the architecture profession closely parallels that of women in medicine.[4]

What about the representation of women and persons of color among architects who are licensed? Here the most reliable source is data from the American Institute of Architects (AIA), the major professional organization in the field. Table 2 illustrates the *dramatic underrepresentation* of women and persons of color in architecture across the board: especially in practice, as AIA members, and as full-time and tenured faculty.[5] As of 1999, 13% of AIA members were women and only 8% were persons of color; of those licensed to practice (i.e., solely regular AIA members, excluding associate and emeritus members), only 10% were women and 8% were persons of color.[6] No woman or person of color has yet received the highly coveted Pritzker Prize, the profession's equivalent of the Nobel Prize.[7]

Astonishingly few African-American architects are licensed to practice in some states. For example, in 1996, twenty-six U.S. states each had a total of five or fewer licensed African-American architects. Delaware, Mississippi, New Mexico, North Dakota, and Rhode Island each had only one. Idaho, Iowa, Maine, Montana, New Hampshire, Vermont, West Virginia, and Wyoming had none.[8]

TABLE 2. Women and People of Color in Architectural Education and Practice

	Total	Women	All People of Color	African American	Asian	Latino	Native American
Architects	194,000	15.7%	—	2.3%	—	4.4%	—
AIA members	64,831	13.0	8.2%	1.3	4.1%	2.6	0.2%
Full-time architecture faculty	2,456	15.8	10.3	3.3	3.1	3.8	0.1
Tenured architecture faculty	1,256	13.9	8.4	2.8	2.7	2.9	—
Architecture under-graduate students	13,701	38.0	29.2	9.1	10.4	8.6	1.1
Architecture graduate students	5,064	43.6	23.7	2.3	12.0	8.4	1.0
Graduates of B.Arch. programs	2,617	28.8	22.1	5.0	9.1	7.5	0.5
Graduates of M.Arch. programs	2,002	37.2	17.4	2.0	9.8	5.2	0.4

No wonder some critics have gone so far as to call African-American architects an "endangered species."[9]

Only 16% of full-time architectural faculty in American colleges and universities are women; just 10% are persons of color. For all tenured architectural faculty—those to whom their institutions have made virtually a permanent, lifetime commitment—the figures are even lower; only 14% are women and 8% are persons of color. About half the women (58%), Latinos or Latinas (50%), and Asian/Pacific Islanders (48%) and one-third the African Americans (34%) among architectural faculty are marginalized in part-time teaching positions, with little or no job security.[10] In the early 1990s, similar statistics prompted an article entitled "Why Aren't More Women Teaching Architecture?" in *Architecture*.[11] In 1992, of the 108 architectural schools in the United States and Canada that grant tenure, 40 schools had no tenured women at all, and 27 had only one.[12] As of the 1997–98 academic year, the 117 accredited architectural schools in the United States and Canada produced only 17 women administrators: 7 deans, 5 chairs, 3 heads, and 2 directors.[13]

Of all undergraduates enrolled in accredited architecture programs in the United States at the close of the 1990s, 38% were women and 29% were people of color. Although these figures represent a substantial increase over earlier ones, the number of students far exceeds the number of those individuals who actually make it into the profession. In accredited graduate architecture programs, women comprise 44% and students of color make up 24%.[14]

The number of African-American architecture students appears to be decreasing slightly, although until 1990 we had no way even to track this information. Prior to that date, the National Architectural Accrediting Board (NAAB) amassed data for "minority" students, but it did not subdivide it by racial or ethnic groups such as African Americans, Latinos/Latinas, Asian Americans, and Native Americans. As of the mid-1990s, African-American architecture students comprised only about 6% of the architectural student body. In 1995 only 32 African-American students across the United States received a master's degree in architecture; by 1999 only 40 had done so. Furthermore, recent figures show a disturbing pattern of *racial segregation* in architectural education. Of the 1,313 African-American students enrolled in architecture schools in North America, 45% were students at the seven historically black schools with accredited architecture programs—Florida A&M, Hampton, Howard, Morgan State, Prairie View A&M, Southern, and Tuskegee—while the remainder were enrolled at the other 96 schools of architecture.[15]

Such disturbing figures raise serious questions about the lack of diversity in the architectural profession today. Statistics like these perpetuate the image of the profession as a private white men's club. To the outside world—and to many within the field—the profession seems incredibly insular and, compared to many other fields, archaic.

WHY DIVERSITY IN ARCHITECTURE?

Why do we need greater diversity among designers? And why is designing for diversity such a paramount concern? *The built environment reflects our culture, and vice-versa.* If our buildings, spaces, and places continue to be designed by a relatively homogeneous group of people, what message does that send about our culture?

Compared to most other countries, our American culture is a rich mosaic of racial and ethnic groups. With the latest waves of immigration, American cities are becoming increasingly racially and ethnically diverse, prompting a 1991 *USA Today* headline, "Minorities a Majority in Fifty-one Cities." The accompanying article noted that during the 1980s, people of color tipped the population scales in seven cities with populations over 500,000, including New York, Houston, Dallas, San Jose, San Francisco, Memphis, and Cleveland.[16] By 1990, Chicago's Hispanics, primarily immigrants from Mexico, Puerto Rico, and Cuba, represented about 18% of the city's population. African Americans were 37%. The Vietnamese have the fastest rate of increase of any ethnic group in Chicago, and Filipinos and Indians are close behind. Historically, the Windy City has had high populations of Italians, Greeks, Germans, Poles, and Irish.[17]

These ethnic groups will eventually assume leadership roles. Several cities have already had African-American mayors and city council representatives: Atlanta, Chicago, Detroit, Los Angeles, New York, and Philadelphia.[18] Yet the architectural profession in these and other cities is predominantly white.

ARCHITECTURE AS A CREATOR AND
REFLECTION OF CULTURE

The lack of diversity in the architectural profession impedes progress not only in that field but also in American society at large. Throughout the world, architects create the places in which we live and work, from those where we are born to those where we die. The built environment is one of culture's most lasting and influential legacies, a fact underscored by Sir Winston Churchill's observation, "We shape our buildings, and afterwards our buildings shape us." Discrimination in the architectural profession can lead to discrimination in how we all use the built environment. In fact, it has done so for years.

Leslie Kanes Weisman's book *Discrimination by Design* provides a thorough analysis of how the built environment has historically reflected and promoted the treatment of women as second-class citizens. Her work examines these issues in American housing, the office tower, the department store, the shopping mall, the maternity hospital, and elsewhere. As Weisman argues:

> Public buildings that spatially segregate or exclude certain groups, or relegate them to spaces in which they are either invisible or visibly subordinate, are the direct result of a comprehensive system of social oppression, not the consequences of failed architecture or prejudiced architects. However, our collective failure to notice and acknowledge how buildings are designed and used to support the social purposes they are meant to serve—including the maintenance of social inequality—guarantees that we will never do anything to change discriminatory design. When such an awareness does exist, discrimination can be redressed.[19]

Women, persons of color, certain ethnic groups, gays and lesbians, and persons with physical disabilities have historically been treated as second-class citizens in the built environment. In effect, their civil rights have been denied. For example, the Jim Crow laws that shaped the landscape of the American South from the late 1880s until the mid-1960s, forcing the construction of separate churches, schools, building entrances, restrooms, cemeteries, and water fountains for African Americans, reflected an oppressive, two-caste spatial system. So did the construction of Nazi concentration camps in Germany and Eastern Europe during the Holocaust, when over twelve million people—including six million Jews, Slavs, gypsies, gays, persons with physical disabilities, and other pariahs—met their deaths. In the United States, approximately 110,000 people of Japanese ancestry living along the West Coast, two-thirds of them American citizens, were forced out of their homes and into "relocation camps" during World War II. No doubt that these are the ultimate modern examples of discrimination by design.[20]

Discrimination by design can be overt or covert. For example, in public places like theaters, stadiums, and airports, we see long lines of frustrated women waiting to use the rest rooms, while men are in and out in a flash. Architects and their clients, as well as building-code officials and others, never noticed that women take longer to use restrooms, and hence women's restrooms need more toilet stalls than do men's rooms. Had women been the architects, clients, and code officials, the built environment would likely be much more user-friendly to women.

Journalists have argued in the *New York Times*, the *Wall Street Journal, Working Woman,* and publications across the country on behalf of gender equity in rest rooms.[21] One of the more vivid accounts appeared in the *New York Times Magazine:*

> I've seen a few frightening dramas on Broadway, but nothing on-stage is ever as scary as the scene outside the ladies' room at intermission: that long line of women with clenched jaws and crossed arms, muttering ominously to one another as they glare across the lobby at the cavalier figures sauntering in and out of the men's room. The ladies' line looks like an audition for the extras in "Les Miserables"—these are the vengeful faces that nobles saw on their way to the guillotine—except that the danger is all too real. When I hear the low rumble of obscenities and phrases like "Nazi male architects" I know not to linger.[22]

In the early 1990s, to accommodate the growing number of women senators, Senate majority leader George Mitchell announced that he was having a women's room installed just outside the Senate chamber in the U.S. Capitol. At that time, only a men's restroom was located there, marked by a sign "Senators Only," an implicit assumption that all senators were men. Senators Nancy Kassebaum and Barbara Mikulski, who did not qualify for admission, had to trek downstairs and stand in line with the tourists. From the U.S. Capitol to fifty state capitols across the country, "potty parity" has often been a pressing issue for women legislators. One New York State assemblywoman reminisced: "We had to tell the doorman whenever we were leaving the floor to visit the rest room—it took so long to get there and back, we were afraid of missing a vote. . . . It was like getting a permission slip from your teacher."[23]

Some state legislators have required architects to design a greater or at least equal number of toilet stalls in women's restrooms, compared to men's, in newly constructed or remodeled public buildings. In 1987, California led the way. State Senator Art Torres introduced such legislation after his wife and daughter endured a long wait for the ladies' room while attending a Tchaikovsky concert at the Hollywood Bowl. The bill became law that same year.[24]

To a certain extent, residential kitchens are also sites of discrimination by design. Instead of standing up, wouldn't it be more comfortable to sit down while washing a sink full of tomato sauce–stained pots and pans? Ironically, we have to be in a wheelchair in order to get architects to design a kitchen that we can use while seated. Many kitchens are designed with cabinets so high that women need step-stools to reach the shelves, placing them in danger of falling onto a hot stove or a hard floor. While American kitchens may feature the latest appliances and the most fashionable interior design, they often pose special problems for Asian-American women, Latinas, and members of other ethnic groups who tend to be shorter than the average white American male.

Even the projects of stellar designers highlight the need for greater sensitivity to the needs of women and other "diverse" users. Many of Frank Lloyd Wright's housing designs featured spacious living areas, yet the kitchens were so dark and tiny that most women—whether the clients or their household help— would have found it unpleasant to cook in them. (We can assume that in Wright's day, men were not doing much of the cooking.) The traditional woman's domain was not Wright's top priority.

Ever since it was built in 1950, the famous glass house that Ludwig Mies van der Rohe designed for his client Edith Farnsworth in Plano, Illinois, has been considered one of modernism's greatest masterpieces. Yet when Farnsworth moved into her showcase house, the roof leaked so badly and the heating system produced such an unsightly film on the windows that a local plumber suggested the house be called "My Mies-conception." When Farnsworth refused to accept delivery of the furniture that Mies had designed for her, she also refused to pay any more bills and soon began legal proceedings, which resulted in a lengthy legal battle fought out in the courts and in the press. In a 1953 interview for *House Beautiful,* she explained:

> The truth is that in this house with its four walls of glass I feel like a prowling animal, always on the alert. I am always restless. Even in the evening. I feel like a sentinel on guard day and night. I can rarely stretch out and relax. . . . What else? I don't keep a garbage can under my sink. Do you know why? Because you can see the whole "kitchen" from the road on the way in here and the can would spoil the appearance of the whole house. So I hide it in the closet farther down from the sink. Mies talks about "free space": but his space is very fixed. I can't even put a clothes hanger in my house without considering how it affects everything from the outside. Any arrangement of furniture becomes a major problem, because the house is transparent, like an X-ray.[25]

A more recent case in point is Ohio State University's Wexner Center for the Arts, the winning entry in a design competition. This building was designed by the world-renowned architect Peter Eisenman and opened in 1989. It attracted enormous national publicity and was hailed as a groundbreaking work in deconstructivist architecture. Purely as a work of art, it is surely that.[26] Paul Goldberger wrote in the *New York Times,* "How well does the building work? Surprisingly well, considering how little its architect professes to care about such things."[27]

There are telling discrepancies between the accolades of the architecture critics and the experiences of everyday users. Jack Nasar, a professor at Ohio State University, has spent years conducting post-occupancy evaluations of this award-winning building.[28] A persistent finding in his research is that the Wexner Center poses special challenges for women users. One serious problem is the threat of crime. A number of women who work in the building, as well as those who must pass by it after dark, find it dangerous because its design offers too many hiding spots for potential criminals. Another problem is the design and location of floor-to-chest-high windows in the building's top-floor offices, a feature that *Time*'s architectural critic referred to as one of several "architectural jokes."[29] To women workers, the windows are no laughing matter. They allow passersby to take a peek up their skirts, hardly a view most women care to expose.

Nasar describes countless examples where elderly people with physical disabilities are not only inconvenienced but endangered by this building. For example, in order to access the Fine Arts Library, visitors must move along a long outdoor aisle that is unsheltered. Marble strips along the walkway become extremely slick whenever it rains. The aisle is a wind trap, making it difficult to walk. When the entrance floor gets wet, it turns slippery. Glare from windows irritates elderly users especially. In order to enter the library, visitors descend a steep stairway into a dark basement, and many have tripped. The building was designed from the perspective of an able-bodied male, without much sensitivity to the different kinds of people who actually use the building. And the public suffers the consequences.[30]

Awarding prizes to buildings like the Wexner Center before the first woman or man has ever set foot in it is ludicrous. And selecting the winners of design competitions primarily on the grounds of aesthetics is an irresponsible use of precious public funds. But Eisenman is not to blame. *Rather it is the architectural profession itself. Its value system, which all too often rewards aesthetics while ignoring the experiences of users—especially diverse users—is simply out of touch with reality.* These scenarios—and countless others—underscore the need for diversity in design.

Controversies about discrimination in architectural education occasionally have made headlines. For instance, when a 1992 report from an ad hoc committee of University of California professors and professional architects critical of Berkeley's Department of Architecture was leaked to Bay Area media, the issue exploded. Three women graduate students at Berkeley's architecture school went public with their complaints of sexual harassment and discrimination.[31] One student had initially complained in 1991 that her professor told her classmates that she had no right to be in architectural school because she was a mother. Yet one of her colleagues contended, "If anything she was remarkable. . . . She had a baby on Thursday and she was back in class on Monday."[32] That same year, several architecture graduate students signed a letter to the dean of the graduate division complaining that architecture professors showed favoritism to males, discriminated against minorities, and treated graduate students in their thirties and forties like juveniles. The ad hoc committee that reviewed the incidents chastised the department.

Two other Berkeley students complained in 1992 that their research supervisor, a graduate student, made sexist and racist remarks, such as "Asian women are inferior to men," and he eventually fired them. One student claimed that the same supervisor had taken a hair tie out of her hand and forcibly pulled it up her leg, saying, "You need a garter belt." The university has since settled the matter, saying that "the appropriate action was taken."[33]

The Berkeley campus was rocked once again a few years later by the lawsuit of Marcy Wong, an assistant professor of architecture, who alleged that she was denied tenure because her white male colleagues were uncomfortable working with an Asian woman.[34] Her saga began in 1985, when members of an ad hoc committee of the architecture department unanimously recommended her for tenure. But the next year, her tenure was denied. Wong and her lawyers claimed that she had been blackballed by an "old boys' club," who felt she did not fit in. Wong filed several unsuccessful grievances with the university before deciding to sue, charging both sexual and racial discrimination. Her case was settled in 1996. Wong and her attorneys were awarded $1 million, of which Wong netted about half. The university contended that it settled the suit because a trial would have been too costly and because the denial of Wong's tenure was justified. As the case dragged on, Wong had three children and started her own architectural office. Yet the lawsuit took its toll on her. She claimed that she fell apart physically, losing weight and suffering severe pneumonia and bronchitis over several winters in a row. She chose not to return to academia. While Wong's legal case is an anomaly in architectural education, her tenure review is not.

Many women have had less successful outcomes, and, like Wong, they chose to flee academia altogether.[35]

In fact, far too many women professors of architecture have been treated unfairly during the promotion process both for tenure and for full professor. Several have needlessly suffered emotional trauma. More often than not, rather than going public and facing retaliation, women architecture faculty suffer in silence.

Another problem underrepresented academicians face is burnout. They are often overworked, required to serve on countless committees, and saddled with administrative tasks. Out of self-preservation they feel they must work as liaisons to the National Organization of Minority Architecture Students (NOMAS), women-in-architecture groups, and other affinity groups. Such commitments are important, but they also cut into precious time needed for research and scholarship, the criteria upon which their evaluations are based.

Two architecture faculty members, Linda Groat and Sherry Ahrentzen, have conducted thorough investigations of gender and racial issues in architectural education. Their 1990 report for the Association of Collegiate Schools of Architecture (ACSA) surveyed 210 women architecture faculty across the United States and analyzed demographics within schools. It documented that women were grossly underrepresented among the ranks of tenured faculty. Even worse, many reported experiencing discrimination on the job, and two-thirds believed that sexism is endemic in architectural education. Over a third of the women faculty surveyed perceived significant inequities in salary, appointments to institutionally important committees, and standards for promotion. Ahrentzen and Groat followed up with extensive interviews of over forty women architectural faculty. Based upon these results, as well as the new agenda called for by the landmark Boyer and Mitgang study, they concluded that women can play special roles in transforming both the mission and practice of architectural education through the ideals of a liberal education, interdisciplinary connections, the integration of different modes of thought, connections to other disciplines through beginning studios, the reformation of pedagogical practices, collaboration, and caring for and counseling students.[36]

In their 1996 study of 650 students at six architecture schools, Groat and Ahrentzen extended their research to examine gender and racial issues for architectural students. Their findings identified the largest and most consistent gender difference as women students' perception that they have to outperform males so that the faculty would take them seriously. They also found that a substantial number of students (43%) in the five Caucasian-dominated schools "believe that students of color must outperform Caucasian students to be taken seriously. . . . These results not only seem indicative of the larger landscape of racial inequities in this country, but they underscore the basis for the extremely low representation of African Americans in the profession generally."[37] The researchers documented women students' perceptions that faculty either ignored or dismissed their work. As the researchers put it, "Such a pattern of dismissal and devaluing leads many women to conclude that there is a tacit double standard whereby male students are perceived by some faculty as inherently more architect-like."[38] Groat and Ahrentzen found that compared to male students, female students were less satisfied with architecture as a career, and among international and Asian-American students, women were much less satisfied with architecture both as a major and as a career. As the researchers suggest, "This generally lower level of satisfaction among women appears to be consistent with anecdotal evidence that there is a high level of attrition of women as they move into their careers."[39] Furthermore, underrepresented students were more inclined to consider switching to alternative careers. Women were more likely than men to consider working for an advocacy or nonprofit firm; an interior design firm; a government agency; in business; and in historic preservation, programming/evaluation, or elsewhere. Over half the Latino students and almost half the Asian-American students considered switching to nonarchitectural careers.[40]

Mark Frederickson has reported on gender and racial bias in design juries, the primary mode of critiquing student design work in architectural education. His extensive research, based on videotaped protocol studies of 112 juries at three American design schools, examined issues such as interruption, opinion polarization, idea building, advisement, questioning, jury kinesis and proxemics, sexual and racial bias, verbal participation rates, among others.[41] Frederickson identified several consistently biased design-jury practices that disadvantage underrepresented students and faculty.

Nevertheless, several years after the publication of my book *Design Juries on Trial,* and after Frederickson conducted his research, design juries remain firmly in place in most architectural schools today. Yet, Boyer and Mitgang found that 58% of administrators and two-thirds of the students agreed that their school should offer alternative ways to evaluate design projects.[42] Resistance to changing design juries is strong, however. In a 1996 article in *AIA Architect,* the architect John Rossi reported that "the traditional jury system in architectural education is effective, its role is valid, and it is not about to be replaced any time soon, agreed a panel of 40 architects, educators, and architecture students that convened at the 1996 AIA New England Conference."[43] Nonetheless, in that same piece, Rossi raised major concerns about counterproductive juries that demoralize students.

DEFINING DIVERSITY

Diversity is a set of human traits that have an impact on individuals' values, opportunities, and perceptions of self and others at work. At a minimum, it includes six core dimensions: age, ethnicity, gender, mental or physical abilities, race, and sexual orientation. But it also includes secondary dimensions such as education, family status, religion, first language, geographic location, military experience, income, communication style, organizational level, work experience, and work style. Although less visible than the core dimensions, the secondary dimensions can exert strong influences on individuals' lives. The core dimensions of diversity can cause some individuals to have more opportunities, greater credibility, and unearned privileges compared to others. As Marilyn Loden, a change management consultant for Fortune 500 companies, argued in her book *Implementing Diversity*, "the recognition of this hierarchy can be the first step towards valuing diversity. For it is only after we appreciate the subtle ways in which one's core identity can help open doors to opportunity—while others with different core identities remain locked out—that we can resolve to value all core identities equally and create a truly level playing field on which to compete and succeed."[44]

A brief discussion of terminology is in order. In fact, the terms "gender," "race," and "ethnicity" are oversimplifications. For conceptual clarity, I often refer to either "women" or "men," or "whites" or "persons of color," but each individual's experience is complex. For instance, social and economic class differences can cause inequities. An African-American woman raised in the South Side of Chicago will likely have a different worldview than her North Shore suburban counterpart, even if only twenty miles separate them. Similarly, an East Los Angeles Latino and his Beverly Hills cousin may feel light-years apart. For another, long-term relationships, marriage, and parenthood color individuals' perspectives. A single mother with three children may well have different priorities than a woman who is married without children.

The terms "race" and "ethnicity" are often interchanged. While "race" refers primarily to one's skin color and physical distinctions, "ethnicity" highlights both physical and cultural differences and is more often used in the sociological and anthropological literature.[45] Note that in describing my survey research results,

I have broken down much of the quantitative data by race (in aggregate form, whites vs. persons of color), while the qualitative data presents a sampling of experiences by ethnicity (for example, African Americans, Latinos/Latinas, Asian Americans). That is because the numbers of respondents in each ethnic category were not high enough to draw statistical comparisons.

Although the term "minority" is frequently used in the architectural profession to define any nonwhite racial or ethnic group, it is offensive to many because it implies a lesser status than that of the white mainstream majority. Nowadays "people of color" is preferable to "minority." No socially acceptable expression accurately links women and persons of color as a group. However, when writers refer to these individuals as managers in organizations, they have often used the term "nontraditional" or "underrepresented." In this book I have adopted the latter as it applies to the architectural profession.

From a theoretical viewpoint, diversity in design can be viewed across a broad spectrum as it relates to: *consumers*–people who use the spaces and places we live in, work in, and pass by every day; *critics*–those who write about design, be they journalists, writers, or researchers; and *creators*–those who design and produce these spaces, be they practitioners, educators, or students–of the environment. Clients inhabit more than one segment of this spectrum, playing dual roles as creators and consumers, for without their financial backing, designers would have no work. *Throughout this book, I will argue that by widening our theoretical viewpoint, and by examining the multiple roles that not only designers, but also consumers, critics, and creators of the environment have played, the contributions of underrepresented persons to architecture come to light.*

Diversity encompasses the concerns of women, persons of color, lesbians and gays, and persons with physical or mental disabilities–almost anyone other than the able-bodied white male. How these individuals relate to the built environment is important. Historically, many have been shut out of the environmental mainstream, and their voices remained silent. The architectural profession has only recently begun to notice them at all.

This cultural lag stems from the fact that for far too long, the voice of the architectural profession has been homogeneous. While consumers of the built environment have always been diverse, its creators and critics have been able-bodied white males. In economic terms, we have witnessed a mismatch between consumers and producers of the built environment. In fact, what the public perceives as architecture's objectivity is merely the construction of white male subjectivity.

Diversity has become an issue of national importance. In 1998, Federal Reserve chair Alan Greenspan–one of the most powerful persons in the United States–proclaimed that diversity "is good for business. It is good for our society. And–it is the right thing to do." He stressed, "Discrimination is patently immoral, but it has now increasingly been seen as unprofitable."[46] That same year, the Securities and Exchange Commission (SEC) held several diversity roundtables in an effort to find ways to boost the role of women and persons of color in corporate America. Arthur Levitt Jr., chair of the SEC, proclaimed, "Fostering diversity is, and will remain, a priority for the SEC."[47]

EQUAL OPPORTUNITY LAWS AND AFFIRMATIVE ACTION PROGRAMS

Equal opportunity laws prohibit workplace discrimination based on race, religion, sex, national origin, age, or disability. By contrast, affirmative action is aimed specifically at race and gender. It is "a set of public policies, laws, and executive orders, as well as voluntary and court-ordered practices designed to promote fairness and diversity." Affirmative action programs spell out guidelines for correcting historic patterns of exclusion and discrimination within organizations. They involve proactive steps to set targets and timetables to improve the gender and racial profiles in specific job categories within an organization. They operate at the federal, state, and private levels.[48]

Set-asides, a component of affirmative action programs, require that on federally sponsored projects, a certain percentage of work be contracted out to persons of color and women. The assumption is that individuals who have had weights placed on their backs cannot run the same distance as easily as someone who is not so burdened. Set-asides and affirmative action programs are attempts to level the educational and economic playing fields.

The political evolution of diversity issues sheds light on the current state of affairs in the architectural profession. Equal opportunity laws and affirmative action programs have played integral roles in this history. They began in the 1960s as an outgrowth of the civil rights movement.

In 1961, President John F. Kennedy issued Executive Order 10925 urging federal contractors to hire more persons of color. While it did not specify enforcement procedures, it did include the phrase "affirmative action." In 1963, the Equal Pay Act was passed. It amended the Fair Labor Standards Act of 1938, which had established nationwide standards for minimum wage, overtime pay, and the employment of children. The new law addressed the need for equal pay for men and women doing work that requires equal skill, effort, and responsibility.

In 1964 President Lyndon Johnson signed into law Title VII of the Civil Rights Act. It barred discrimination because of race, color, religion, sex, or national origin in hiring, firing, promoting, compensating, and other terms, privileges, and conditions of employment. Only if a finding of discrimination was made did the act require court-imposed affirmative action. That same year, the Equal Employment Opportunity Commission (EEOC) was established.[49]

In 1965, Executive Order 11246, also signed by President Johnson, required federal contractors to adopt goals and timetables to achieve proportional representation. The order pertained exclusively to race and made affirmative action the purview of the U.S. Department of Labor. At that time, the Office of Federal Contract Compliance was established. Two years later President Johnson issued Executive Order 11375, adding the category of sex to the areas protected by affirmative-action orders. In 1972 the Equal Employment Opportunity Act empowered the EEOC to take legal actions in federal courts to enforce Title VII of the Civil Rights Act. At that time, the Equal Pay Act was amended to cover administrative, executive, and professional employees, and Title VII of the Civil Rights Act was broadened to include higher education faculty. In 1978 the Pregnancy Discrimination Act extended existing short-term disability or sick leave to pregnant women and made it illegal to discriminate on the basis of pregnancy.

President George Bush signed the 1991 Civil Rights Act, making it possible for victims of intentional discrimination based on sex, religion, or disability to recover compensatory and punitive damages. Prior to this time, such remedies pertained only to race-based discrimination cases. That same year, Title II of the Civil Rights Act, the Glass Ceiling Act, established a bipartisan twenty-one-member Glass Ceiling Commission charged with preparing recommendations on "eliminating artificial barriers to the advancement of women and minorities (to) management and decision-making positions in business."

In 1993, President Bill Clinton signed into law the Family and Medical Leave Act (FMLA), offering men and women job-protected, unpaid time off to recover from a serious illness or to care for a new child or sick relative. Under the FMLA, a person who works for a company that employs fifty or more workers is entitled to up to twelve weeks of unpaid, job-protected leave to care for a newborn, a newly adopted child, or a seriously ill child, spouse, or parent.[50]

Soon after affirmative action programs were established, they unleashed a strong public backlash. Charges of reverse discrimination surfaced nationwide, as white males argued in the courts that affirmative action programs had denied them equal opportunity on the job. Many cases were successful.

By the mid-1990s, serious efforts to dismantle affirmative action programs were underway. In 1995 Governor Pete Wilson of California issued an Executive Order to End Preferential Treatment and to Promote Individual Opportunity Based on Merit. This ended all state affirmative action programs not required by law or by a court decree. That same year, the University of California Board of Regents voted to end affirmative action in admission, hiring, and contracting at all of its campuses beginning in 1997. In 1996 the anti–affirmative action California Civil Rights Initiative passed in a statewide election. It was later challenged by the courts, and the decision was upheld. California served as a bellwether for other states to place anti–affirmative action initiatives on their ballots. Although in certain states, affirmative action programs have been scaled back significantly, and recent Supreme Court decisions have limited their scope, they remain intact in most of the nation.

At the time of this writing, the debate over the proposed Employment Non-Discrimination Act (ENDA) remains unresolved. This measure would provide federal legislation to prohibit discrimination against gays and lesbians in the workplace. However, even if ENDA were signed into law, lesbians and gays would still not have as much legal protection as that currently offered to women and persons of color.

How have equal opportunity laws and affirmative action programs affected architects in the United States? The results are mixed. Without a doubt, the greatest achievement has been in the educational arena, where the legislation and programs have opened the doors of colleges and universities that had historically excluded women and persons of color, either explicitly or implicitly, from studying architecture. As a result, they allowed a more diverse constituency to trickle into the field. In the professional arena, affirmative action programs offered women- and minority-owned businesses countless opportunities that would otherwise have been impossible to gain.

On the downside, some beneficiaries of affirmative action programs find themselves viewed as tokens, pigeonholed into particular types of work. This is true not only in architecture but in other professions.[51] Such programs are double-edged swords. Some architects are quick to point to firms that abuse the intent of set-aside programs, that is, firms that claim to be woman- or minority-owned but where those individuals serve as a cover for a white male who essentially runs the company.

In the academic world, university-wide affirmative action programs have long pressured architecture departments to hire women and persons of color as faculty. Colleagues often resent having to hire so-called "affirmative action candidates," and throughout their university careers, many underrepresented faculty receive little or no departmental support and may feel as if their credentials are viewed as suspect.

How has the Family and Medical Leave Act affected architects? Since few architectural offices hire more than 50 employees, its effect has been minimal. As of 1996, only 9% of architectural firms employed 20 or more employees; 10% had 10–19 employees; 26% had only 2–4 employees, and another 34% were offices of solo practitioners.[52] Apart from such statistical evidence, anecdotal accounts have revealed blatant subversion of the intent of FMLA. Some women architects have returned to their jobs after maternity leave only to be laid off after a week.[53]

Rule of Conduct 1.401 of the AIA's Code of Ethics and Professional Conduct clearly states, "Members shall not discriminate in their professional activities on the basis of race, religion, gender, national origin, age, disability, or sexual orientation."[54] Violation of any rule of conduct is grounds for disciplinary action by the institute. Ethical Standard 5.1 in the AIA's code of ethics also has implications for underrepresented architects; but as a standard rather than a rule, it is not considered mandatory. Instead, it is one of many goals toward which members should strive in professional performance and behavior. This standard states, "Professional Environment: Members should provide their associates and employees with a suitable working environment, compensate them fairly, and facilitate their professional development."[55] *Yet as my survey results reveal, women architects are not compensated fairly—and the profession provides little recourse.*

In connection with Rule of Conduct 1.401, the AIA issued an advisory opinion entitled "Discrimination against Employees Based on Gender."[56] Rules must apply to all professional activities of AIA members, including dealings with clients, colleagues, employees, and others. This advisory opinion describes a troublesome case, which I summarize here.

A woman was repeatedly harassed by a male coworker in their architectural office. He sent her malicious notes; consistently rearranged items on her workstation; removed equipment from her workstation and replaced it with inferior substitutes; and demeaned her education, competency, and professionalism, making disparaging comments in front of her and her coworkers. Although she had been at the firm six months longer than he and was two years further along in her preparation for the Architect Registration Examination (ARE), he was paid $3,500 a year more than she. He was also offered training in Computer Aided Design (CAD), which she was denied even though she had expressed a desire to learn it.

Her attempts to discuss this harassment with the offending coworker were to no avail, as were her repeated discussions with her supervising architect. Her boss made matters worse by meeting with the offender as well as all other male employees in the studio. This resulted in tension between her and other male coworkers, with whom she had never experienced problems. Furthermore, her supervisor explained that he had done all he intended to do, and that she should learn to expect this behavior if she continued to work in a "man's profession."

After contacting her local AIA component and asking the staff to intercede in what she perceived to be a violation of the institute's Code of Ethics and Professional Conduct, she was referred to a local council on human rights. Council personnel, while sympathetic, warned her of being blackballed in the local architecture community if she filed a complaint. During her annual evaluation at her firm, wherein she received a favorable review, she advised her supervising architect that the harassment had not stopped. He indicated that he could do no more to help her. She subsequently passed the registration exam. But the harassment soon escalated and recurred regularly over three weeks. She once again attempted to discuss her case with her supervisor, asking him to stop further harassment.

A few days later, she was suddenly informed that her services would no longer be required, effective 5:00 P.M. that same day, due to a work slowdown. She was fired. Yet just days after that, the same firm offered a job to a male architect whose education, job experience, and licensing status were almost identical to hers. He was told that he was needed immediately because so much work had to be done.

This case clearly outlines a pattern of harassment that never ceased, one that the supervising architect implicitly condoned by failing to recognize and deal with it, even after the woman's repeated complaints. Because he told her that she had better get used to this kind of behavior if she intended to continue working in a "man's profession," he overtly condoned and aided in the harassment. Furthermore, by paying her substantially less than a male colleague with considerably less experience and less seniority in the firm, and by offering her fewer training opportunities, the supervising architect overtly discriminated against her. Considering all of this, and the fact that her annual reviews had been positive, the legal analysts concluded that "it is difficult to ascribe her employment termination to anything other than overt discrimination based on her gender." The hiring of a male with similar training and experience, within days of the woman's termination due to a supposed work slowdown, made the case of gender discrimination even stronger. This case is a preview of some of the shocking stories that women architects recounted to me in the course of my research.

MANAGING DIVERSITY

By the mid-1990s, many organizations discovered that the equal opportunity laws and affirmative action programs of the 1960s were of limited effectiveness. They came to believe that valuing differences and managing diversity, two out-growths of the earlier developments, are more successful ways to address in-equities in the workplace. These new approaches seek to maximize the potential of every individual by helping organizations create a level playing field and a supportive environment for all employees.

Valuing differences and managing diversity do not merely satisfy legal requirements. They represent a paradigm shift that fundamentally changes the corporate culture. Profile improvement may still fall under their canopy, but it is not an end in itself. Managing diversity is a new strategy that holds organizations responsible for creating an environment in which diversity not only survives, but thrives. This management model is a giant leap beyond affirmative action. As Marilyn Loden writes, "The basic aim of valuing diversity is to create a more flexible, diversity-friendly environment where the talents of all employees can flourish and be leveraged for individual, work team, and organizational success."[57]

In his book *Beyond Race and Gender* and numerous other publications, R. Roosevelt Thomas Jr. underscores the need for organizations to manage diversity.[58] Formerly a professor at Harvard University, Thomas now heads the American Institute for Managing Diversity (AIMD). He cites countless examples where organizations with good intentions have been ineffective at achieving diversity. The result has often been no more than politically correct rhetoric or occasional small-term gains. According to Thomas, managing diversity must be a long-term goal, and organizations take years to achieve it. People in many levels of management must engage in a consistent, consolidated effort. Organizations must conduct a culture audit in order to assess the current state of affairs at their workplaces, to identify critical issues, and to begin to address them in a holistic way. *The Guide to Culture Audits,* published by AIMD, elaborates on how these work.[59]

With this political context in mind, what would it mean to value differences and manage diversity within the architectural profession? No longer can we tell underrepresented designers to either sink or swim and offer them no life raft. Managing diversity calls for a systematic, holistic approach to revamp what many underrepresented architects would call a "chilly climate" or an "inhospitable corporate culture."

LOSING FROM INTOLERANCE AND
GAINING FROM DIVERSITY

There is no doubt that diversity is good for society. But humanitarian reasons are not enough. What are the costs of intolerance? And what are the benefits of incorporating diversity programs into the architectural profession?

Whether aware of it or not, every organization pays a hefty price when it fails to provide a supportive work environment for underrepresented employees. Teamwork can not flourish. Sales may be lost. Innovation may be limited. Productivity is reduced. Absenteeism can rise. And turnover can skyrocket. Among the other costs are: (1) worker alienation resulting from misunderstandings of values and behaviors; (2) unnecessary termination stemming from communication breakdown and misinterpreting employee behavior; (3) managers' reluctance to hire and work with diverse workers; (4) racism and discrimination resulting from misinterpreting the behaviors of others; (5) costly discrimination suits arising from poor communication and worker alienation.[60]

Virtually all employers fear lawsuits, especially those resulting from an intolerance of workplace diversity. Multimillion-dollar racial discrimination suits like those against Denny's restaurants and Texaco tarnish the reputations of organizations in the eyes of clients, customers, investors, potential employees, and the public. Such cases often lead to boycotts, lost revenues, huge settlements, and just plain bad publicity.

Still other practices result in social and psychological costs—and ultimately economic costs as well. *Ethnocentrism* involves assuming that the behaviors of others, no matter what their origins, can be interpreted according to the rules and values of one's own culture. *Stereotyping* entails using inflexible statements about a category of people, applying them to all members of a group without regard to individual differences. As my research demonstrates, both of these can be found in the architectural profession.

Culture shock is a state of mind that occurs when people are immersed in a strange culture. It happens generally in three ways: an individual's behaviors are not getting the response to which he or she is accustomed; an individual realizes that he or she no longer knows the cultural rules of the game and does not understand how to behave; or, finally, an individual no longer receives appropriate credit for achievements, skills, or ideas. When underrepresented architects enter the traditional architectural office, two worlds collide. Like immigrants, the underrepresented workers are trying to build a permanent home in a new land.

Marga Rose Hancock, executive director of AIA Seattle, makes a strong case that architectural firms ought to be proactive in promoting diversity. She argues that those firms who engage in racist or sexist practices are asking for trouble, as employees once treated unfairly become corporate executives or public officials elsewhere who steer valuable contracts away from them.[61]

If principals of architectural firms allow a high incidence of internal harassment to occur and do little or nothing about it, if they treat coworkers in a disrespectful manner, or if they are uncomfortable dealing with gay or lesbian coworkers, how can they feel confident that these are not problems with clients, consultants, subcontractors, and others outside the firm? What kinds of business opportunities may be lost from groups against whom they have particular biases?

Among the demonstrated benefits of successful corporate diversity programs are an increase in the number of women and persons of color contributing to patents; reduced absenteeism; and improved promotion and retention numbers for underrepresented employees.[62] Managing diversity also provides a competitive advantage, setting some architectural firms above others—attracting a new breed of clients and users in a more globally diverse marketplace. Ethnic marketing efforts can be made. Architects respond more effectively to various subcultures, whose spending power is rapidly increasing. Consequently, customer service will be greatly improved, and the public's image of the architectural profession will be enhanced. A nonarchitectural example serves as a case in point: when Aetna, a major insurance company, wanted to expand into a Hispanic market, they tapped into their network of Hispanic employees, who advised them about where to advertise in newspapers and radio programs.[63]

MODEL WORKPLACES FOR DIVERSITY

Several model workplaces foster and thrive on diversity. *Diversity: Business Rationale and Strategies,* a report published in the mid-1990s and based on information from thirty-four companies and fifty-three organizations, provides examples of successful diversity programs.[64] It reveals that the most critical elements for a successful diversity strategy are, in order of importance: (1) management commitment, leadership, and support; (2) integration of diversity initiatives into business and organizational objectives; (3) communication and continuing dialogue among all employees; (4) education and training; and (5) accountability with consequences, especially for senior and middle management; and (6) employee involvement.

Successful corporate practices include: (1) incorporation of diversity into mission statements; (2) diversity action plans; (3) accountability in business objectives; (4) employee involvement from all levels and functions; (5) career development and planning; (6) community involvement and outreach; and (7) long-term initiatives directed at overall culture change.

What do diversity programs such as these accomplish? Their aims are varied. They teach managers to ensure that their companies comply with affirmative action programs and equal opportunity laws dictated by the federal government and by the state. They teach people from different backgrounds to value their individual differences and work together. They recruit employees from underrepresented communities. They offer employees flexible work schedules to enable them to meet obligations at work as well as at home.

Roosevelt Thomas describes a number of pioneering organizations that have taken significant steps toward managing diversity. Avon is one of the most successful. Its current progress in promoting minorities and women goes back to the mid-1980s. The company hired a consultant to undertake a multicultural planning research project. A five-year implementation plan produced several new multicultural initiatives. Critical to its success is a partnership between human resources and line management. At its core is a management philosophy of employee empowerment.[65]

Marilyn Loden believes that members of an organization occupy any one of five segments on what she calls a Diversity Adoption Curve. At one end of the curve are innovators and change agents, with pragmatists and skeptics in the middle and traditionalists at the other end. Those at the innovation end of the scale perceive greater opportunities and fewer risks in adopting diversity practices in the workplace, while those at the traditionalist end of the scale see decreased opportunities and increased risks.[66] She outlines an elaborate strategy for creating a workplace environment in which different types of people are approached about diversity in different ways. Beginning diversity programs with those who are likely to be most receptive–the innovators–helps foster an atmosphere in which others, such as the pragmatists, are likely to participate later on. But Loden cautions that forcing everyone to participate unwillingly is a prescription for disaster.

She also warns that diversity programs can spark a harsh backlash, a predictable reaction to any new idea. Some individuals may react toward diversity programs with denial, dread, hostility, cynicism, and contempt. Among the most commonly mentioned reasons for resisting diversity programs are suspicion of "otherness," hiring quotas, reverse discrimination, a shrinking economic pie, divisiveness, lowering of quality and performance standards–all of which share a common motivation: fear.

According to Loden, ignoring the mainstream can lead to calamitous consequences. If diversity benefits only underrepresented employees, then others are much less likely to buy into it. Viewing such programs as no more than affirmative action, they are likely to feel alienated and marginalized. Hence white males must be included in the planning, decision-making, and implementation processes in order for diversity programs to be effective. Similarly, those who promote diversity in the workplace must avoid sounding self-righteous and morally superior. Spreading blame and guilt simply won't work. Advocates of diversity must be open to those who oppose it. Silencing the opposition will simply worsen what may already be an adversarial environment. Open discussion and dialogue are essential.

Who should conduct diversity awareness training programs? Simply having employees undertake this role can leave them floundering to answer questions and control the discussion, placing them in an awkward and dangerous position. Gender, racial, and multicultural issues can become volatile and explosive. Calling in an outside expert can result in a program that sounds like "one size fits all," too canned to be credible. A model of internal and external trainer pairs is a good alternative. The external trainer has the group facilitation skills, and the internal trainer has the corporate knowledge and experience. Together, the two balance each other.

As a result of continuing education requirements instituted at the AIA, architects now are required to complete thirty-six learning units of continuing education per year in order to maintain their professional licenses. Since diversity issues are not part of the required curricula for architectural school, enrolling in diversity continuing-education classes is one way to help educate a profession that has lagged behind other fields. Principals, partners, personnel managers, human resource specialists, and others in leadership positions are ideal candidates for such courses.

Ever since 1987, Catalyst, a nonprofit research organization that works with businesses to advance women, has issued an annual award showcasing exemplary initiatives.[67] Throughout the year, a committee conducts a thorough evaluation, including interviews and focus groups with a wide range of employees, along with two-day audits of finalist companies. Among the criteria evaluated are senior management commitment, measurable results, accountability, replicability, and originality. *The Catalyst Guide to Best Practices* discusses winning programs in detail, covering such issues as mentoring, recruitment, compensation, performance evaluation, sexual harassment programs, workplace flexibility, work/life balance, diversity, women's networks, and career development.[68] Recent award winners included Procter and Gamble, the Sara Lee Corporation, the Allstate Corporation, and Avon Mexico. Catalyst offers advisory teams that are hired by companies and firms to create more supportive environments for women employees. Its information center serves as a national clearinghouse for women and work, offering a myriad of valuable resources. Catalyst's awards winners and their diversity initiatives can be adapted as models for design practice.

In order to meet the changing needs of employees and their families, a few architectural offices have already paid special attention to diversity issues. Chicago's Ross Barney + Jankowski Architects has long been one of the most female-friendly firms in the country. Carol Ross Barney has routinely assigned women as project architects and encouraged them to advance professionally on the job. Her office has been the launch pad for many women's successful architectural careers. At Boston's Stull and Lee, one of the oldest African-American architecture firms in the United States, over half its employees are women and persons of color. The office has a strong affirmative action policy along with an informal mentoring system. It accommodates flexible work hours and encourages its employees to travel and take continuing education courses.[69]

At Steffian Bradley and Associates of Boston, over 65% of its sixty staff are women or persons of color. Of ten principals, two are women, and of six associates, four are women. The firm offers flexible hours, excused absences when employees or their children are sick, and both maternity and paternity leave.[70] Another family-friendly firm is Leers, Weinzapfel Associates, Inc., of Boston, where over half of thirty members are women. Its employee review process asks its staff to evaluate their future career development and that of the firm.[71]

Ann Beha Associates of Boston has made the development of its professional staff a top priority by hiring an outside business consultant. Their joint efforts helped Beha value the contributions of staff at all levels, encouraged her to cultivate leadership, and reinforced her efforts to make team collaboration a hallmark of the firm's work. The coach trained three principals who passed on their knowledge to the rest of the office. Beha's office has distinguished itself with an unusually diverse client constituency, from small community groups with limited resources and many age groups to larger institutions. She has specialized in starting new cultural initiatives such as community performing arts centers and design work for Native American cultures.

A British firm, Waldman and Jim, offers alternative part-time or flex-time contracts to women employees who need them. Gail Waldman, a partner in the firm, has no difficulty informing clients if their project architect is not in. She explains, "After all, even full-timers are not accessible all day."[72]

In sum, managing diversity clearly produces dividends in the workplace, and the architectural profession is no exception. Chapter 8 highlights in greater detail how architectural firms can effectively manage diversity. When women, persons of color, gays and lesbians, and persons with disabilities work side by side with white male architects, they are better able to respond to the complex environmental needs of diverse clients and users.

Chapter 2

WOMEN AS CONSUMERS, CREATORS, AND CRITICS OF THE BUILT ENVIRONMENT

Sexism, racism, classism: architecture's got the lot.
—Naomi Stungo

The star system, which sees the firm as a pyramid with a Designer on top, has little to do with today's complex relations in architecture and construction.
—Denise Scott Brown

HISTORY HAS MUCH TO TEACH US about the complex relationships between gender and architecture. If asked to name the giants of architectural history, students would likely cite Frank Lloyd Wright, Le Corbusier, and Mies van der Rohe. But if asked to name women luminaries in architecture, they would likely draw a blank. In fact, most architectural history textbooks have long ignored the female gender altogether. Even today, when students enter my course in gender and race in architectural studies, they are usually unable to name even one woman architect, dead or alive. The star system has obscured the major roles that women have played on the architectural stage–as clients, preservationists, designers, and critics of the built environment.

WOMEN CLIENTS

It was often the foresight of women clients–progressive, upper-class consumers– that provided opportunities for white male architects to flourish in their careers. For example, in the eighteenth century, the visionary nature of Catherine the Great of Russia catapulted the Scottish architect Charles Cameron into a most successful career, one that he would probably not have had otherwise. In built form, his architectural prowess reflected the grandiose dreams of the empress. She was inspired by the palaces of England, Scotland, Ireland, France, and Germany and wanted her Russian architecture to be even grander than that of Rome.[1]

Three outstanding nineteenth-century women reformers made significant contributions to British housing. The heiress Angela Burdett-Coutts, using Charles Dickens as her advisor and Henry Darbishire as her architect, built tenements for the poor in the East End of London in the 1850s and 1860s. From the 1860s on, Octavia Hill became a landlady and agent for other landlords; her objective was to house the poor more decently by offering inducements such as house repairs, improvements, and other rewards. A generation later, Henrietta Barnett founded Hampstead Garden Suburb, reflecting the ideology of the garden city movement inspired by Raymond Unwin and Barry Parker.[2]

British women continued to have a significant input into housing design. Their influence peaked in 1918 with the work of the Women's Advisory Housing Subcommittee to the Ministry of Reconstruction, just as World War I was drawing to a close. The subcommittee was set up at the urging of a politicized British women's movement, still exultant over winning the vote. Its mission was to visit specimen houses built by the Ministry of Munitions during the war and to advise on various proposed plans for postwar houses for the working class, with special attention to the convenience of the housewife. The subcommittee members were, in effect, consultants to the government.

During the eighteenth and nineteenth centuries, several women housing reformers called for drastic changes in American housing planning and design. A few innovative schemes for ideal communities were implemented that reflected feminist ideas about housing and housework. They often featured communal housing where kitchen and eating facilities were shared. Several books have been written about the accomplishments of these ambitious domestic reformers.[3]

The Dana-Thomas house in Springfield, Illinois, a masterpiece designed by Frank Lloyd Wright, would not have been possible had not Susan Lawrence Dana (1862–1946), later known simply as Susan Lawrence, been willing to pay the bill for Wright's services. Susan Lawrence's father, Rheuna D. Lawrence, had been mayor of Springfield, president of the State National Bank, president of the Springfield Board of Education, and highly prominent in local business and social circles. At his death in 1901, Susan Lawrence Dana inherited the family estate, valued at $3,000,000, a terrific fortune at that time. Between 1902 and 1904 she commissioned a project to remodel her family home. Although it is not clear exactly why she selected Wright to be her architect, it is possible that his aunts, Ellen and Jane Lloyd-Jones of Spring Green, Wisconsin, may have introduced her to his work.[4]

When designing the Dana-Thomas house, Wright was only thirty-five years old. This project was one of his first open-ended commissions, offering him the freedom not only to design the building, but also to create appropriate furnishings for it. As the *Springfield News* reported on March 14, 1903, "The magnitude and magnificence of the new residence begins to come out of the chaos and the indications are that the home will be a mansion unlike any other in the city for size, finish and cost." When it was finally completed, and for about two decades thereafter, the house served as a hub for Springfield's social, cultural, and charitable activities. The Dana-Thomas house is one of the most brilliant examples of Wright's designs anywhere in the United States.

Wright was only one of several prominent male architects whose careers were enhanced by female clients. As Alice Friedman argues in her book on women clients and twentieth-century architecture, women often served as collaborators in design or as catalysts for architectural innovations. Friedman points to Truus Schröder's house (1924), designed by Gerrit Rietveld in Utrecht, Holland; the Villa Stein–de Monzie (1927) at Garches, designed by Le Corbusier for Michael and Sarah Stein, their friend Mme Bagrielle de Monzie, and her adopted daughter; Dr. Edith Farnsworth's weekend house (1945–51) in Plano, Illinois, the work of Ludwig Mies van der Rohe; Constance Perkins's house (1955) in Pasadena, California, designed by Richard Neutra; and the celebrated house (1963) in Chestnut Hill, Philadelphia, that Robert Venturi designed for his mother.[5]

In the early 1900s, women across the United States established many clubs that provided centers for recreational, educational, and civic activities, and they often hired women architects to design them. For example, in Southern California, the Wednesday Club of San Diego hired Hazel Wood Waterman (1865–1948) to design buildings for service organizations.[6]

The prolific career of architect Julia Morgan (1872–1957), described in more detail below, was largely made possible through her association with a network of women clients. First and foremost among them was Phoebe Apperson Hearst, wife of Senator George Hearst and mother of William Randolph Hearst, owner and editor of the San Francisco *Examiner*, who eventually built an empire in newspaper, radio, and film. The Hearst family fortune was made from Senator Hearst's copper, silver, and gold mines, along with investments in millions of acres of land in Mexico and California. When the elder Hearst died in 1891, his will provided that his wife inherit his $20 million fortune because he considered their only son to be a hopeless spendthrift; he proved to be right.

Phoebe Hearst's accomplishments included founding schools and libraries in the mining areas developed by her husband; establishing kindergartens in California and in Washington, D.C.; and helping the University of California, Berkeley, to become the "Athens of the West." With $200,000, she sponsored the International Competition for the Phoebe A. Hearst Architectural Plan for the University of California, which drew international attention to Berkeley and provided the campus with a comprehensive plan for its future.[7] Hearst contributed funds for the Hearst Mining Building and a woman's social center and gymnasium known as Hearst Hall; she also underwrote the Departments of Archaeology and Anthropology, founded what is now the Phoebe Apperson Hearst Museum of Anthropology, and became the university's first woman regent. In 1890, she cofounded the General Federation of Women's Clubs; in 1897, the National Congress of Mothers, which later became the Parent-Teacher Association; and in 1917, the Travelers' Aid Association. Her support for the national Young Women's Christian Association (YWCA) and its many buildings throughout the country reflected her desire to help the new class of young working women.[8] By the time she died in 1919, Hearst had donated over $1.5 million to the university.

Although Phoebe Hearst is the most famous female benefactor of the University of California's Berkeley campus, other women played important roles by sponsoring major built projects there. Two of that campus's best-known landmarks, Sather Tower and Sather Gate, were funded by Jane Krom Sather, who donated over half a million dollars to the campus between 1900 and 1911, the year of her death. Sather Tower was modeled after the campanile in the Piazza San Marco in Venice, Italy. Visible from miles away, the tower has symbolized the university for students, faculty, alumni, and residents of the San Francisco Bay Area. Other women who donated funds for major building projects on the Berkeley campus include Elizabeth Josselyn Boalt ($100,000 for Boalt Memorial Hall of Law, dedicated in 1911); Mary McNear Bowles ($350,000 for Bowles Hall, the university's first student residence hall, in 1929); Rosalie Meyer Stern ($250,000 for Stern Hall, the university's first residence hall for women, which opened in 1938); and Rhoda Haas Goldman ($23.75 million from the Walter and Elise Haas Fund toward the construction of the Haas School of Business, which opened in the 1990s).[9] Berkeley is only one of many university campuses across the nation that have benefited from the generosity of women benefactors.

The Women's Rights National Historical Park, run by the National Park Service and located in Seneca Falls, New York, was established on the site of the first Women's Rights Convention, held in 1848. Here, for the first time, women came together as a political force to begin the long struggle to win the right to vote. About three hundred men and women attended the convention, and before it ended, sixty-eight women and thirty-two men signed the Declaration of Sentiments drafted by Elizabeth Cady Stanton. The park was authorized by Congress in 1980 and consists of about six acres of land, encompassing the Wesleyan Chapel, the actual site of the convention, as well as Declaration Park, the Stanton home, a visitors center, and an education and cultural center.[10]

Two women, Ann Wills Marshall and Ray Kinoshita, won a national design competition to restore the chapel and adjacent park, which was dedicated in 1993. They worked on the competition while finishing their architecture degrees at Harvard University. Their design preserves the bare remains of the Wesleyan Chapel, stabilizing its roof as a symbol of the building's historic importance. Although the design is minimalist, its emotional impact is strong. The chapel sits on the edge of a sloping lawn, where a honed bluestone wall, constantly washed with a thin veil of water, features the text from the Declaration of Sentiments and the names of the one hundred people who signed it.[11]

Out of over 130 submissions, the team of Weiss/Manfredi Architects won a competition for the design of the Women in Military Service for America Memorial in Washington, D.C. The first memorial of its kind, it captures the previously undocumented history of American servicewomen, honoring all women who have enlisted in the U.S. armed forces. It sits in an unusually prominent location at the entrance to Arlington National Cemetery, where it was inserted into a 1927 neoclassical hemicycle designed by McKim, Meade and White, on axis with the Lincoln Memorial across the Potomac. Groundbreaking took place on June 22, 1995, before an estimated crowd of six thousand, including President Bill Clinton; his wife, Hillary Clinton; and women veterans from World War I through the present. The memorial officially opened in 1997. Its design incorporates a reflecting pool in the plaza fronting the curved gateway and an arc of glass tablets on the upper terrace. The upper terrace provides visitors with a panoramic view of Washington, D.C. The memorial includes a 33,000-square-foot Education Center, which houses a theater, computer registration center, Hall of Honor, conference center, and exhibit gallery. *Washington Post* architecture critic Ben Forgey called the memorial "a perfect gesture in a proper place at a fitting moment."[12] The memorial project had special significance for architect Michael Manfredi, whose mother, Dorothy Manfredi, served in the Army Nurse Corps during World War II. Marion Weiss, the other architect of the project, said that the memorial "is about an assumption that the true power in architecture begins not with the architect, but with a site and the aspirations of an enlightened client. . . . [The project] is about a site perceived as a remnant in spite of its central location on the monumental axis, and a set of individuals perceived as peripheral in spite of their critical role in the military service of this country."[13]

WOMEN PRESERVATIONISTS

The public is largely unaware of the pioneering roles that women have played in historic preservation movements across the United States.[14] As early as the 1850s, the Mount Vernon Ladies' Association (MVLA), a volunteer organization led by Ann Pamela Cunningham, spearheaded the preservation of Mount Vernon, the Virginia home of George Washington. Cunningham soon came to be recognized as a national leader among women, and almost every early preservation group had ties to the MVLA.

The Daughters of the American Revolution (DAR), organized in 1890, also became a significant women's force for historic preservation. It became the first national organization to protect historic sites throughout the United States. In 1892, DAR chapters organized to preserve the Betsy Ross House in Philadelphia, now open to the public as a museum. Countless other projects followed. Since then, the DAR has also placed bronze markers at numerous historic sites across the country. Historically, many women's clubs throughout the United States engaged in preservation interests. In 1916, the National Association of Colored Women (NACW) vowed to preserve the home of Frederick Douglass in Anacostia, a section of Washington, D.C.

In addition to preserving individual sites of national significance, women's groups served as trailblazers by protecting buildings threatened with demolition in urban areas. In 1909, Susan Pringle Frost, an active member of the Charleston Federation of Women's Clubs, began purchasing architecturally significant real estate in Charleston, South Carolina. She was one of the first to recognize the potential of Charleston as a restored historic district.

In 1926, Christine Sterling became interested in Los Angeles's historic Olvera Street. She persuaded the city to begin its historic preservation efforts here, and much later, in 1952, the forty-acre district was designated as a state and city park. During this same period, in 1930, Elizabeth Thomas Werlein organized the Vieux Carré Property Owners Association in New Orleans to restore and preserve the historic homes in the French Quarter, which had become a center for the city's speakeasies and prostitutes during Prohibition. One can only speculate about how Charleston and New Orleans would look today without their colorful historic districts.

Not long after her husband, John F. Kennedy, became president of the United States, Jacqueline Kennedy took the lead in restoring the White House to its original design and also in preserving historic Lafayette Square across the street.[15] Mrs. Kennedy had been educated at Vassar College during the late 1940s, spent a year in Paris at the Sorbonne studying art history, and received her degree in American history from George Washington University in 1951. Her academic background brought her an appreciation for historic art and architecture. As first lady, her preservation efforts garnered national attention, and her televised tour of the White House in 1962 won her many points with both the ratings and the critics.

Were it not for Jackie Kennedy's spearheading the historic preservation movement in the nation's capital, Lafayette Square would likely have been bulldozed. Preliminary plans called for the small-scale, historic residential buildings there to be replaced with a modernist office design similar to those of large U.S. government buildings constructed abroad. Plans to raze the historic Executive Office Building and replace it with high-rise towers were already underway when Mrs. Kennedy voiced her objections. Millions of dollars in architects' fees had already been paid, and during the summer of 1961, President Kennedy formally approved some of the plans. Yet Jackie stepped directly into the controversy over intentions to redevelop Lafayette Square in February 1962, urging those involved to revisit the designs. She stated, "The wreckers haven't started yet, and until

The late Jacqueline Kennedy played a pivotal role in spearheading the historic preservation movement across the United States when she was first lady. Here she is shown with architect John Carle Warnecke reviewing a scale model of Lafayette Square in Washington, D.C., in 1962. Photograph #KN24273, John F. Kennedy Library.

they do, it [the square] can be saved."[16] In a letter to Bernard L. Boutin, administrator at the General Services Administration, the first lady pleaded, "They are now planning to put up a hideous white modern court building. All architects are innovators, and would rather do something new than in the spirit of old buildings. I think they are totally wrong in this case, as the important thing is to preserve the 19th Century feeling of Lafayette Square. So you do as Mr. Finley suggests—write to the architects and tell them to submit you a design which is more in keeping with the 19th Century bank on the corner. It should be the same color, same size, etc."[17]

Regarding the Old Court of Claims building, now the Renwick Gallery, on the corner of Seventeenth and H Streets, also bordering Lafayette Square, the first lady wrote to Boutin:

> It may look like a Victorian horror, but it is really quite lovely and a precious example of the period of architecture which is fast disappearing. I so strongly feel that the White House should give the example in preserving our nation's past. Now we think of saving old buildings like Mt. Vernon and tear down everything in the 19th century—but in the next hundred years, the 19th century will be of great interest and there will be none of it left; just plain glass skyscrapers. The Fine Arts Commission and the architects want to tear this down and put a Park in its place because they think it makes the block look more symmetrical. . . . I hope you will use all of your influence to see that this building is preserved and not replaced with a few trees.[18]

In her high regard for Victorian architecture, Jacqueline Kennedy was ahead of her time; handsome Victorian buildings were not restored in San Francisco and other American cities until several years after her initiatives. The final plan for Lafayette Square, developed by the architect John Carl Warnecke, showed Jackie's strong influence. It included two tall office buildings as background architecture, while in the foreground, and as a low-rise screen, there was to be a series of new brick-clad, nineteenth-century-style rowhouses that tied in with the existing historic buildings. It was one of the first designs of its kind, producing modern architecture while addressing the past, and it has since served as a prototype for defining the concept of adaptive reuse at the federal level. Yet the first lady's actions were scorned by some. Ralph Walker, a member of the Commission of Fine Arts who reviewed the resulting plan, complained, "I just hope Jacqueline wakes up to the fact that she lives in the twentieth century."[19]

Jacqueline Kennedy's brief tenure as first lady inspired a greater appreciation of the arts nationwide. Yet her contributions to the preservation of Lafayette Square were not widely recognized until after her death. At a dinner in 1993, the historian David McCullough, seated next to her, acknowledged her key role in saving Lafayette Square, adding that he was certain that she had been thanked many times before. "'Mr. McCullough,' she responded, 'I have never been thanked.'" As Richard Moe, president of the National Trust for Historic Preservation, and Leonard Zax, trustee of the D.C. Preservation League, later acknowledged, "In a very real sense, Jackie Kennedy had a greater effect on the shape and spirit of the historic heart of the nation's capital than any architect or developer."[20]

Jackie also propelled the revitalization of Pennsylvania Avenue, one of the most important streets in Washington, D.C. She sparked the renovation of older buildings for theater and the arts along and near that thoroughfare, and she worked hard to ensure that adaptive reuse was a key component in the revitalization plans. In urging the passage of the National Historic Preservation Act in 1966, members of Congress pointed to Mrs. Kennedy's preservation efforts as a model not only for Washington, D.C., but also for communities throughout the nation. Following President Kennedy's assassination in 1963, Mrs. Kennedy protested the demolition of New York City's historic Penn Station, and, later on, she helped preserve that city's Grand Central Terminal.

Lady Bird Johnson, wife of President Lyndon B. Johnson, also played a major role in improving the quality of the physical environment when she was first lady.[21] Not only did she plant flowers in public spaces, but she also planted environmental values in the minds of the country's leaders and citizens. She often wrote in her personal diary about her interest in natural resources and environmental issues. Although many sources inspired her work, she was especially impressed by the work of Jane Jacobs, author of the classic text *The Death and Life of Great American Cities,* who influenced a generation of architects and planners. Johnson had heard her speak at a luncheon in 1964 and was especially struck by her comments about the lack of money "for the upkeep of an existing park."[22]

Lady Bird's most significant legislative achievement was the Highway Beautification Act of 1965. Her experiences campaigning with her husband across Texas and around the United States—and seeing the bleak highways, junkyards, and billboards blighting the countryside—inspired her to help improve the national landscape. Without her influence, the highway beautification bill would never have become law at that time. Her involvement in this legislative process sparked both high praise and sharp criticism. In Montana, for example, a billboard appeared calling for the "Impeachment of Lady Bird." Despite this, she continued to oversee the implementation of the Highway Beautification Act from its passage in 1965 until she left the White House in early 1969.

Like her predecessor in the White House, Lady Bird Johnson was a strong proponent of preservation. She lent her public support to the National Trust for Historic Preservation and fostered a favorable climate that led to passage of the National Historic Preservation Act in 1966. She also guided an effective campaign to improve the monuments, parks, and public vistas of Washington, D.C. In 1982, as she approached her seventieth birthday, she donated $125,000 and sixty acres of land east of Austin, Texas, to establish the National Wildflower Research Center. The center, which includes 300,000 square feet of research space, cosponsors symposia on wildflower research and, along with highway departments in other states, examines how roadside wildflowers reduce mowing and maintenance costs by millions of dollars annually.

Lady Bird Johnson was a pivotal figure in the history of the environmental movement. As one of the first champions of environmental values to shine in the national spotlight, Lady Bird Johnson legitimized environmental issues in the eyes of the public.

For decades, the architect Beverly Willis played a major role in revitalizing many of San Francisco's postwar neighborhoods. Her renovation of two major buildings on Pacific Avenue in the early 1960s was a catalyst for the renaissance of Jackson Square. Around the same time, owners of three Victorian buildings in historic Cow Hollow approached Willis. Instead of tearing the structures down, she devised an innovative scheme to jack them up, renovate them, replace the crumbling foundations with a new story underneath, and create a miniature mall. The overwhelming success of this commercial complex led to the rebirth of Union Street. Her prolific design work in the Bay Area and elsewhere has continued to stimulate urban revitalization. Willis wrote about her ideas and her career in the book *Invisible Images*.[23]

Since the late 1970s, Ann Beha has given new life to historic buildings in New England and elsewhere. Her firm, Ann Beha Associates, has built a national practice focusing on the contribution of museums, historic sites, and civic and academic institutions to American culture. Among her most notable projects are the preservation master plans for the Massachusetts State House, Trinity Church in Boston, that city's Symphony Hall, and the Fogg Museum at Harvard University. In 1995 the firm completed the award-winning renovation of Jordan Hall at the New England Conservatory of Music.

Beverly Willis, FAIA, of Beverly Willis Architects, designed the Union Street Stores in San Francisco, completed in 1963, a major renovation that sparked the revitalization of several city blocks. Photograph courtesy Beverly Willis.

Architect Ann Beha has played a major role in restoring historic buildings such as this 1995 award-winning renovation of Jordan Hall at the New England Conservatory of Music. Photograph courtesy Wheeler Photographics.

WOMEN DESIGNERS

Women designers have been around for centuries, but only recently have their contributions to the built environment been recognized. In South Africa, women of the Transvaal Ndebele tribal group were the primary designers, builders, and decorators of vernacular housing. In fact, this is still the case for many African tribal groups.[24]

Native American women played a major role in fabricating tipis. Among the Blackfeet, who dominated the upper Great Plains north of the Missouri River and east of the Rocky Mountains, women depended on men to hunt buffalo, but men depended on women to transform the buffalo hides into shelter. Women constructed these tipis cooperatively, usually completing them during the course of a day. More often than not, early male anthropologists failed to acknowledge that the role of Native American women in their tribe was not only important, but essential.[25] In fact, women were designers and builders in many Native American tribes.[26]

Another early trace of women designers can be found as far back as the fifteenth century in Florence, Italy. In 1436, a woman submitted a model to a design competition for the lantern of the Duomo. She was apparently a member of the Gaddi family, a wealthy, influential lot, which included artists of great distinction in Florence. Six submissions were received and Brunelleschi's model was ultimately selected, but only five of the contestants were named in documents. The sixth was referred to simply as an "Anonimo Fiorentino."[27] Brunelleschi's biographer, Antonio Manetti, remains silent about one submission by "una femina."[28] Almost three hundred years later, Plautilla Brizio (or Bricci) became the first known woman professional architect; she practiced in Rome during the 1760s.[29]

Most likely the first European country in which women graduated from architectural school in a university was Finland (the first country to give females the right to vote), where they can be traced back to the 1890s. At the time, women could be admitted to the university there, but only by special permission, petitioning for "exemption of her sex." Yet in most countries, women were not allowed into architectural schools until the late nineteenth and early twentieth centuries. In Russia, the first private design school for girls, called the Women's Architectural Classes, opened around 1899 in Odessa; in Moscow, the Women's Construction Courses offered training in design and construction beginning in about 1906. Yet neither school offered an academic degree. It was not until the 1917 Revolution that Russian women were allowed to enroll in architectural schools. In Austria, Martha Bolldorf-Reitstaetter was the first woman to graduate in architecture from the Vienna Academy of Fine Arts, but not until 1934.

In the United States, land grant universities were open to both women and men from the time that their architectural programs began. But they were not open to African Americans, Native Americans, Mexican Americans, and other students of color, male or female. Cornell University and Syracuse University opened the doors of their architecture programs to both genders in 1871, and the University of Illinois in 1873. Mary Page and Margaret Hicks were the first women to graduate from architectural school; Page from the University of Illinois in 1878 and Hicks from Cornell in 1880. Yet not all Ivy League schools were as enlightened as Cornell. By 1915, Harvard University still did not admit women into its architectural program. In that year, when Katherine Brooks Norcross wanted to study at Harvard's Graduate School of Landscape Architecture but was denied admission, two Harvard instructors, Professors Henry Frost and Bremer Whidden Pond, offered to teach female students. Although some of the Harvard men referred to it as the "Frost and Pond Day Nursery," or "The Little School," Norcross and other women students were serious, and in 1916, the Cambridge School was founded. It operated until 1942.[30]

The first published design by an American woman architect was an 1878 student project for a workman's cottage by Margaret Hicks (1858–1883). In 1888, Louise Blanchard Bethune (1856–1913), who entered the male-dominated profession through an apprenticeship at a Buffalo, New York, architectural office, became the first woman elected to membership in the American Institute of Architects. At a speech to the Women's Educational and Industrial Union in 1891, she stated: "Women have entered the architectural profession at a much earlier stage of its existence even before it received legislative recognition. They meet no serious opposition from the profession nor the public. Neither are they warmly welcomed."[31]

One of the most prominent figures in American architectural history is Sophia Hayden (1869–1953), the first woman to graduate in architecture from the Massachusetts Institute of Technology. She designed the Woman's Building at the World's Columbian Exposition of 1893 in Chicago, a structure decorated by three women artists, Mary Cassatt (1844–1926), Mary MacMonnies (1858–1946), and Candace Wheeler (1827–1923). The building provided a tangible incentive for more women to pursue architecture as a career.[32]

The second female graduate of MIT's architecture program was Marion Lucy Mahony (1871–1961). She and her husband, Walter Burley Griffin, enjoyed successful careers both in the United States and in Australia. (For further discussion about her accomplishments, see the section on husband-wife designer teams, below.)

The most prolific woman architect of twentieth-century America is Julia Morgan. She enrolled at the University of California, Berkeley, in 1890, at age eighteen. She was the only woman student in the engineering program there at that time, and she graduated in 1894. During her years as a student at Berkeley, she worked with Bernard Maybeck, one of the leading figures in the California Arts and Crafts movement. Struck by her talents, Maybeck encouraged her to pursue studies in architecture, passing on a rumor that the Ecole des Beaux-Arts in Paris might be ready to accept women. In 1898, she became the first woman to enroll at that school. On the stiff entrance examination, Morgan ranked thirteenth; only ten French students and two other foreigners were ahead of her. In 1904, she became the first woman architect registered in the state of California.

Morgan is best remembered for her twenty-five-year professional association with William Randolph Hearst. It culminated in the outstanding design for Hearst Castle, the magnate's extravagant home in San Simeon on California's central coast. One of that state's most popular tourist attractions, it is often compared to the palace at Versailles. At the time, it was one of the nation's most significant architectural commissions. From 1920 through 1938, during the building's design and construction, Morgan traveled to the site almost weekly by train and taxi from her San Francisco office, two hundred miles to the north. Throughout her forty-seven-year career, Morgan designed approximately seven hundred buildings in California and elsewhere, almost all of which were built. Her projects included single-family houses, residential apartments, churches, schools, college buildings, stores, hospitals, and YWCAs.[33]

Mary Colter (1869–1958) left a lasting legacy in the American Southwest, where she was inspired by the architecture of the Native Americans as well as by Spanish colonial buildings. Among her most well-known works are those along the South Rim of the Grand Canyon, in Grand Canyon National Park: Hopi House, an interpretation of an Indian pueblo; Desert View Watchtower, which resembles a prehistoric ruin; Bright Angel Lodge, an inn in the rustic style; and Lookout Studio and Hermit's Rest. Bright Angel Lodge took two years to build and cost $500,000 in 1935–37. Its interior featured a "geological fireplace" constructed from rock found on the South Rim and laid in the actual order of its geological formation, from bottom to top.[34] To understand this magnificent landscape, Colter descended the canyon on a construction cableway. A pioneer of the architectural style later labeled National Park Service rustic, Colter inspired many other architects.

In Winslow, Arizona, she designed La Posada, a sprawling hotel and railroad station in the Spanish Colonial Revival style, which opened in 1930. Her client was the Fred Harvey Company, which employed her for almost half a century.

Mary Colter designed the Bright Angel Lodge located along the South Rim of Grand Canyon National Park, Arizona. It was one of the most significant architectural commissions to be given to a woman at that time. This photo was taken c. 1937. Photograph courtesy Grand Canyon National Park, #9675.

Other designs to her credit include ornate interiors at La Fonda Hotel in Santa Fe, New Mexico; and Union Station in Los Angeles, which featured a blend of Southwestern design elements and art deco geometry. Five of her buildings are currently National Historic Landmarks, and several have been or will soon be restored. In an article in *Preservation* magazine spotlighting Colter's career, Arnold Berke asks why her works at the Grand Canyon are well known, while she, herself, is not. Berke writes, "Many explanations come to mind but fail to explain the silence—why, for example, one can search in vain for her name in nearly every history of American architecture. (She was almost the exact contemporary of Frank Lloyd Wright and Julia Morgan. . . .) Mary Colter waits outside the pantheon, a rara avis even in the rosters of also-rans."[35]

Marcia Mead (1879–1969) planned housing for African-American war workers in Washington, D.C., during World War I. She also designed numerous YMCA buildings and was a member of the United States Housing Commission. Ida Annah Ryan (1883–1960) researched and designed what she proposed to be the model tenement. Lois Howe (1884–1967), who had a Boston firm, specialized in the design of low-income public housing. The work of these American architects reflects their commitment to social concerns and especially to low-income housing. As Milka Bliznakov has written, "Close collaboration between user and architect, careful adjustment of the space to the user's needs, personalizing and humanizing the built environment often expressed users' preferences rather than the architect's design philosophy."[36]

In 1910, Lilian Jenette Rice (1889–1938) was one of the first women to graduate from the School of Architecture of the University of California at Berkeley.[37] A native of San Diego, she returned there and began her career in the architectural office of Hazel Wood Waterman, a talented designer previously associated with the well-known architect Irving Gill. Later Rice worked for Richard Requa, architect of the 1935 California Pacific International Exposition at San Diego's Balboa Park. In 1922 his firm, Requa and Jackson, received a commission to design and supervise the construction of a planned development in northern San Diego County. The commute proved difficult for the principals, who had more lucrative projects downtown, so they turned the project over to their associate, Lilian Rice, who worked on it for five years.

As resident architect of Rancho Santa Fe, Rice was inspired by the site's rolling hills and eucalyptus groves, and she designed an environment that blended architectural, landscape, and urban design. She created clusters of residential and commercial structures along a wide, landscaped street. Arcades covered the sidewalks, and white-walled townhouses were topped by red-tiled roofs. Entrance gates led to intimate patios and courtyards overflowing with colorful bougainvillea, banana and pepper trees, and stately palms. Rice's regional style—a form of Spanish Colonial architecture with adobe wall construction—draws from the natural beauty of the area as well as its historic associations recalling the early days of Rancho San Dieguito. Among Rice's most notable accomplish-

Lilian Rice designed and supervised the construction of Rancho Santa Fe, a new community north of San Diego, California. As resident architect, she created an environment that blended architectural, landscape, and urban design. Pictured is the Inn at Rancho Santa Fe which she designed; completed in 1923. Photograph courtesy Rancho Santa Fe Historical Society.

ments there are the Inn at Rancho Santa Fe, a school, a library, and numerous commercial structures and private residences. By 1927, despite the fact that many San Diegans viewed Rancho Santa Fe as "in the middle of nowhere," over 80% of its land had been sold. In the following year, its homeowners formed an association to ensure the protection of their community. Rancho Santa Fe had become a prototype for future developments. Rice opened her own firm in the late 1920s, and in 1931 she was one of the few women to gain membership into the AIA. She continued her architectural work until her sudden death after emergency surgery in 1938. Years later, her legacy lives on. Nine of her buildings at Rancho Santa Fe are listed on the National Register of Historic Places.

Although a horticulturist rather than an architect, Kate Sessions (1857–1940), one of Rice's contemporaries, figured prominently in the design of San Diego's urban environment. Long before the terms became popular, she was one of California's first environmentalists and conservationists. Through an extensive network of contacts in South Africa, Asia, Spain, Australia, New Zealand, Mexico, and South America, Sessions imported hundreds of plant species and grew them from seedlings at her nursery. Among these were the Bird of Paradise, Bracelet Bottle Brush, and Poinsettia shrubs; Star Jasmine vines; Banyan and Twisted Juniper trees; and a wide variety of palm trees. Never before had they been seen in Southern California. In 1892, in exchange for leasing thirty acres of City Park, Sessions was required to plant a hundred trees in the park and another three hundred ornamental trees throughout the city every year. As a result, Sessions left her mark throughout the region, and she soon became known as the "Mother of Balboa Park."[38]

During World War I and World War II, increasing numbers of women enrolled in architectural schools, particularly throughout Eastern Europe. The new states there provided stipends and fellowships for academic education to their top students, both women and men. Moscow's first State Architectural Office, founded in 1918, included four women who were then working on their architectural degrees at Moscow Polytechnic Institute: M. Markuse, E. Altgausen, I. Danilova, and S. Abramova. In the 1920s, many women graduated in architecture from the Higher Art and Technical Studios, formerly known as the Moscow Free Studios. From this time on, particularly in Eastern Europe, according to Milka Bliznakov, women were instrumental in helping to transform the profession from a "gentleman's aesthetic preoccupation of stylistic concerns to a social commitment for public welfare. . . . Architects were no longer decorators of cultural artifacts but creators of culture."[39]

In the Weimar Republic, Czechoslovakia, Poland, and Russia, the works of the architectural avant-garde—which included many women—exemplified this new-found social significance. In 1929, the Russian architect Lidia Konstantinovna Komorova was elected to the editorial staff of *Contemporary Architecture (SA)*, the magazine of the Society of Contemporary Architects. Her career included both design and research, and in 1937 she completed her Doctor of Architecture degree. Similarly, Maria Kruglova's career also drew upon both design and research, and in 1941 she began teaching at the Moscow Engineering-Construction Institute and she later taught at the Moscow Architectural Institute. Luibov Zalestskaia, who worked on designs with Kruglova, also engaged in a teaching and research career at the Moscow Architectural Institute. Nonetheless, the work of Russian women architects remains relatively unknown. As elsewhere, their work was rarely published, their buildings have often been destroyed, early records have disappeared, and their contributions have been overlooked.

In the United States, the Arts and Crafts movement sparked the emergence of interior design as a profession. According to the critic Aaron Betsky, it "marked the entrance of women into the design world—but only in a limited arena and according to principles originally set by men."[40] By the 1920s, women were designing more than just domestic interiors. Their arena had expanded to stores and restaurants as well. This marked an important distinction: men continued to design spaces for work and production, while a few pioneering women began to delve into the design of spaces for work and consumption. Eileen Gray (1879–1976), who collaborated with Le Corbusier, and Florence Knoll, who in 1946, with Hans Knoll, cofounded Knoll Associates, one of the most successful furniture design companies in the world, flourished in this era. Nonetheless, they remain isolated examples.

Women's enrollment in American architectural schools has increased significantly since the 1960s. In the late 1960s, women comprised under 6% of all architectural students nationwide; that figure more than doubled during the 1970s and quadrupled during the early 1980s.[41]

As the women's movement evolved, and as more women began to enter the ivory tower as architectural faculty, the 1970s witnessed the advent of a series of books addressing gender issues in architecture. Among the earliest works were Doris Cole's *From Tipi to Skyscraper: A History of Women in Architecture* and Susana Torre's edited volume *Women in American Architecture: A Historic and Contemporary Perspective*.[42]

Around that same time, journal articles spotlighting the recent accomplishments of women and people of color began to appear. In 1981, the journal *Heresies* published a special issue entitled "Making Room: Women and Architecture." In 1985, a volume edited by Gisela Ecker, entitled *Feminist Aesthetics,* was published, followed foue years later by Ellen Perry Berkeley and Matilda Mc-Quaid's anthology, *Architecture: A Place for Women.*[43] Both the January–February 1991 issue of *Inland Architect* and the October 1991 issue of *Architecture* magazine were devoted to women in architecture. *Landscape Architecture*'s May 1995 issue highlighted the work of women landscape architects.

Norma Sklarek wrote a fascinating essay in 1990 that included several brief biographies of women architects in the United States and abroad.[44] Among the American architects spotlighted were Natalie de Blois, Kate Diamond, Sarah Harkness, Jane Hastings, Denise Scott Brown, Margot Siegel, Cathy Simon, Virginia Tansmann, Anne Griswold Tyng, and Beverly Willis. Other noteworthy publications of the 1990s included Clare Lorenz's *Women in Architecture: A Contemporary Perspective,* featuring profiles of international women architects; Leslie Weisman's *Discrimination by Design: A Feminist Critique of the Man-Made Environment;* and three anthologies: *The Architect: Reconstructing Her Practice; Architecture and Feminism;* and *The Sex of Architecture.*[45]

The American Institute of Architects has undertaken surveys of women in architecture from time to time. Its 1983 study revealed that the overwhelming majority of the nearly one thousand women architects surveyed had been discriminated against primarily in advancement, work assignments, and salary. Such discrimination has led to problems with self-esteem and self-confidence for some women architects, thus slowing their career progress. In 1983, the average woman architect had eleven years of experience and earned $27,000 annually, compared to $40,500 for her male counterpart.[46] Based on survey responses from twenty-nine firms in the Detroit area, a 1985 article published in the journal *Women and Environments* pointed out discrimination in hiring, salary, and relative position in firms.[47]

A 1989 *Progressive Architecture* reader poll, "Women in Architecture," revealed that most of the 1,300 respondents believed that women have fewer opportunities and receive fewer rewards than men with the same levels of experience. In a 1991 *Progressive Architecture* reader poll, nearly a quarter of the 734 respondents reported evidence of habitual sexual or racial harassment in their offices. Other empirical research includes Karen Kingsley and Anne Glynn's 1992 study of women architecture alumni of Tulane University, and Anne McDermott's master's thesis based on surveys from the group Chicago Women in Architecture.[48]

The dilemmas faced by diverse designers are not unique to the United States. In many countries, women's roles in the architectural profession paralleled the

American experience. This was the finding of Blanche van Ginkel, the first female president of the Association of Collegiate Schools of Architecture, who traced the history of women in architecture in Canada.[49] Across the Atlantic, Lynne Walker provided a fascinating account of the entry of women into the architecture profession in Britain. She argued that although women were actively involved in architecture as designers, builders, craft workers, estate managers, as well as writers, theorists, and clients, the role of women in the profession has been virtually ignored in standard histories of British architecture.[50]

Opposition to women's entry into professions in the United Kingdom was strong. Women were barred from entry into architecture "for their own good"; because of fear that women in architects' offices would lead to the dreaded "commingling of the sexes"; and because there were no "facilities" for the ladies.[51] Still other prohibitions centered around the unsuitability of women to inspect buildings, mount ladders and scaffolds, and deal with workmen and clients. Ironically, this view did not extend to working-class women, who often made the bricks and forged the nails for the nineteenth-century building industry. What was often acceptable for working-class women was not acceptable for women of the upper class.

Although the Royal Institute of British Architects (RIBA) was founded in 1834, it was not until 1898 that the first woman, Ethel Charles, was admitted. In 1900 her sister, Bessie Ada Charles, was allowed in. Together they built a successful architectural practice and went on to receive numerous awards and prizes.[52] Only in 1917 were women first admitted to the Architectural Association, the center for formal architectural training in Britain. Throughout the twentieth century, British architectural schools remained male-dominated institutions; by the late 1980s only 3% of the faculty was female. And by the 1990s, women architects were still few, prompting Martin Pawley to write in the *RIBA Journal,* "Like Sasquatch, Bigfoot and the Abominable Snowman, it seemed that the species 'woman architect' is . . . rarely sighted."[53] Nonetheless, many British women architects have made major contributions to well-known contemporary buildings, including the Joseph shops in West London (Eva Jirincna, 1984 and 1986), Heathrow Airport Terminal 4 (Ann Gibson of Scott, Brownrigg and Turner, 1985), and the Manchester Crafts Village (Gillian Brown of the Manchester City Architects Department, 1982).[54]

Elsewhere the picture varies greatly, country by country. For example, in Japan, by the mid-1980s, only 3% of architecture students were women, and by 1990, fewer than 1% of Japan's Architectural Association (JAA) 7,000 members were women.[55] By contrast, in China, as of 1990, women made up 30% of students in architectural schools as well as architects in practice. At the same time, Beijing had its own women's Architectural Association with over 100 members.[56] The percentage of women in architecture schools in India soared to 50 in 1987 from 10 in 1970.[57]

In Norway, by 1990, about 50% of the students at Oslo School of Architecture were women, but the majority of them did not go on to practice as architects. By contrast, at the same time in Finland, one-third of the country's 1,500 architects were women.[58]

In Russia and elsewhere in the former Soviet Union, a similar ratio can be found; as of 1990, one-third of practicing architects and one-half the students in Russia's architectural schools were women.[59] Despite the oppression that the Communist regime imposed on virtually every segment of society, there were employment opportunities for women that were unavailable in many other parts of the world. While women and men had only minimal personal rights, they did have equal professional status.[60] This level of equality was also reached in Argentina, where as of 1986 almost half of all architects were women.[61]

HUSBAND-WIFE PARTNERSHIPS

Marrying couples have traditionally vowed to remain together "for better or for worse, for richer or for poorer, in sickness and in health," and many women navigate their way through the architectural profession with a marriage partner. Some marry architects and work in joint practice while others work in separate firms. In fact, husbands and wives and/or life partners in the same field are fairly common; many find their mates as students in graduate school or later on as professionals in their place of employment. Although at the time of this writing the AIA does not maintain data on the number of husband-wife teams in architectural practice, it is clear that husband-and-wife architectural partnerships are on the rise. The increased enrollment in architectural schools since the 1960s is one reason for this. For some architects, demanding working conditions, long hours in confined spaces, the intense pressure of meeting deadlines, and a passion for the field are the perfect prescription for romance.[62]

Marriage to or partnership with another architect presents both obstacles and opportunities. Whether married to their male business partners or not, many women designers have been overshadowed by them. Women have often been eclipsed in this way because of the phenomenon of misattribution, one of many subtle forms of discrimination. They do not receive credit where credit is due, and their achievements are attributed to another person. This is by no means unique to architects. For centuries, the accomplishments of many women artists and scientists have been ignored, while their husbands enjoyed fame and fortune.

The architectural profession has long had a tradition of misattribution, and until only recently it has remained a secret. But misattribution is only part of a broader phenomenon: the star system, which routinely credits only a single individual with the accomplishments of many. Countless architects—both men and women—have become forever lost in their stars' shadows as a result. But for women, the problem has been chronic. For instance, in a passage from his autobiography, Nathaniel Owings (1903–1984) candidly described the role of Natalie de Blois (1921–   ), an architect who had to settle for relative anonymity in Owings's well-known firm of Skidmore, Owings, and Merrill (SOM), where she was employed for thirty years. According to one description, she was "Natalie de Blois. Long, lean, quizzical, she seemed fit to handle all comers. Handsome, her dark straight eyes invited no nonsense. Her mind and hands worked marvels in design—and only she and God would ever know just how many great solutions, with the imprimatur of one of the male heroes of SOM, owed much more to her than was attributed by either SOM or the client."[63]

A historical analysis of the partnering phenomenon is revealing. Notable design partnerships throughout the twentieth century have included Charles Rennie Mackintosh (1868–1928) and his wife, Margaret Macdonald (1864–1933); Walter Burley Griffin (1876–1937) and his wife, Marion Mahony Griffin (1871–1961); Ludwig Mies van der Rohe (1886–1969) and his longtime companion, Lilly Reich (1885–1947); Le Corbusier (1887–1965) and his gifted design assistant, Charlotte Perriand (1903–   ); Charles Eames (1907–78) and his wife, Ray Eames (1912–88); and Louis Kahn (1902–74) and his collaborator, Anne Tyng (1920–   ), who worked together for almost three decades, from 1945 until his death in 1974.[64] Behind the scenes, "invisible" women such as Elissa Aalto (1922–94) and Mary Barnes contributed significantly to the work of their famous husband-architects, Alvar Aalto (1898–1976) and Harry Elmer Barnes (1889–1968). The founding members of one of America's most successful architectural firms, the Architects Collaborative (1945–65), were two couples: John and Sarah Harkness, and Norman and Jean Fletcher.[65]

It is no surprise that the reevaluations of Margaret Macdonald, Ray Eames, and other women designers have taken place against the backdrop of the women's movement, gender studies, a questioning of modernism, and a greater appreciation for "subordinate" elements of the firmly entrenched hierarchy of the arts. In that hierarchy, architecture (largely the purview of males) was—and still is, to a large extent—more highly regarded than the so-called "decorative arts" (largely practiced by females).[66] It also comes as no surprise that many of the published works that have reassessed these women are by women themselves.

Well before she ever married Charles Rennie Mackintosh, Margaret Macdonald and her sister, Frances Macdonald (1873–1921), had successful artistic careers of their own. Yet soon after the talented Scottish couple was wed, art critics were instrumental in constructing Mackintosh as the genius-creator and romantic hero, while criticizing Macdonald's collaboration with her husband. Janice Helland, biographer of Margaret Macdonald, admits that

> while they worked together in partnership, Margaret Macdonald is most often remembered only as Charles Rennie Mackintosh's wife, and her art is most often discussed as an addendum to his more important works. Macdonald's designs, usually made into gesso panels, beaten metal panels or embroidered hangings, functioned as decorative postscripts to Mackintosh's architecture or interiors. Thus, in keeping with established art historical hierarchies, architecture retains its lofty position while design assumes a more subordinate role; and in keeping with society's patriarchal structure, the architect is usually perceived of as male, the designer female.[67]

Once Mackintosh was acknowledged, Macdonald was shoved to the margins of discourse surrounding him, "silenced by the fate of her husband's career." In fact, Mackintosh has been the subject of more books, papers, and articles than any other twentieth-century British architect or designer, and his work has been the focus of countless exhibitions, conferences, films, television programs, and educational projects.

Macdonald was not just a contributor to her husband's designs. More than anyone else, Macdonald encouraged her husband to view himself as an artist-architect not just in the Glasgow building trade, but in the creation of a new European architecture.[68] Her correspondence reveals that she handled all the couple's finances, and that he would have been lost without her. In fact, Mackintosh was always proud to acknowledge his wife's strong influence on his work. Toward the end of his life, he wrote her: "You must remember that in all my architectural efforts you have been half, if not three-quarters of them." And he admitted that "I had talent, but Margaret had genius."

Soon after their deaths, a prominent London art critic, P. Morton Shand, publicly disapproved of the role Macdonald had played in her husband's work. He repeated damning comments about her, concerned that a 1933 memorial exhibition of Mackintosh's work, held in Glasgow, should not "give the impression that Mrs. Mackintosh was in any sense considered her husband's equal or his 'alter ego.'"[69] Shand insisted that her work "never could have had any permanent value."[70]

Shand set the pace for critics who followed him. Even into the 1990s, publications about Mackintosh continued to glorify his individual genius while minimizing his wife's collaborative role. Only recently have biographies like Helland's begun to acknowledge that women's contributions to these classic design partnerships were crucial.

Throughout most of her lifetime, Marion Mahony Griffin's accomplishments were eclipsed by those of her husband, Walter Burley Griffin.[71] After graduating from MIT, Marion Mahony returned to her native Chicago, where she became the first woman licensed to practice architecture in the state of Illinois. Early in her career, she landed a job at Frank Lloyd Wright's studio in Oak Park, Illinois, where she worked from 1895 to 1910. In 1911, she married Griffin, then an apprentice in Wright's studio. Although best known for her outstanding renderings of Wright's designs, she played an active role as a designer in Wright's studio as well. One of her best designs is the Adolph Mueller house in Decatur, Illinois, built in 1910.

In 1912, Marion Mahony Griffin's talents as a graphic artist helped her husband win an international competition to plan Canberra, the new capital of Australia. The couple moved "Down Under," remaining there for two decades. Walter went on to achieve international fame and fortune. Marion continued to work at his side, but in his shadow. While their designs were listed in his name, she served as a source of their ideas, a critic of his designs, and the renderer and interpreter of their visions. Yet only occasionally did she affix her own initials on certain drawings. Sources close to the couple contend that some of Walter's major projects in Melbourne, Australia, were actually his wife's: the Australia Cafe (1914), the Capitol Theatre (1922–24); and, along the banks of Sydney's harbor, the Castlecrag Community.

Lilly Reich maintained her own atelier throughout most of her life and left a clearly identifiable legacy.[72] She began her career as a designer of clothing, furniture, and interiors. From about 1920 on she expanded into exhibition design. Her groundbreaking exhibit for the International Frankfurt Fair of 1926 received much critical acclaim and captured the attention of Ludwig Mies van der Rohe, whom she had first met in 1924. The two developed a personal and professional relationship, often collaborating on exhibition projects. Two of Reich's major works were the artistic direction of the exhibition halls at the 1929 Barcelona International Exposition and the 1931 German Building Exposition in Berlin.

Yet Reich's work was eclipsed by Mies's, most notably his German Pavilion of 1929, at Barcelona. As Mies's partner, Reich received the contract for the furnishings in his apartment house in Stuttgart's Weissenhof Housing Settlement, thus becoming the only woman there to design the interior of an entire dwelling. Mies van der Rohe became director of the famous Bauhaus in Dessau in 1930, and in 1932 he offered Reich a position as director of the weaving studio and interiors workshop. She was one of the few women of her generation to obtain a teaching position at an art school.

During the reign of the Nazis, Reich's career took a nose dive. Nazis urged women to forgo their careers in favor of their roles as mothers and housewives. The only way that women artists could carve out careers was to pattern their art and their lives in accordance with Nazi philosophy. As Reich's biographer, Matilda McQuaid, points out, "She was also ignored and excluded because she was a woman. . . . For the most part women were simply banished from public life and the arts."

To make matters worse, Mies received an invitation to teach in the United States, where he emigrated in 1938, leaving Reich behind. She visited him in Chicago the next year but then returned to Germany, where she served as his business representative until 1947. Mies's career soared to its zenith, while Reich's plummeted. Toward the end of World War II, Reich was working at the office of Ernst Neufert on standards for residential buildings, jobs that were far beneath her expertise. Tragically, as the bombs were dropping in Berlin in 1945, Reich fled, losing most of her personal and professional papers, records, and documents. She died two years later, at age sixty-two, following a long illness.

Many critics consider Charles and Ray Eames to be among the most important American designers of the twentieth century.[75] Although most famous for their innovative furniture designs, which became classics of mid-century modernism, their architecture, exhibition design, products, films, and multimedia presentations also brought them international acclaim. In fact, they designed very few buildings, the best known of which was their own house in Pacific Palisades, California (1945–49). Their biographer, Pat Kirkham, contends that much of the existing literature about the Eameses "overprivileges the contribution of Charles in relation to Ray, who, like so many female designers before her, has not always been given due recognition for her many and considerable achievements. To give Ray full credit, however, is not to deny the titanic achievements of Charles but rather to reassess their partnership. . . . The retrieval of Ray Eames from the margins of history forms part of a wider feminist project of studying the lives of and work of women formerly 'hidden from history.' "

Kirkham argues that while stellar contemporaries such as Buckminster Fuller often referred to Charles as a genius, "much of what they admired was his joint work with Ray." By 1940, while Ray Kaiser was enrolled at Cranbrook, she had already been committed to modernism for many years, and she was more avant-garde than Charles Eames had been when he entered the same school in 1938. While many historians view Charles as the force behind the couple's modernist products designed after their marriage in 1941, Ray deserves equal credit. In their early years together, the connection between them was emphasized by their attire. The couple often wore coordinated outfits; their 1944 Christmas card featured them in matching black tee shirts and similar poses, and in a 1947 photograph they were wearing matching gingham shirts. Throughout their partnership, their sense as a couple remained strong, and they enjoyed what was probably the most exciting design practice in the United States at the time. Shortly after the exhibition "Connections: The Work of Charles and Ray Eames," which opened in Los Angeles in 1976, Ray was named "Woman of the Year" by the California Museum of Science and Industry. Yet despite her many accomplishments, in her 1988 obituaries, "most of the assessments of her work . . . were less than generous."

The relationship between Louis Kahn and Anne Tyng was both personal and professional. The twosome collaborated on such seminal works as the Yale University Art Gallery and the Trenton Bathhouse.[74] In 1953, after seven years with Kahn, Tyng left for Rome. She went there on a Fulbright fellowship, but she was also pregnant with Kahn's child. As Tyng explained, "While Louis Kahn began to experience well-deserved recognition for his work, I was the sole passenger on a freighter that was heaving through rough seas on its way to Rome. I felt confident that concepts and buildings Lou and I had developed together were significant achievements for bringing him the fame that he longed for, but on a personal level I had never felt more alone, uncertain, and filled with misgivings. Having Lou's baby was not the breaking-away I was thinking of when I applied for a Fulbright."

During this period, when their daughter, Alexandra, was born, Kahn, who was still married at the time, wrote weekly letters to Tyng in Rome, fifty-three of which were later published in a book. Kahn wrote to Tyng on October 29, 1954, "To be working with you again would be not only marvelous to feel again but good for buildings."

In 1960, when Tyng realized that Kahn was involved with someone else, she suggested to him that their relationship become platonic. "This occurred not long before Lou's and my proposed City Tower was about to be in the Museum of Modern Art exhibit *Visionary Architecture*. I did not get an invitation to the opening. When I asked our secretary about it, she said my name might not be on the credit label. I immediately asked Lou if my name was credited. He answered no, so I suggested it might be better if he called the museum than if I called. . . . He simply called and my name was added. I was profoundly shocked that Lou would do such a thing." Tyng added, "I could not believe that his desire for recognition would erode his integrity, since sharing credit with me would not necessarily diminish his fame."

These cases underscore the fact that misattribution has run rampant throughout the history of the architectural profession. But equally troubling is the fact that the same problem persists at the dawn of the new millennium. About three-quarters (74%) of the respondents in my survey agreed with the statement, "In firms where both men and women are principals, men are perceived as being in charge."

Denise Scott Brown was one of the first women architects to speak out about this injustice. An article in *US News and World Report* described how Scott Brown was "famously snubbed by the architectural establishment" in 1991 when her husband, the architect Robert Venturi—but not she—was awarded the Pritzker Prize for lifetime achievement, despite the fact that the couple collaborate on everything. "We both design every inch of a building together," Scott Brown explained.[75] Elsewhere she confessed, "It's really very difficult to tease us apart, or say 'She does this and he does that.' Such attributions are usually inaccurate. They scant the fact that in joint creativity two plus two don't make four, they may make five. This can't be understood by assigning roles."[76] In 1993, Robert Venturi refused to accept the nomination for the AIA's Gold Medal, among its most prestigious awards, unless it was jointly extended to his partner. It was not. In a 1997 interview, Scott Brown speculated: "The question of being a woman will be in the air forever in my case. If I had not married Bob, would I have gone further or not? Who can tell? But the same question holds for him. If he had not married me, would he have gone further?"

Venturi easily recognizes that "inspiration can be dual," and their collaboration goes far beyond their design work. Both have been prolific writers as well. Yet here too, Scott Brown admits, "I found that no matter whose name was first, if I wrote with Bob, readers presumed Bob wrote it."

Only recently did the architectural press begin to pay much attention to the husband-wife/partnering phenomenon. Martin Filler, author of a 1996 *Architecture* feature article on "Husbands and Wives," admits that, "As recent studies of the early Modernists reveal, they did not work alone—and some of their most important collaborators were women."[77] The topic must have struck a nerve, as soon thereafter, a 1997 issue of *Practices* featured articles highlighting the work of such husband-wife design partnerships as Margaret McCurry and Stanley Tigerman (Tigerman McCurry Architects, Chicago); Robert Venturi and Denise Scott Brown (Venturi, Scott Brown and Associates, Inc., Philadelphia); Tod Williams and Billie Tsien (Tod Williams Billie Tsien and Associates, New York); Marion Weiss and Michael Manfredi (Weiss/Manfredi Architects, New York); and others. The same issue included a large section entitled "Between the Sheets: Partners on Partnering," with pieces by Elizabeth Plater-Zyberk and Andres Duany; Betsy Olenick Dougherty and Brian Paul Dougherty; Brenda Scheer and David Scheer; Frances Halsband (reflecting on her career and that of her husband, Robert Kliment); and other design pairs.[78]

In fact, some of the best known contemporary women architects are part of husband-wife teams. Visibility is a distinct advantage of working in tandem with an architect-husband, especially if the husband is already well known. Yet Deborah Dietsch, former editor-in-chief of *Architecture* magazine, aptly notes that women-owned firms, although increasing in number, have received little attention in the press compared to women architects in partnership with men, especially husband-and-wife teams.[79]

If today's architecture students can name any contemporary women architects at all, those in husband-wife partnerships would likely come to mind. But what about the rest? In an article for *Florida Architect*, Linda Dunyan used a musical analogy to bring the point home: "The 'symphonic syndrome' is . . . , unfortunately, not music to women's ears. While the players in the design and construction process may be able to accept the participation of a woman as the second seat oboist, a woman as maestro is a bitter pill to swallow. The fact is that an architect is trained to conduct the show, but the woman architect is not easily accepted as leader of the team. Old ways, after all, die hard."[80]

One-fifth of my survey respondents (20%) had a spouse or "significant other" who was also an architect. Compared to men, women were almost three times as likely to marry another architect; over a quarter (27%) of the women surveyed, compared to only 10% of the men, had an architect as a spouse. When architects surveyed were asked to describe their mentors, a few cited their spouses.

What are the benefits and costs of working with an architect spouse? It can help both members of the pair become professionally established in the field. Since women are disadvantaged by their underrepresentation in the field, working with a partner or spouse can offset the difficulties of starting out on one's own. My respondents were asked to rate where they thought women architects have the greatest chances for career advancement. Running a husband-wife firm was rated near the top of the list, just under interiors and government work.

Because each partner benefits from the other's ideas, their practice is often greater than the sum of its parts. For instance, Andres Duany credits his own awareness of issues in regional planning to his wife's interest in the subject. Conversely, his understanding of town-planning history influenced Elizabeth Plater-Zyberk.[81] Almost every architect interviewed in the 1997 issue of *Practices* acknowledges the strong symbiotic relation of partners.

Another clear benefit is that many of these women are spared the day-to-day injustices that surfaced throughout my research. Male employees are unlikely to treat a woman architect unfairly when she happens to be their boss. (Note, however, that many women partners face unequal treatment in other spheres, such as with clients and with the press.) Husband-wife teams are less bound by the traditional work-home split; they are forced to find a way to accommodate their family's needs. Many architects who practice with their spouses, including several interviewed in *Practices,* cite this as a major attraction. Frances Halsband wryly describes the initial years of her joint architectural practice with her husband, Robert Kliment: "We moved from the leisurely pace of 80 hours a week to working all the time. Within three years, our income had risen to zero." Later she adds, "It may well turn out that the 'norm' for those vocations that require and thrive on full-time commitment is the dedication of the whole person and the whole family to the task."[82] Yet this raises a host of troubling issues: Must marriage to an architect be a prerequisite for women to succeed? What about those women who prefer not to marry architects—or not to marry at all? What about those women—and men—who can't afford to work all those grueling hours for free?

Partner-architect arrangements have their downside. When work and home are two separate spheres, each spouse or partner has another world in which to escape. But not so when work and home life are meshed. Elizabeth Diller and her partner, Ricardo Scofidio, both live and work in the same space in New York. Her assessment of this arrangement: "We have given up privacy, the ability to call in sick; we have nowhere to go. The boundary [between living and working] is constantly being traversed."[83]

One dilemma faced by husband-wife teams is the ever-present danger that the marriage may dissolve, and then what? Most marriages do not end overnight. Divorce is usually preceded by marital strife and separation. What impact can this discord have on one's architectural practice? What kinds of stress can this place on the workplace—on employees, clients, contractors, consultants, and the firm as a whole? In small offices, especially, where coworkers are more likely to know about each other's personal lives, what effects can marital discord have? In some cases, might employees feel torn, placed in a position of "taking sides" with either husband or wife?

In fact, a number of husband-wife business partnerships have disbanded as a result of broken marriages. Some partners may rebound professionally very quickly, while others may never recover.

Yet another difficulty may arise when one member of the team dies. One of the white women architects (#166, age forty-eight) in my survey struggled to reestablish herself professionally: "When my husband died, our client assumed he was the architect and I was the helper—much of my work disappeared. Then one of our competitors asked me to practice with him—my clients returned. Eventually I went back out on my own."

WOMEN CRITICS

Until only recently the world of architectural criticism, especially in the popular media, has been dominated by white males. One should stop to ask: Who have been the editors of architectural magazines, our architectural critics in local newspapers, and our design critics in national magazines? Whose voices are heard by the public, and whose are missing? For decades, Ada Louise Huxtable was one of the pioneering women architectural critics. More recently, Deborah Dietsch exerted strong critical influence. In 1996, out of twenty-six architectural critics or reporters who wrote for major newspapers or magazines, nine were women.[84] By 2000, of 73 architecture critics, writers, reporters, and editors, 38 (52%) appear to be women, as suggested by their names.[85] While this trend is encouraging, the voices of architects of color are still rarely heard in the world of architectural journalism.

Although their numbers historically have been few, women critics have written some of the most inspiring works about architecture.[86] For example, in the nineteenth and early twentieth centuries, Catharine Beecher and Charlotte Perkins Gilman were two important theorists on domestic architecture, analyzing the need to improve women's economic role in the home.

In the 1860s, Melusina Fay Peirce was among the first to argue that women were oppressed because their work in the home was unspecialized and unpaid, a theory that feminists today would also espouse. Around the time of World War I, women gained prominence as housing reformers. For many years, Edith Elmer Wood was concerned that so many of the nation's poor lived in inadequate housing. In 1935, her *Slums and Blighted Areas in the United States,* published by the Public Works Administration, provided President Franklin D. Roosevelt with the famous line from his 1937 inaugural address: "I see one third of a nation ill-housed, ill-clad, ill-nourished." Wood's goal to improve housing conditions for the nation's underclass was realized with the passage of the National Housing Act of 1937, the impetus for the country's first federally constructed public housing units. Similarly, Catherine Bauer Wurster's writings played a significant role in improving the nation's low-income housing stock. Yet her important contributions were often overshadowed by those of her well-known husband, the architect William Wilson Wurster.

In 1961 Jane Jacobs catapulted to fame with the publication of her book *The Death and Life of Great American Cities.* Now a classic text, her book turned the field of urban planning on its head by calling upon professionals to design places that encouraged "eyes on the street," forcing residents to interact directly with their urban environment, and mixing residential and commercial uses. Jacobs's writings turned her into an icon of renewed interest in cities. In 1997, an international conference entitled "Jane Jacobs: Ideas That Matter" was held in Toronto to honor her work. As the architect Cesar Pelli reflected, "She's had an impact that is still being absorbed. . . . She has shifted the focus from a purely idealistic and theoretical conception of the city to seeing things how they really are, how people actually behave instead of how they are supposed to behave."[87]

It was only during the last quarter of the twentieth century that women were allowed to scale the ivory towers. As women faculty edged their way into the architectural academy, the doors of the publication world cracked open, too. Many took advantage of these new opportunities by pursuing active roles as scholarly writers and critics. Influential writers and their seminal works include: Gwendolyn Wright, *Building the Dream: A Social History of Housing in America;* Dolores Hayden, *The Grand Domestic Revolution* and *The Power of Place;* Clare Cooper Marcus, *House as a Mirror of Self;* and Galen Cranz's *The Chair: Body, Culture, and Design.*[88] These and other books, scholarly articles, and conference presentations by women have enriched the discourse of the field. In 1988, Diane Ghirardo became the first female editor of the *Journal of Architectural Education,* long a bastion for male architecture professors. Soon afterward, she became the second woman to serve as president of the Association of Collegiate Schools of Architecture.

Ever since its founding in 1968, the Environmental Design Research Association (EDRA), a professional organization of environmental designers and social scientists interested in the relationship of people and the built environment, has included large numbers of women. Many works written by EDRA members, both male and female, have called for architects to be more accountable to the public and to design spaces that more clearly respond to users' social, psychological, and cultural needs. Among the more notable women writers whose works have appeared routinely in EDRA's annual *Conference Proceedings* and publications (*Environment and Behavior, the Journal of Architectural and Planning Research;* the *Journal of Environmental Psychology;* and the *Design Research Newsletter*) are Sherry Ahrentzen, Clare Cooper Marcus, Galen Cranz, Kristen Day, Roberta Feldman, Karen Franck, Linda Groat, Min Kantrowitz, Lynda Schneekloth, Amita Sinha, Sharon Sutton, Sue Weidemann, and Polly Welch. Several have analyzed women's use of the built environment, examining such issues as gender divisions in the home—whereby women are typically relegated to the inner sphere and men to the outer realm—and the lack of safety for women in urban streets.

Although most writings on diversity in design have appeared in the scholarly literature and in professional trade journals, the popular press has occasionally picked up on these issues, most often in articles by women journalists who share an interest in architecture. A handful of major city newspapers have highlighted women architects in their feature articles.[89]

A 1996 article in *US News and World Report* written by Jill Seider featured several women architects and their projects: Cathy Simon and the San Francisco Main Library, Kate Diamond and the air traffic control tower at the Los Angeles International Airport, and Denise Scott Brown and the Sainsbury Wing of the National Gallery in London. Seider argues that "women architects . . . are beginning to step out from the shadows cast by their more dominant male colleagues. . . . many of them, now established professionals and respected college educators, are putting their stamp on American architecture."[90]

SEXISM AND THE STAR SYSTEM

Women have played significant roles as consumers, critics, and creators of the built environment throughout history, yet many of them remain invisible. In her disturbing 1989 essay, Denise Scott Brown was among the first to protest what she called "sexism and the star system in architecture."[91] Her essay provides a stinging comparison of her own professional success with that of her "star" husband, Robert Venturi, in their professional design practice: "But, as sexism defines me as a scribe, typist, and photographer to my husband, so the star system defines our associates as 'second bananas' and our staff as pencils."[92]

In their dual roles as consumers and creators, women clients sparked the professional development of talented male designers who may not have been discovered otherwise. Women served as wealthy benefactors for major educational institutions, civic organizations, and other entities. They spearheaded the creation of spaces commemorating significant events in women's history. As preservationists, women led the way in saving countless buildings from the wrecker's ball. Some of our nation's most cherished historic districts were saved through the efforts of dedicated groups of women. And some of our nation's first ladies pioneered what we now know as the preservation movement.

For centuries, women have designed and built works of architecture around the globe. But when architecture officially became a profession requiring professional education and licensure, the doors were slammed shut to women. A handful of daring women began to pry them open. A less-than-welcoming educational environment and a hostile work environment awaited them. As they attempted to establish themselves professionally, they encountered tremendous prejudice and discrimination. Their accomplishments were laudable. Yet they remained undocumented, unpublished, and unrecognized. Until recently, most women designers who established practices with their husbands or male business partners worked in their shadows. More often than not, they toiled away behind the scenes while their male partners rose to fame and fortune.

Historically, gatekeepers of the architectural publishing world have excluded all but white males. Only recently have the gates opened to a new breed of architectural scholars. These individuals have played increasingly important roles in the profession by raising issues that their white male counterparts had long ignored. As more women entered the academy, a new type of scholarship began to emerge. A history once lost was now discovered. The accomplishments of previously unknown women architects have now came to light. In addition, social issues such as low-income housing have become the focus of many women writers. Other female critics have pressed architects for a greater social conscience, pleading with them to integrate user needs—including those of women and children—into their designs. They were the first to call for diversifying the profession and to examine the challenges faced by those underrepresented in the field. The voices of diversity added resonant notes to the chorus of architectural critics.

The recent wealth of publications about feminist issues in architecture has prompted other observers to take a look at the role of masculinities in architecture.[93] No matter whether the writers are women or men, they have found that investigating how gender relates to space and place is now fertile ground for analysis.

In retrospect, the civil rights and women's movements of the 1960s were turning points in the history of diversity in design. Slowly but surely, the numbers of women architects began to increase. Gender barriers to the architectural profession began to break down. Progress has been substantial. Despite significant gains, however, women remain marginalized in the architectural profession.

Chapter 3

SEXUAL ORIENTATION, RACE, AND ETHNICITY

I possessed natural skill at drawing and an instinctive interest in the design of buildings. I determined, when I was still in high school, to become an architect. When I announced that intention to my instructor, he stared at me with as much astonishment as he would have displayed had I proposed a rocket flight to Mars.

—Paul Revere Williams

JUST AS ARCHITECTURAL HISTORY TEXTS have traditionally ignored women, they have also overlooked other actors on the architectural stage. Homophobia, racism, classism, and the star system kept gays, lesbians, African Americans, Asian Americans, Latinos/Latinas, and other ethnic groups out of the profession. But in fact, members of these underrepresented groups have long been instrumental in reshaping our American landscape. They have played essential roles as clients, consumers, creators, and critics of the built environment.

GAYS AND LESBIANS IN DESIGN

Until recently, relatively little had been published about the experiences of lesbians and gays in architecture–their roles as consumers or creators of the built environment. But lately some fascinating work has begun to emerge. First, consider gays and lesbians as *consumers* of the built environment. For decades, gay and lesbian bars remained secret, purposely hidden from public view. This was mainly for safety reasons to prevent those who frequented them from danger and persecution.[1] Only in the latter portion of the twentieth century did these venues become more visible.

The environmental psychologist Maxine Wolfe has traced the history of lesbian bars in the United States, their meanings for lesbians in different communities, their relationship to lesbian culture, and the emergence of the lesbian and gay political movements. She notes that most literature on women and environments has overlooked the role of lesbian spaces, thus reflecting a heterosexist bias. Wolfe describes how lesbian bars as public meeting places for so-called "deviant" women historically have been subject to police raids, closings, and arsons. The women who frequented them were targets of humiliation, arrests, rapes, and beatings by the police as well as by heterosexual men in bar raids and other disruptions. She argues, "The felt need to 'be in the closet,' even in 1992, is because one can still be fired from one's job, lose one's housing or children, be discharged from the military, or thrown out of one's family, if one's identity as a lesbian or gay man is known. Only three states and 60 cities have even limited anti-discrimination legislation and there is none on the national level."[2]

Aaron Betsky has analyzed the characteristics of spaces and places designed or used primarily by gays and lesbians in his book *Queer Space*.[3] He discusses how clubs, salons, tearooms, and bathhouses reflected society's attitudes towards gays. His analysis explains the symbolic quality of remaining "in the closet," which contains both "the secret recesses of the soul and the masks you wear." Comparing lesbian and gay communities such as Mission in San Francisco and Park Slope in New York, Betsky finds those of lesbians to be longer-lasting, less exclusive, and more flexible. Gay communities are characterized by ghetto-like isolation. Like the settlements of immigrant populations of the past, queer spaces have spread from Silver Lake to West Hollywood in Los Angeles; Castro to Noe Valley to Twin Peaks in San Francisco; and from the West Village to the East Village and Chelsea in New York. Betsky argues that the AIDS epidemic virtually destroyed queer space, and that "virtual communities" on the Internet, along with the anonymity of the suburbs, have all but replaced it.

A few cities have issued tour guides and maps pointing out significant places in the gay and lesbian civil rights movement. Along with the Boston Area Lesbian and Gay History Project, the Boston Chapter of Gay and Lesbian Architects and Designers (BGLAD) has issued a map of the Boston area highlighting important sites in gay and lesbian history. Among the sites included are Playland, Boston's oldest continually operating gay bar; Other Voices, the city's first gay bookstore; New Words, the major lesbian/feminist bookstore in the Boston area;

and the Meetinghouse Coffeehouse, a popular cafe for gays in the mid-1970s. On the Harvard and Radcliffe campuses are places where "a roster of queer luminaries" taught or studied, including Gertrude Stein, Horatio Alger, Adrienne Rich, Frank O'Hara, Ralph Waldo Emerson, and Barney Frank, the openly gay Massachusetts congressional Representative.[4]

In many cities, gays and lesbians were urban pioneers who gentrified run-down neighborhoods. In San Francisco, Polk Street, Fillmore Street, and the Castro Street districts underwent a metamorphosis with the influx of gays.[5] Once nondescript commercial strips, they were transformed into lively neighborhoods of bars, restaurants, and shops. Here gays and lesbians assumed important roles not only as designers, but also as citizens and clients who assumed financial risks to invest in questionable parts of town. The revival and restoration of Victorian architecture in San Francisco and other cities across the United States beginning in the 1970s was, in large measure, sparked by gay and lesbian home-owners.

Only recently have we begun to see the homes and interior spaces of gay or lesbian couples identified in mainstream magazines like *Architectural Digest, Metropolitan Home,* and *Elle Decor.* The August 22, 1996, issue of the *New York Times* featured Wisconsin congressional Representative Steve Gunderson and his partner, Rob Morris, an architect, in its "At Home With" column. As Jonathan Boorstein points out, "Four years ago, it was unheard of for gay or lesbian couples to have their homes or interiors identified as such in design journals, shelter magazines, or newspaper lifestyle sections. . . . The simple fact that our homes are being presented just as their homes are gives us an odd sort of equality and legitimacy."[6]

Next, consider gays and lesbians as *creators* of the built environment. In San Diego, Jesse Shepard, an accomplished musician who also had a prolific literary career under the name Francis Grierson, designed Villa Montezuma, completed in 1887.[7] Scholarly experts on the villa speculate that Shepard may have been gay, as he never married and had a live-in friend and companion, Lawrence Waldemar Tonner, for over forty years. Villa Montezuma features turrets, an elaborate roof design, unusual woodwork, and exquisite stained-glass windows. As the most prominent example of Victorian architecture in the region, the mansion is now owned by the San Diego Historical Society and it has become a popular tourist attraction.

Aaron Betsky contends that the postmodern movement, which challenged modernist architecture in the 1980s, was spearheaded by gays. Only then, he argues, did interior design become a fashionable concern of architects: "It feminizes architecture and makes decoration and the design of the interior a more masculine pursuit."[8]

It may surprise readers to learn that some of the top names in the architectural profession were gay. But how public were these practitioners about their sexual orientation? Until recently, not very. Jonathan Boorstein has identified a number of historical and contemporary designers and architects he believed to be gay, including Arthur Erickson, Bruce Goff, Frank Israel, Philip Johnson, Charles Moore, and Michael Taylor. Lesbian designers and architects include Elsie de Wolfe, Eileen Gray, and Julia Morgan.[9] (Note, however, that others disagree with his assessment of Morgan's sexuality.) Among gay couples who made their careers in design partnerships are Peter Stamberg and Paul Aferiat; Percier and Fontaine; Jed Johnson and Alan Wanzenberg; and Rodolfo Machado and Jorge Silvetti. Boorstein has identified what he terms a "queer design aesthetic." "Queer design deploys three characteristics: *camp,* or an ironic, subversive point of view; *drag,* or dressing things up to get a theatrical effect or desired result; and *bricolage,* or the assemblage and appropriation of elements—real or referential—to build queer identity for one's self or to identify one as queer to others."[10]

Boorstein raises a number of questions that have yet to be explored. For example, what effects do one's age, class, religion, ethnicity, or geographic region have on queer spaces? How are queer interiors influenced by those popularized in books, movies, theater, and television? What is the result when straights design for gays or lesbians, or when gays or lesbians design for straights?[11]

Lesbians and gays face a unique set of issues in the workplace, and the design community is no exception. In socially liberated areas these problems are less likely to occur, but in smaller towns, and in smaller architectural offices, they may be exacerbated. Forced to listen to distasteful jokes about "fags" and "dykes," gays and lesbians routinely face discomfort in their work environments. While coworkers display photographs of spouses, partners, and children, gay and lesbian employees who have not revealed their sexual orientation at work hesitate to do so. Many may feel uneasy discussing their social lives, caught in a "lie of pronouns": where "I" (instead of "we") went over the weekend, or what "she" (instead of "he") gave me for Christmas. Many opt for silence or lie about their holiday or vacation plans. When employee staff directories list spouses, they may prefer to leave a blank by their names.

The AIDS epidemic has left a devastating trail of death and destruction, wiping out a large portion of the design community. The challenges for designers and partners with AIDS can be gut-wrenching. For instance, if a gay architect's partner is diagnosed with AIDS and his boss doesn't even know his sexual orientation, he may never consider asking for a leave from work. A gay worker who loses a partner needs to take off time to grieve, yet if coworkers are unaware of his home life, he may return to work before he is emotionally ready to do so. A 1994 article in *Progressive Architecture* described a firm that laid off staff members diagnosed as HIV-positive.[12] Although such actions are prohibited under the 1990 Americans with Disabilities Act, they still occur.

For gay and lesbian architects, coming out is an ongoing process, one that occurs over and over with every new social situation. As one woman put it, "Bringing it up is like opening a curtain and letting someone have a look at a world that they have never seen before, with you as their guide. The dynamic that results can seem a lot like teaching the course 'Gay Life 101' to your colleague, who may be a peer or a supervisor or even the company president. It feels awkward, and I feel self-conscious as I start to guide them through my world."[13]

Some coworkers will openly let gays and lesbians know that they can accept their sexual orientation as long as they don't talk about it. Yet to many gays and lesbians, keeping quiet about their personal lives means that they can't be accepted at all. As a result, many feel isolated and alienated in the workplace.

Another corollary to their invisibility is their apparent interchangeability with other lesbians or gays. In fact, this pattern is seen with all underrepresented groups in the workplace—whether they be gay or straight. When there are so few of any one kind of individual, people tend to mentally put them in the same box, mistaking one for the other.

Some workers tend to confuse supporting equal rights for gays and lesbians or speaking out against homophobia and being gay or lesbian oneself. Many heterosexual employees fear that supporting a gay or lesbian colleague may lead others to perceive them as homosexual. Afraid of "guilt by association," they are likely to remain silent. Some gay and lesbian employees avoid each other at work for this reason.

What are the consequences of "coming out" in a small architectural office today? Can gays and lesbians be covered on their partners' insurance policies? What are the unique experiences faced by lesbians, as compared to gays? In an architectural work environment dominated by men, does a gay male have a professional advantage over a lesbian? And what about gay and lesbian *critics* of architecture? How often are their voices heard, and do we even know who they are? Such issues merit serious exploration.

CLIENTS OF COLOR

Historically, African Americans, Latinos/Latinas, Asian Americans, and other racial and ethnic minorities were most likely to serve as clients of architectural work for religious structures. Around the country, churches, temples, and mosques were built as part of ethnic communities. Community centers have also been built to meet the needs of ethnic groups. In cities with high ethnic concentrations, as in San Francisco's Chinatown, as their economic positions improved, persons of color hired architects, interior designers, and others to build and remodel restaurants, shops, housing, and other building types.

The latter part of the twentieth century saw renewed interest in the historic preservation of racial and ethnic districts around the country, a testament to the commitment to designing for diversity.[14] A case in point is Memphis's Beale Street, a historic district that celebrates the contributions of African Americans to that city. Before the Civil War, it was the home of the region's few free African Americans, and by the beginning of the twentieth century, it had become a bustling business and entertainment center for African Americans throughout the South. W. C. Handy, the "Father of the Blues," began his musical career here, and Beale Street, with its pawn shops, theaters, saloons, banks, clothing stores, and professional offices, became a center for black America well before the civil rights movement of the 1960s. Although many structures in the area were cleared for urban renewal in the 1960s, Beale Street was named a National Historic Landmark in 1966. Ever since, it has undergone a renaissance. Throughout Beale Street there are markers noting significant historical events and architectural structures.[15]

Other noteworthy ethnic districts include Chinatowns in San Francisco, Oakland, New York, Philadelphia, and Washington, D.C.; Los Angeles's Olvera Street, a historic district that celebrates the contributions of Mexican Americans to Southern California; San Diego's Little Italy; and Little Havana in Miami, Florida.[16] In preparation for the 1996 Democratic National Convention, Chicago's Greektown, a lively commercial strip along Halsted Street, underwent a major facelift. A new Hellenic Cultural Center will serve as its focal point. Plans are now underway for a revitalized "Byzantine-Latino Quarter" in Los Angeles, near St. Sophia, a Greek Orthodox cathedral.

In Houston's Third Ward, Project Row Houses was an initiative to renovate twenty-two shotgun houses in a predominantly African-American neighborhood in that Texas city. Currently used for rotating art, photography, and literary projects, the buildings are intended to create a positive presence in the black community.[17]

The 1980s and 1990s saw the construction of some notable museums documenting discrimination of racial and ethnic groups. The Martin Luther King Jr. Center for Nonviolent Social Change, completed in 1981, is the hub of a twenty-three-acre National Historic Site and Preservation District in downtown Atlanta, Georgia. The district encompasses the Victorian home where the civil rights leader was born–the first birth home of an African American to be placed on the National Register; Ebenezer Baptist Church, where King served as co-pastor with his father; King's tomb; and several other residences and shops in Sweet Auburn, one of the United States' most historic African-American cultural and business districts. The King Center promotes the elimination of poverty, racism, and war through research, education, and training in nonviolence. It draws more than 3.5 million visitors each year.[18]

The National Civil Rights Museum opened in 1991 on the site of the former Lorraine Motel in Memphis, Tennessee, scene of the 1968 assassination of Martin Luther King Jr. Its goal is to instill in visitors an appreciation of the history, struggle, important events, and personalities of the civil rights movement. Its 10,000 square feet include exhibits, an auditorium, courtyard, gallery, gift shop, and administrative offices. An exhibit of the Montgomery bus boycott of 1955–56 features a city bus restored to its appearance during that turbulent period. The motel room and balcony where King was shot form the emotional focus and historical climax of the exhibits.[19]

The Birmingham Civil Rights Institute in Alabama opened in 1992, capturing the spirit and drama of those who dared to confront racial discrimination and bigotry. Its Barriers Gallery features fourteen venues conveying the quality of life under segregation from 1920 to 1954, including replicas of a mine entrance, segregated streetcar, newspaper office, shotgun house, classroom, courtroom, and church. Three exhibits in its Confrontation Gallery depict the climate of violence and intimidation that reinforced segregation.[20]

Since its opening in 1993, the world-renowned United States Holocaust Memorial Museum in Washington, D.C., has become one of the most popular tourist attractions in the nation's capital. As of 2000, over 15 million visitors had seen the museum, an average of about 2 million visitors annually. The museum tells the story of the Nazis' systematic efforts between 1933 and 1945 to exterminate the Jews as well as the gypsies, the physically disabled, homosexuals, Polish intellectuals, Soviet prisoners of war, and others.[21]

The Simon Wiesenthal Center Museum of Tolerance in Los Angeles houses original letters of Anne Frank, artifacts from Auschwitz, artwork from Theresienstadt, and bunk beds from the Majdanek death camp. Its Multimedia Learning Center provides visitors with unprecedented access to the history of World War II and the Holocaust. Its "Tolerancenter" features thirty-five hands-on exhibits, one of which, "Understanding the Los Angeles Riots," explains different perspectives on the 1992 uprisings.[22] Such museums educate the public about the physical, social, and cultural consequences of racist societies and totalitarian regimes.

The late twentieth century witnessed the proliferation of museums and cultural centers celebrating the history of particular racial, ethnic, and cultural groups. For example, the Mexican Museum in San Francisco, established in 1975, was the first to focus on the work of Mexican and Mexican-American artists. Originally located in the city's Mission District, a largely Latino neighborhood, it has since moved to Fort Mason along San Francisco Bay, where it has become a popular tourist attraction. The Jewish Museum of San Francisco, designed by Daniel Libeskind, is to open a new building next door to the Mexican Museum in 2002.

Detroit, Michigan, offers numerous structures commemorating the role of African Americans in that city. Its Charles H. Wright Museum of African American History, founded in 1965, moved into a new building in 1985, and in 1997 moved into yet another structure. To date, it is the world's largest African-American history museum and cultural center. The $33 million-dollar facility features a soaring rotunda, one hundred feet in diameter and fifty-five feet from its floor to the top of its dome. Its architectural form symbolizes how African people relate the earth to the sky; the dome has reflective glass and is lit from underneath, enabling visitors to look up to the stars and see themselves reflected on the ground. It was designed by Sims-Varner and Associates of Detroit. Annual celebrations held at the museum include Children's Day, Kwanzaa, and an African World Festival that draws an average attendance of one million over a three-day weekend. African, Caribbean, Creole, American soul, and other international foods are served as part of this event.[23]

Detroit's Graystone International Jazz Museum opened in 1974, celebrating the contributions of jazz artists, largely African American, to the American music scene. That same city's Motown Historical Museum provides a fascinating glimpse into the world of African-American music stars from the world famous recording company. The museum opened in 1988 and underwent a major restoration in 1995. Here fans can rock to Motown sounds, view the elaborate sequined gowns of Brenda Holiday and other female artists, marvel at the costumes of the Temptations, and purchase a look-alike of Michael Jackson's famous glove.

In Atlanta, the APEX (African-American Panoramic Experience) Museum is housed in a beautifully restored 1910 building. Exhibits chronicle the history of the Sweet Auburn area of the city and include a ride on a fifty-seat trolley car, a replica of a turn-of-the-century tram that ran along Auburn Avenue. The museum provides an excellent environment for visitors to learn about the local homes and businesses, many of which are being restored to their original 1920s appearance.

The San Diego Chinese Historical Museum opened in 1996.[24] San Diego's Chinese Historical Society spearheaded the $1.2 million restoration of the old 1927 Chinese mission building. The building served the Chinese community until the 1960s. Today it is the centerpiece of the Asian Pacific Thematic Historic District adjacent to San Diego's historic Gaslamp Quarter. The museum's mission is to collect and preserve documents, photographs, and artifacts about Chinese-American history and to provide an ongoing educational program to help Chinese Americans learn about their heritage, foster cultural exchange and understanding between the Chinese and other ethnic groups, and encourage multicultural diversity. Located on a small corner site in an urban neighborhood, the restoration of the building under the direction of the architect Joseph Wong is simple and stunning. The museum's Asian Garden, designed by Alexander Chuang, now executive director of the museum, and refined by Joe Yamada, a local landscape architect, features a waterfall, stream, small bridge, fish pond, stone path, and decorative rocks. A large bronze statue of Confucius adorns its courtyard.

The museum's exhibits include a permanent display about the history of Chinese and Chinese-Americans in California. The exhibits depict the contributions of Chinese laborers to the construction of the historic Hotel Del Coronado in the 1880s and other major projects. They also highlight the roles of the Chinese in fishing, manufacturing, farming, and service industries as launderers, cooks, servants, and gardeners. The display describes the impact of the Chinese Exclusion Act of 1882 (not repealed until 1943); the Scott Act of 1888, which put an end to the Chinese fishing industry; and the anti-Chinese movement. Special exhibits have focused on hand-painted silk Chinese kites and on bronze sculptures by a young artist from China.

In its short lifetime, the museum has already received numerous honors and awards. In 1996, San Diego's Gaslamp Quarter Foundation presented its Land-

The San Diego Chinese Historical Museum opened in 1996 and now serves as the centerpiece of that city's Asian Pacific Thematic Historic District. It has received numerous design and preservation awards. Museums like this one, focusing on the cultural heritage of special ethnic groups, have sprouted up across the United States. Photograph courtesy San Diego Chinese Historical Museum.

mark Award/Good Neighbor Award to recognize the museum's significant contribution to historic preservation and revitalization. It also received the prestigious Orchid Award for Historic Preservation from the Orchids and Onions Community Awareness Program, where the public votes on its favorite and least-favorite buildings, interiors, parks, public art, graphics, and local planning projects throughout the region.[25]

The National Museum of the American Indian is one of the most recent projects to celebrate designing for diversity. Located on the historic Mall in Washington, D.C., and scheduled to open in 2001, the museum is part of the Smithsonian Institution. It is the culmination of years of meetings with Native American communities throughout the Western Hemisphere. GBQC Architects of Philadelphia in association with Douglas Cardinal are the lead architects, and Jones and Jones Architects and Landscape Architects of Seattle, Washington, are the lead design consultants on architecture and site. Cardinal is a Blackfoot from Alberta, Canada. He also designed the Canadian Museum of Modern Civiliza-

The Longhouse Education and Cultural Center at Evergreen State College in Olympia, Washington, was designed by Johnpaul Jones, a Native American architect, and completed in 1996. It was intended to sustain the relationship between the college, its students, and Native American residents from surrounding Puget Sound communities and Northwest Coast tribes. Jones and Jones of Seattle, Washington, has designed several award-winning buildings for Native American causes. Photograph courtesy Jones and Jones.

tion in Ottawa and the Space Center in Edmonton.[26] A spirit of diversity is embodied in several projects designed by another Native American, Johnpaul Jones, and the firm Jones and Jones, in which he is a partner along with husband-and-wife architects of the same surname, Grant Jones and Ilze Jones: Bosque Redondo Memorial in Santa Fe, New Mexico; the Institute of American Indian Art–Campus Master Plan, also in Santa Fe, New Mexico; the Longhouse Education and Cultural Center at Evergreen State College, Olympia, Washington; the Makah De'aht Tribal Elders' Activity Center, Neah Bay, Washington; and the Spokane Tribe Cultural Learning Center in Willpinit, Washington. At the Institute of American Indian Art in Santa Fe, the "broken circle concept," a recurring theme among Native peoples signifying that "nothing is perfect," is incorporated into the design of the great Center Circle Plaza around which most of the campus is organized.[27]

DESIGNERS AND CRITICS OF COLOR

The history of racial and ethnic groups as designers and critics of the built environment is rich and varied. This section focuses specifically on the roles of African Americans, whose history in the field of architecture has only recently begun to be documented. Latino/Latinas, Asian Americans, and others have made significant contributions to the built environment throughout American history as well. While architectural literature provides scant documentation, some historical accounts have been recorded elsewhere.[28] The contributions to architecture made by people of color is a topic ripe for research and scholarship. One of the most insightful analyses of the African-American experience in architecture is the 1996 essay by Bradford Grant. He compares the experiences of blacks in three historical periods: the era of slavery, the Jim Crow era, and the period of the civil rights movement and beyond.[29]

In a 1997 critique of the work of three prominent African-American architects—Julian Francis Abele, Hilyard Robinson, and Paul R. Williams—Max Bond raised some penetrating questions about why they had remained in obscurity for so long. Color aside, he argues, none of them fits the "mythic masterbuilder mode." Bond blames the profession's narrow, elitist criteria for judging architectural work. The field is so preoccupied with aesthetics that socially responsible design is often overlooked.[30]

African-American slaves played a major role in both the design and construction of plantations all across the American South in the eighteenth and nineteenth centuries.[31] Upon recognizing their talent, some urban slave owners hired out or loaned their slave artisans to work on other plantations. A 1787 contract between Robin deLogny and Charles, a free African-American carpenter, woodworker, and mason, indicated that some free African-American architects were active at that time. Horace King, a slave architect, designed some of the best constructed bridges in Alabama in the 1800s; when one such bridge was constructed in 1873, spanning 614 feet across the Chattahoochee River, it was the longest of its type. In addition to free African-American artisans, African-American planters built large plantation homes and mansions.

Many unknown African Americans designed and built housing for themselves while slaves before the Civil War and as free persons afterward.[32] Slave quarters generally featured a severe, plain design, smaller rooms, and fewer windows than the housing of whites. While porches were added to most houses in the post-slavery period, they were smaller in blacks' houses than in those of houses built for whites in the same vernacular tradition.

Four cultural sources–Spanish, French, British, and American–inspired the dwellings of the African-American slave culture. Pre–Civil War African-American housing in the Southeast was influenced largely by American (British heritage) and French Creole sources. Some housing types influenced by the African-American tradition spread outside the southeastern United States by the late nineteenth century. The shotgun house, in particular, originally developed by African Americans, was prefabricated and shipped outside the region by railroad from New Orleans and Atlanta. Among the variants of the shotgun, or "low house," were the double shotgun, the camelback, the North Shore house, and the lateral wing shotgun. Another housing type developed by African Americans, the "high house" with two-tier front galleries, can still be found along the Gulf Coast, especially in Port Arthur, Texas.

While the shotgun house was an urban vernacular entity that spread from formerly French areas, cottages of black Anglo-Americans are found in the rural landscape along the East Coast, in areas once occupied by the British colonies. In Charleston, South Carolina, the famous two-story "single houses," which faced the side yard rather than the street, were in part influenced by the Jamaican urban house dating back to the eighteenth century. Today, much African-American folk and vernacular housing is fast disappearing from the southeastern United States.

Formal training for African Americans eventually offered opportunities for architectural or technical education. The first industrial arts school for African Americans opened in 1868.[33] Located in Hampton, Virginia, it was originally known as Hampton Normal and Agricultural Institute and is known today as Hampton University. By 1881, Tuskegee Institute in Tuskegee, Alabama, another institution of higher education specifically for blacks, had opened its doors. Its earliest buildings were designed by its African-American faculty, and many of its subsequent structures were designed by Robert Robinson Taylor, hired in 1892, the first African American to graduate in architecture from the Massachusetts Institute of Technology. In keeping with the philosophy of Tuskegee's founder, Booker T. Washington, most of the school's major buildings were built by its students. In 1893 Tuskegee became the first black school to offer training in architecture, and in 1957 it first offered its Bachelor of Science degree in the discipline. In 1911, however, Howard University had become the first predominantly black university to offer a Bachelor of Science degree in architecture, and in 1950 its School of Architecture first became accredited. Howard's location in Washington, D.C., helped make it the capital of African-American architects.

With or without recognized credentials, black architects had long made their mark on the American landscape. In the 1790s Benjamin Banneker, an African-American architect, assisted Pierre Charles L'Enfant in the planning and design of Washington, D.C. Early in the next century, Joseph Francis Mangin, another African American, served as the principal designer of New York's City Hall.[34]

In 1899, John A. Lankford became the first known African American to run an architectural office, located in Jacksonville, Florida. In 1901, after moving to Washington, D.C., he designed a major office and social building in that city, the Pythian Building, which was also constructed by African Americans. Lankford was the first of his race to write a book on architecture, entitled *Artistic Churches and Other Designs* and published in 1923. In 1906, William S. Pittman won a competition for the design of the "Negro Building" at the Jamestown Exposition, the world's fair held in Virginia in 1907. He established his office in Washington, D.C., and later moved to Texas, where he became the first African American to practice architecture in that state.

In 1910, Moses McKissack founded the architectural firm of McKissack and McKissack, now the nation's oldest black-owned architectural and construction firm. From that office, Hilyard Robinson designed the army base adjacent to Tuskegee Institute, where African-American fighter pilots received segregated training. Robinson studied at the University of Pennsylvania and received his bachelor's degree (1925) and master's degree (1931) in architecture from Columbia University. Robinson had served in World War I and later returned to Europe to study the work of the Bauhaus and the Dutch modernists, and he also traveled to Russia. He completed the Langston Terrace Public Housing project in 1936, an early example of low-income housing in Washington, D.C., and the first venture between an African American and a white architectural firm (Erving Porter and Associates). In 1987 Langston Terrace earned a listing on the National Register of Historic Places, and in 1988 it was the subject of a television documentary. It incorporated well-designed open spaces and sensitively scaled details, along with artwork from the "social realism" school, popular in Europe and Latin America at the time; such art depicted working-class figures in heroic poses. Robinson also designed the fine arts complex at Howard University and the Communications Building at Hampton Institute (1960), both of which incorporated sophisticated technology for speech instruction, theater, and broadcasting. According to Max Bond, "Robinson demonstrated a strong commitment to serving and celebrating Afro-America without harboring any sense that such a commitment conflicted with his other, outreaching impulse to assimilate the architectural languages of his time and the broad cultural imperatives of a shared American identity."[35]

Described in *Philly Talk* as a "Forgotten Black Designer," Julian Francis Abele was the first African American to graduate from the University of Pennsylvania School of Architecture, as well as from the Ecole des Beaux-Arts in Paris in 1906; he followed Julia Morgan at the Ecole by only a few years. There he studied Greek and French classical styles, traditions that influenced both his painting and his architecture. He served as chief designer for Horace Trumbauer from 1909 until that firm dissolved in 1938. Trumbauer had embraced a black protégé "despite opposition from within and outside the firm."[36] Along with a technical colleague, William Frank, Abele designed homes for many prominent Philadelphians, and he served as architect for several buildings on the Duke University campus in North Carolina. Ironically, at the time, "Negroes" were barred from that campus. Among Abele's most prominent projects were the Duke townhouse in New York City (1909), now New York University's Institute of Fine Arts; Widener Library at Harvard University (1913); the Free Library of Philadelphia (1927); and the Philadelphia Museum of Art, whose building opened in 1928.[37]

In 1926, thirty-eight years after Louise Bethune broke the gender barrier at the American Institute of Architects, Paul Revere Williams (1894–1980) broke the racial barrier, becoming the first African-American member of the AIA. Karen Hudson's book about her grandfather, *Paul Revere Williams: A Legacy of Style,* provides a visual analysis of this prolific African-American architect's work. He overcame racial discrimination and made a significant imprint on the American landscape, particularly in the Los Angeles area, from which he hailed.[38]

Some contemporary scholars view Williams as a controversial figure. His article, "I Am a Negro," when read in today's context, sounds unduly apologetic and deferential to the white mainstream and even insulting to some African Americans. Nevertheless, his ability to succeed in the architectural profession at the time was laudable.

Although Williams was told early on by his teachers at Los Angeles Polytechnic High School that "only white people hire architects, and they won't hire you," he ultimately proved them wrong.[39] After working his way through school and studying architecture at the University of Southern California, and following an additional two years' study at the Beaux-Arts Institute in New York, in 1915 he became registered as an architect in Los Angeles. He got his first job by copying the names of all architects in the Los Angeles telephone book and seeing them one by one until he found one who would hire him. In 1923, after working for others for several years, Williams decided to go out on his own. The 1920s building boom in Southern California sparked a need for architects. Yet even in the Los Angeles area, where the social climate was more liberated than else-where, clients coming to his office and seeing that he was African American were often taken aback and ready to leave. But here Williams's "tricks" came into play. Once clients were in his office, Williams asked them what kind of budget they had to spend. He would then say that he rarely took on projects with that low a figure, but that perhaps he could offer them some suggestions "free of charge." This served as the bait that drew them in. He would ask them to dis-cuss what kind of "dream home" or building they had in mind. While he sat opposite them during their discussion, he adeptly began to sketch out their ideas—upside down. This enabled them to see their ideas immediately come to life, and, literally, from their own point of view. This unusual ability won him scores of clients.

Paul Revere Williams soon became known as the "architect to the stars," de-signing homes for such film stars as Lucille Ball and Desi Arnaz, Lon Chaney, Betty Grable, Cary Grant, William Holden, Martin Landau, Tyrone Power, Frank Sinatra, and Barbara Stanwyck, among others. Among his other well-known clients were Walter Winchell, reporter and broadcaster in the 1930s and 1940s, and E. L. Cord, manufacturer of Cord automobiles. Another of his landmark structures is the Theme building at the Los Angeles International Airport, with its famous circular restaurant. His work also included modest homes for low-income families, hotels, department stores, and hospitals. By the end of his ca-reer, he had designed over three thousand residences and commercial build-ings. He also published two books, *Small Houses of Tomorrow* (1945) and *New Homes for Today* (1946). Ironically, his race prohibited him even from enter-ing some of the projects that he had designed, such as the Polo Lounge at the Beverly Hills Hotel.[40] In 1939, Paul Revere Williams became the first African-American architect to win a Merit Award for Design Excellence from the AIA, for the Music Corporation of America Office Building in Beverly Hills, Califor-nia. In 1957, Williams broke yet another mold by becoming the first African-American architect elected to the AIA College of Fellows.

In 1929, Cornelius Henderson, a black engineering graduate from the Uni-versity of Michigan, designed the first all-welded-steel factory building in the United States. A decade later, William Moses won a design competition for the state of Virginia's exhibition building at the 1939 World's Fair in New York City. Although he received his prize money, his design was never implemented.

The civil rights movement of the 1960s marked a turning point in the history of African-American architects, cracking open doors that had been slammed shut. In 1965, Harvey B. Gantt became the first African American to graduate from Clemson University. With strong support from the National Association for the Advancement of Colored People (NAACP), and following a controversial court order requiring racial integration, he was admitted to that campus in January 1963. His case made national headlines. Gantt has had a distinguished architectural and political career. In 1984 he was elected mayor of Charlotte, North Carolina.

In 1966 Norma Merrick Sklarek became the first African-American woman member of the AIA. In 1980 she became the first African-American woman elected to its College of Fellows, following Paul Revere Williams by twenty-three years. Also by the 1980s, Sklarek had become vice president and project director for Welton Becket Associates, a major architectural firm in Santa Monica, California. She later went on to work at the Jerde Partnership in Los Angeles. Her designs include a downtown plaza for Sacramento, California, and the Fashion Institute of Design and Merchandising in Los Angeles, both with the Jerde Partnership; the Pacific Design Center in Los Angeles, the San Bernardino City Hall in San Bernardino, California, the Commons and Courthouse Center in Columbus, Indiana, and the United States Embassy in Tokyo, all with Gruen Associates; and Passenger Terminal One at the Los Angeles International Airport, with Welton Becket Associates.[41]

J. Max Bond Jr. became one of the most accomplished African-American architects of the latter part of the twentieth century. He began his professional career in the late 1950s. In the 1960s, Bond spent four years in Ghana designing village libraries, outdoor amphitheaters, and other structures. When he returned to New York City, he helped establish the Architects Renewal Committee in Harlem, cofounded Bond Ryder and Associates, and served as partner in Davis, Brody and Associates.[42] Best known for his work on the Martin Luther King Jr. Center for Nonviolent Social Change, in Atlanta, Georgia, Bond summarized his design philosophy: "I have generally worked for people with little power, rather than those who can afford to build monuments to themselves. In attempting to give form to the strivings of average people, I have sought to contribute to progress and popular empowerment rather than to the status quo and institutional power."[43]

Other African-American architects whose careers flourished in the 1960s and beyond include: Walter Blackburn, Wendell J. Campbell and Susan M. Campbell, Ronald Garner, Robert Kennard, Charles F. McAfee and Cheryl L. McAfee, Harry L. Overstreet, Harry G. Robinson III, William J. Stanley and Ivenue Love-Stanley, Donald L. Stull and M. David Lee, Sharon E. Sutton, Lou Switzer, Jack

Travis, and Roberta Washington. Roberta Washington was one of twenty-six African-American students invited to attend Columbia University on full scholarship in response to its 1968 campus riots. After receiving her degree and later spending four years in Mozambique working on hospital and housing projects, she returned to New York City in 1983 to open her own firm. Her projects include the conversion of a factory to an alcohol crisis center, the Harlem Hospital, and a single-room occupancy hotel renovation.[44]

A number of professional organizations in the architectural field have benefited from the expertise of African Americans. In 1968, Whitney M. Young Jr., director of the National Urban League, delivered the keynote address entitled "Man and His Social Conscience" at the AIA National Convention. (More about this galvanizing speech and the subsequent founding of the National Organization of Minority Architects in 1971 can be found in chapter 4.) In 1970 Robert J. Nash became the first African American to hold a national office in the AIA when he was elected vice president. Six years later, John Henri Spencer became the first person of color to serve as president of the National Architectural Accrediting Board, and in 1978 James C. Dodd became a member of the AIA's board of directors.

In 1983 Howard University held its first conference on the roles of women of color in the field, entitled "Minority Women in Architecture: A Sense of Achievement," with about one hundred African-American women students, interns, and licensed architects in attendance. Another Howard symposium, "Black Women Architects: Looking toward the Future," featured an exhibit on black women architects, panel discussions on the themes "Race, Culture and Gender as Factors in Design Theory" and "Herstory Stories–On Being a Black Woman Professional in the Construction Industry," slide presentations, and workshops on preparing for graduate school and the professional world. At the time of the symposium, in 1992, only forty-nine African-American women were licensed to practice architecture in the United States.[45]

Jack Travis's 1991 book *African American Architects in Current Practice* was the first to document the work of contemporary African-American architects. Travis was inspired to edit this book after the release of the hit film *Jungle Fever*, directed by Spike Lee. Its lead character, Flipper Purify, is an African-American architect struggling to succeed in a large white firm in New York City. The film sparked a flurry of interest in real-life figures resembling the protagonist. (In fact, Travis had designed a home for Lee.) Travis's interviews with thirty-five African Americans in architecture are revealing. He writes:

It is evident that racism is still of paramount concern. The lack of talented, young blacks to fill positions and carry on the legacy of these existing black firms was another major concern. I found that only one firm, that of Lou Switzer, could boast that all of its clients came from the private sector. All of the other firms rely on at least 55% (most of them 85% or more) of their produced work from the public sector. . . .

Yet, these firms endure. Their work attests to the fact that these men and women of color, having to do better than their white counterparts at each juncture of their lives, are indeed special. They have persevered against prejudice, fear, and ignorance to achieve prominence.[46]

Two other works addressing concerns of designers and critics of color are Thomas Dutton's anthology, *Voices in Architectural Education: Cultural Politics and Pedagogy,* which appeared in 1991, and Thomas Dutton and Lian Hurst Mann's anthology *Reconstructing Architecture: Critical Discourses and Social Practices,* published in 1996.[47] In 1990, John Morris Dixon, then editor of the now defunct *Progressive Architecture* magazine, had urged his readers to bring the accomplishments of underrepresented professionals to his attention. After participating in the twentieth annual conference of the National Organization of Minority Architects (NOMA), he recognized that African-American architects had been overlooked by *P/A* and its competitors. Dixon since published several articles on this topic. In 1992, along with several African-American architects, he served as a juror for NOMA's annual honor awards.[48]

A 1990 report of a focus group on "Today's Minority Architect," sponsored by the AIA Minority Resources Committee, pointed out that few role models existed for underrepresented architects and that businesses owned by such individuals had received limited exposure and attention. This may help explain why so few persons of color enter the field.[49]

A 1991 article by Jane Holtz Kay in *Architecture* magazine speaks specifically to the invisibility of African-American architects: "the sort of racial blindness acquired through success has not come to America's black architects. . . . No black architectural history has figured in the canon of Eurocentric architectural education. Neither the vernacular heritage of the black community nor the architecture of Africa are studied in most schools. Only a handful of architects or educators are acquainting blacks with their past as builders."[50]

Two educators, Bradford Grant and Dennis Mann, produced the first dedicated listing of black architects, *Directory: African American Architects,* in 1991. This was followed by a second edition in 1995, listing 1,158 licensed African-American architects. Today it is available on the Internet. When the first directory was sent out to subscribers, Grant and Mann included a short survey asking African-American architects to identify specific issues requiring further research. A total of 101 individuals responded. Among the issues they identified were the need for data on African-American architects in public service versus private practice and on African-American owned firms, and encounters with the glass ceiling for African-American architects in private firms. Grant and Mann pursued this research agenda in a follow-up survey entitled "The Professional Status of African American Architects," in 1995. They sent out surveys to 980 African-American licensed architects and received responses from 382, a 39% response rate. All respondents remain anonymous. Grant and Mann's pioneering survey was one of the first empirical pieces of research to study the perceptions of African-American architects.[51]

Among their key findings: African-American women architects comprise one of the most underrepresented groups in the profession. Of all African-American architects surveyed, over a third (37%) reported receiving their first professional degrees from a historically black university. Almost one out of five respondents (19%) received their architectural degrees from Howard University. The researchers raise a number of questions about why this is so. By contrast, most predominantly white schools of architecture demonstrate a weak rate of matriculation for African-American students. Over half of those architects surveyed (55%) owned their own firms (a figure far higher than the percentage of AIA members who, at the time the study was conducted, owned their own firms—only 33%); 20% were employed in the private sector; and 17% worked in the public sector. The rest were either full-time faculty, retired, or unemployed. Very few African-American-owned firms reported joint venturing with white-owned firms. Such findings lead one to believe that to a large extent, African-American architects practice in a largely racially segregated environment.[52]

Several persons of color who are critics—among them Carl Anthony, Milton Curry, Darrel Fields, Kevin Fuller, Eugene Grisby, Edward Soja, and Camilo Jose Vergara—have focused on environmental design issues concerning the urban community and communities of color. Architects and Designers Opening the Border Edge of Los Angeles (ADOBE LA), a Latino-based group of architects, artists, and designers, has been documenting the Latino presence in the Los Angeles urban landscape. Artists and critics associated with the Cultural Explainers, an interactive public art project, have been collaborating to promote cross-cultural understanding through their art and sculpture in Los Angeles's Koreatown, Pico-Union, and South Central LA.[53] While some of their work is readily available in the popular press, other essays or articles can be found only in alternative publications.[54] As Bradford Grant, himself an African-American architect, expressed the problem, "Critics of color are often not heard beyond the academic arenas or the 'minority' communities. . . . We are very strong and articulate critics of the urban and physical environments, although the dominant society or the established environmental design field may not listen or read our critiques."[55]

Other people of color who are social critics have addressed issues that bear directly on the architectural experience. For example, Cornel West questions the political legitimacy of architectural critics by asking, "Why are they trained as they are, how are they reproduced, and what set of assumptions about history, economics, culture and art inform the curriculum and faculties that educate them?" He also argues that architectural critics hesitate to engage in serious analyses of the complex relationships between corporate firms and architectural practice and the system of social patronage that distinguishes architecture from the other arts.[56]

Based on his interviews with scores of African-American middle-class professionals as well as other research, the African-American journalist Ellis Cose argues that these individuals face rampant racial discrimination but their problems have been overshadowed by accounts of the problems of less-privileged African Americans that dominate the news.[57] Discrimination is often subtle but no less painful. Intense pressures for African Americans to serve as ambassadors of their race result in their weariness with being the "first" and the "only." Would-be trailblazers become disillusioned when they discover that a good education, hard work, and high performance are not enough to determine how high one can rise. Racial discrimination often gets in their way. In many professions, African Americans feel isolated and neglected. Many accomplished professionals complain of "not being in on things," left out of the informal communications network, and without anyone who takes a supportive interest in their careers. All too often, they watch people pass them by, moving into jobs they thought they should have. Although their credentials get them in the door, after just a few years their supervisors offer no more than fuzzy feedback, unsubstantiated with examples. Despite high salaries, many are pigeonholed in race-related jobs dealing with affirmative action, community relations, or "minority affairs." Several believe their careers are being stymied; rather than running into a glass ceiling, they hit one made of cement and steel. The experiences Cose describes mirror those of many African-American architects who participated in my research.

In his book *Reflections of an Affirmative Action Baby*, Stephen Carter candidly discusses his mixed emotions as an African-American law professor who has both benefited and suffered from affirmative action. Although an intellectual, Carter feels that he lives in a box—one formed by the assumptions that others make when they find out he is black. Depending upon whom he meets, the label on that box varies from "Caution: Black Left-Wing Activist, Handle with Care or Be Accused of Racism," to "Careful: Discuss Civil Rights Law or Law and Race Only," to "Warning! Affirmative Action Baby! Do Not Assume That This Individual Is Qualified!"[58] Labels like these may well be applied by others to African-American architects.

RACISM, CLASSISM, AND THE STAR SYSTEM

Members of racial and ethnic groups have always been clients, consumers, creators, and critics of the built environment. Yet they have been historically marginalized by the collective forces of racism, classism, and the architectural profession's star system. Only recently have their contributions to the built environment begun to be recognized.

Ever since the tumultuous civil rights movement, the accomplishments of African Americans in all walks of life have been more fully recognized. But when asked to name even one architect of color, most of today's architecture students are still likely to draw a blank. Would music students have trouble identifying at least one African-American musician? Would law students fail to recognize one African-American lawyer? In this respect, architecture remains an anomaly, adrift in some other place and time. Architectural education draws almost exclusively upon the study of building types in white America, Europe, and other parts of the Western world; hence contributions from elsewhere tend to be downplayed. Most students graduate with no exposure to them at all.

While racist admissions policies once prohibited African Americans from studying architecture at many mainstream colleges and universities, some African-American institutions began to offer architecture as a field of study. Many architects launched their careers there. Like their female counterparts, male African-American architects faced a hostile work environment where they routinely encountered prejudice and discrimination. Ironically, some African-American architects such as Paul Revere Williams designed spaces in clubs, buildings, and neighborhoods from which they, themselves, were banned. Other African Americans commissioned and designed significant religious, community, and civic structures throughout the United States. They and other ethnic groups spearheaded the preservation of historic buildings and urban districts that formed the hub of their own subcultures. More recently, architects of color have been instrumental in designing museums and cultural centers focusing on ethnic groups across the country.

Unlike the world of entertainment and sports, however, where African Americans have long held starring roles, the architectural profession in the United States has all but excluded persons of color from its pantheon. Until only recently the architectural press has failed even to cover their work, and their projects still are rarely featured on the covers of journals such as *Architectural Record* or *Architecture*.

Any discussion of marginality must recognize the role of economic status. In fact, cost prohibits many members of poor families from studying architecture. For a poor student without a scholarship, the journey through architecture school is all but impossible. In architectural practice, too, individuals with lesser economic means are disadvantaged, lacking the network of social contacts that can benefit them professionally. Architects who can afford to join country clubs are able to socialize with wealthy homeowners, developers, and business persons with the means to build new residences and offices. Their paths are likely to cross while playing on the golf course, mingling at parties, or watching their children compete in the swimming pool. Until recently, many such clubs remained bastions of white Anglo-Saxon Protestants, barring African Americans and other racial and ethnic groups as members. Without such opportunities to develop professional contacts, the playing field for racially and ethnically diverse architects has long been uneven, and to a certain extent it remains so today.

Chapter 4

NETWORKS OF POWER

Only Girl Architect Lonely: Wanted—To meet all of the women architects in Chicago to form a club.

—Want ad

A WANT AD WAS POSTED IN 1921 in a Chicago newspaper by Elizabeth Martini, a female architect who felt isolated amidst her male coworkers. Martini later formed the Chicago Women's Drafting Club. By 1932, the club included all fourteen women architects in the area.[1]

Faced with obstacles of sexism, racism, classism, homophobia, and the ever-present star system, underrepresented architects turned to each other for support. While majority architects sought their professional identity from the American Institute of Architects, others found that the organization lacked commitment to the special needs of diverse constituents. Hence underrepresented architects formed groups of their own. These new networks of power helped many struggling architects find a professional home where they felt not only welcome but valued and supported. Unlike the AIA, with its impressive headquarters located around the corner from the White House in Washington, D.C., most of these organizations have no permanent office space. And unlike the AIA, which has scores of professional full-time staff members, most of these organizations are run by volunteers who meet on evenings and weekends. Despite their meager resources, or perhaps because of them, their achievements have been remarkable.

Diverse designers gradually have been changing the face of the architectural profession. In the Los Angeles region, for example, the Equal Opportunity Department of the Community Redevelopment Agency in 1990 listed 126 minority-run architectural service firms: 29% (37 firms) male Asian, 29% (36 firms) African-American male, and 9% (11 firms) Hispanic male. In that same listing, another 29% (37 architectural service firms) are run by women: 6 Asian, 2 African American, and 29 non-minority; none is Hispanic. As Ann Moore, a writer for *L.A. Architect,* put it, "The common denominators for minority and women architects are numerous. They possess intense creative energy. They contend with the fact of difference, and all of them are hungry for work. Their hunger is partly economic, but they also want to participate in the building of the region, and they want to express that impulse through the same medium that they collectively see as the traditional province of white men."[2]

During the last few decades of the twentieth century, new avenues offered diverse designers the opportunity to speak out on gender and racial issues in the architectural profession. In professional organizations, meetings, conferences, and exhibits, their voices have been forceful.

Professional organizations have provided a steady, strong vehicle for consciousness-raising and camaraderie, as their leaders have encouraged participants to raise controversial issues, share experiences with others, and challenge their workplaces to be more receptive to a diverse constituency. Ann Moore reports that Roland A. Wiley, a Los Angeles African-American architect, views the American Institute of Architects as useful for professional development but feels that specialized organizations support "'cultural development.' They provide their members with a deeper understanding of their own ethnic, racial, or gender identity, he believes, and give them an arena for developing ways to overcome their peculiar sets of obstacles."[3]

In architecture such affinity groups include local women's architectural organizations, the National Organization of Minority Architects (NOMA), the Organization of Black Designers (OBD), and the Organization of Lesbian and Gay Architects and Designers (OLGAD). Among their goals are: (1) advancing the status of their members in the profession; (2) increasing the visibility of their members in architecture by promoting activities and exhibiting members' work; (3) networking for job placement and career advancement; and (4) lobbying for issues of special concern to their members in the profession.[4]

WOMEN IN ARCHITECTURE ORGANIZATIONS

Women's architecture organizations in the United States and abroad have been active for several decades. (See table 3.) In 1915, women architectural students at Washington University in St. Louis and at the University of Minnesota formed local groups. In 1922, midwestern women architects and students held a convention in St. Louis, forming a national organization, Alpha Alpha Gamma. In 1948, it was reorganized at the San Francisco convention and renamed the Association of Women in Architecture.[5]

TABLE 3. Chronology of Women-in-Architecture Organizations (Twentieth Century)

1915	Women architecture students at Washington University and University of Minnesota form local organizations
1917	Cambridge School of Architecture and Landscape Architecture opens in Massachusetts
1921	Elizabeth Martini forms Chicago Women's Drafting Club
1922	Midwestern women architects and students hold a convention in St. Louis and form a national organization, Alpha Alpha Gamma
1938	Women's Architectural Club publishes magazine, *Architrave*
1942	Cambridge School of Architecture and Landscape Architecture closes
1948	Alpha Alpha Gamma reorganized at a San Francisco convention and renamed Association of Women in Architecture
1963	Union Internationale des Femmes Architects (UIFA) founded in Paris
1972	Women in Architecture, Landscape Architecture, and Planning opens in Cambridge, Massachusetts
	Organization of Women in Architecture founded in San Francisco
	Alliance of Women in Architecture (AWA) established in New York City
1974	Chicago Women in Architecture (CWA) is founded
	Women's School of Planning and Architecture (WSPA), a national summer program, is established
1978	CWA initiates exhibit "Chicago Women Architects: Contemporary Directions"
	"Women in Architecture: A Historical and Contemporary Perspective" exhibit travels nationally
1981	American Institute of Architects (AIA) Archive of Women in Architecture is initiated
1983	AIA begins collecting data on gender and race of its membership
	Constructive Women Architecture and Design Archive formed in Cammeray, Australia
1985	International Archive of Women in Architecture (IAWA) is established in Virginia
	AIA renames Women's Task Force the Women in Architecture Committee
1988	Three California organizations for women in architecture hold their first joint conference
1988–91	Exhibits "That Exceptional One" and "Many More" make a nationwide tour

TABLE 3. Con't.

1989	AIA's Women in Architecture Committee publishes its first newsletter
1990	California Women in Environmental Design (CWED) is formed
	AIA issues its first Speakers' Bureau focusing on women and minority architects
	Women's Task Force of the Association of Collegiate Schools of Architecture (ACSA) issues its report on the status of women in architectural education
1991	Exhibit "Women's Work: Architecture and Design" showcased in San Francisco at CWED conference
1992	AIA establishes Diversity Task Force and National Diversity Program
	L. Jane Hastings becomes first woman chancellor of the AIA College of Fellows
1993	Susan Maxman becomes the first woman president of the AIA
	"More Than the Sum of Our Body Parts" by Chicks in Architecture Refuse to Yield (CARY) exhibited in Chicago
1994	AIA holds its first National Diversity Conference in Washington, D.C.
1995	"ALICE (Architecture Lets in Chicks, Except . . .) THROUGH THE GLASS CEILING" displayed in San Francisco
1996	"Shattering the Glass Ceiling" exhibit displayed at the AIA National Convention in Minneapolis
1998–99	Art Institute of Chicago hosts "Women in Chicago Architecture" exhibit
	CWA celebrates its 25th anniversary with a series of gala events
2000	"D2K: Connecting the Dots," a series of diversity workshops cosponsored by Arquitectos, CWA, and Illinois National Organization of Minority Architects, held in Chicago

The Union Internationale des Femmes Architectes (UIFA), known in English as the International Union of Women Architects and Town Planners, was founded in Paris in 1963,[6] where it held its first conference. Conferences followed every three years in Monaco; Budapest; Paris; Berlin; Washington, D.C.; Copenhagen; Capetown, South Africa; and other sites. Through exhibitions and workshops, the UIFA routinely promoted the work of its members, who hailed from over fifty countries. The Association of Women Architects, Landscape Architects, Planners, and Women in the Building Industry is based in Australia. The Constructive Women Architecture and Design Archive was formed in 1983 in Cammeray, Australia, and has 150 members.

It was not until 1972 that professional organizations for women in architecture became more widespread throughout the United States. That year saw the opening of Women in Architecture, Landscape Architecture, and Planning in Cambridge, Massachusetts; the Organization of Women in Architecture in San Francisco; and the Alliance of Women in Architecture in New York City. In 1974, Chicago Women in Architecture (CWA) was formed. The Women's School of Planning and Architecture (WSPA), the first such school to be founded, financed, and run entirely by women, was also begun in 1974.

Women-in-architecture organizations in the United States have fallen into two camps: (1) regional components connected with chapters of the AIA and (2) groups not affiliated with the AIA. While they share many goals, they differ primarily in philosophical stance toward the AIA itself. Affiliates of the AIA believe that gender issues can best be addressed as more women join and participate in the institute. Those not affiliated with the AIA contend that it is not sufficiently proactive. Three non-AIA-affiliated California organizations—San Francisco's Organization of Women Architects, Los Angeles's Association of Women Architects, and San Diego Women in Architecture—joined together as California Women in Environmental Design to hold their first joint conference in 1988. In 1989, Women in Architecture, a Denver group not allied with the AIA, claimed that the institute did not address equal pay for equal work, parental leave, and set-aside contracts for women-owned firms.[7]

In the 1970s the AIA formed its task force on women. The AIA Archive of Women in Architecture was initiated in 1981 to collect biographical data on women in the profession.[8] The AIA began collecting data on the race and gender of its members in 1983. In 1985, a complementary but independent archive, the International Archive of Women in Architecture (IAWA), was established to collect and preserve archival material by and about women architects around the world. It is a joint program of the university libraries and the College of Architecture and Urban Studies at Virginia Polytechnic Institute and State University in Blacksburg, Virginia. The archive consists of over 140 collections of papers from women architects and organizations.

In 1985 the AIA's task force was named the Women in Architecture Committee. Four years later, under the leadership of the Chicago architect Carol Ross Barney, it published its first newsletter in an attempt to reach women architects nationwide. Subsequent newsletters were published from 1989 to 1994, after which they were absorbed into AIA's mainstream monthly publication, *AIArchitect.*

In 1991, the AIA Women in Architecture Committee met in Chicago, where it mounted the exhibits "That Exceptional One: Women in American Architecture, 1888–1988," "Many More: Women in American Architecture, 1978–1988," and "Women's Choices, Women's Voices" and held a symposium entitled "Fitting In or Making a Difference." At that meeting the committee reviewed over two hundred submissions from women architects throughout the United States for a special issue of *Architecture* (October 1991) on women architects. All were added to the institute's Archive of Women in Architecture.[9]

A milestone was reached in 1993 when Susan Maxman, principal of her own architectural firm in Philadelphia and recipient of a 1991 AIA honor award, became the first woman president of the AIA since its founding in 1857. Prior to that time, only two women had even come close to the top post: Sarah Harkness and Anna Halpin, each of whom served as AIA vice president, in 1978 and 1980, respectively. Maxman, who, as an undergraduate, had been educated as both an architect and an interior designer, returned to school for a master' degree in architecture while in her thirties and raising six children. She graduated in 1977, worked for several firms in the Philadelphia area, and founded her own practice in 1980.[10]

Another turning point in the history of the AIA was reached in 1992 when L. Jane Hastings of Seattle became the first woman chancellor of the AIA College of Fellows.

CHICAGO WOMEN IN ARCHITECTURE (CWA)

During CWA's first meeting, in 1974, about a dozen women sat on the floor in a small room at Gertrude Kerbis's office.[11] Some came because they felt isolated in their work environment, where they were often the only women professionals in the office. Some came to discuss discrimination, affirmative action, and the challenges of combining architectural work with family responsibilities. Others came simply out of curiosity. Their meetings soon moved to the home of Natalie de Blois, an architect who worked at the Chicago office of Skidmore, Owings, and Merrill for thirty years and was its first female senior designer. By the end of the year, CWA's membership had reached about forty and included practitioners, educators, and students. CWA's inaugural newsletter was soon issued, and regular meetings followed.

One of the organization's earliest activities was the production of a videotape, *Shadows on the Landscape,* aimed at women high-school students interested in a career in architecture. In recognition of their efforts, the producers received a service citation from the Illinois Council of the AIA. The group also established an honors award program to aid outstanding women architectural students at local universities.

In 1978 CWA's exhibit entitled "Chicago Women Architects: Contemporary Directions" provided the first opportunity to publicly display its members' work. It was shown at Chicago's ArchiCenter contemporaneously with a national traveling exhibit called "Women in Architecture: A Historical and Contemporary Perspective." The exhibits drew two thousand visitors and received two awards.[12]

CWA has long been intellectually active. Issues of its bimonthly newsletter,

The Muse, have discussed the debate on affirmative action; spotlighted Gae Aulenti, the Italian architect who completed the interior design of Paris's Musée d'Orsay; and featured profiles of inspiring women architects of the past. In 2000 its committees included Book Club, Education, Membership, Networking, Programming, Public Relations, Women's Business Enterprise, Women in Architecture Task Force, and Newsletter, reflecting the many areas of interest in the group. That same year, the organization celebrated its twenty-fifth anniversary with a yearlong series of special events.[13]

ORGANIZATIONS FOR ARCHITECTS OF COLOR

The American Institute of Architects received a wake-up call when Whitney M. Young Jr., then executive director of the Urban League, one of the nation's largest African-American organizations, addressed the AIA national convention in 1968. (See table 4.) "You are not a profession that has distinguished itself by your social and civic contributions to the cause of civil rights," he proclaimed. "You are most distinguished by your thunderous silence and your complete irrelevance."[14] His harsh words struck a chord with the audience.

Two years later, the AIA created the Minority/Disadvantaged Scholarship program to attract young students from minority and/or disadvantaged backgrounds to pursue professional degrees in architecture. The 1970s also saw the formation of the AIA task force on minorities, which in 1985 became the Minority Resources Committee (MRC). It published its first newsletter in 1989. That same year the AIA sponsored a focus group and roundtable discussion with the MRC. Among the major concerns raised were set-aside work, difficult certification procedures, inconsistent enforcement, and uneven program management; difficulties in securing private-sector commissions; and negative perceptions about underrepresented architects.[15]

At that time, the national MRC steering committee established a network of regional contacts across the United States. Its purpose was to disseminate information about the AIA and current MRC programs, to foster communication among minorities nationwide, and to encourage membership and participation of minority architects in the AIA and in the profession.[16]

Concurrent with these efforts was the establishment of two other fact-finding bodies, the AIA College of Fellows Task Force on the Entrance of African Americans into the Profession and the Association of Collegiate Schools of Architecture (ACSA) African American Task Force. ACSA's task force developed

TABLE 4. Chronology of Organizations for Architects of Color
(Post–Civil Rights Era)

1968	Whitney M. Young Jr. addresses AIA national convention
1970	AIA creates Minority/Disadvantaged Scholarship program
1971	National Organization of Minority Architects (NOMA) is formed in Detroit
1983	AIA begins collecting data on gender and race of its membership
1985	AIA renames Minority Task Force the Minority Resources Committee (MRC)
1989	AIA MRC publishes its first newsletter
	AIA sponsors focus group and roundtable discussion with the MRC
	AIA College of Fellows Task Force on the Entrance of African Americans into the profession is established
	AIA holds its first Minority Fellows reception at its National Convention in St. Louis
	Association of Collegiate Schools of Architecture (ASCA) African American Task Force is established
1990	African American Architectural Archive established at Howard University in Washington, D.C.
	The Organization of Black Designers founded
1992	AIA establishes Diversity Task Force and National Diversity Program
	Los Angeles NOMA members join the Coalition of Neighborhood Developers to help restore South Central L.A., devastated by the Rodney King riots
1993	NOMA president Robert Easter meets with administration officials at the White House
	Exhibit "Design Diaspora: Black Architects and International Architecture, 1970–90" displayed in Chicago
1994	AIA holds its first National Diversity Conference in Washington, D.C.; African-American architect Harvey Gant addresses attendees
1995	Survey conducted on Professional Status of African American Architects, by Bradford C. Grant and Dennis Alan Mann
1996	Raj Barr-Kumar becomes first architect of color to be elected president of the AIA
2000	NOMA annual meeting held in New Orleans
	Directory of African American Architects available online
	Symposium entitled "African American Designers: The Chicago Experience Then and Now" organized by the University of Illinois at Chicago and the DuSable Museum of African American History

proposals addressing three major issues: (1) increasing the numbers of African-American faculty members and visiting critics/lecturers; (2) attracting and retaining additional African-American students into the study of architecture; and (3) providing broad exposure of existing, successful programs or projects designed to attract minorities into the profession. Two other landmark events occurred in the 1980s and 1990s. The 1989 AIA National Convention in St. Louis marked the first time that the AIA hosted its Minority Fellows reception, and in 1996, Raj Barr-Kumar, originally from Ceylon, was elected president of the AIA, the first person of color to be elected to this position.[17]

The National Organization of Minority Architects (NOMA) was formed in 1971, sparked by those attending the AIA national convention in Detroit. A reception hosted by the Michigan Black Architects was the first such event to be included on the convention's program agenda. It was held at the mansion of the legendary Berry Gordy of Motown Records. Twelve African-American architects were cofounders of NOMA.[18]

NOMA soon began its annual conferences, along with its newsletter, *NOMA News.* Its conferences feature expositions, workshops, seminars, symposiums and panel discussions, exhibits, tours, and special events for students. NOMA's awards programs include its Excellence in Architecture Award for professionals, along with student design competitions. In 1990, Howard University established its African-American Architectural Archive. Its purpose is to collect, preserve, and document the work, accomplishments, and involvement of black American architects in the profession.[19]

A unique feature of NOMA conferences has been its "Bro's Arts Ball," a take-off on the formal Beaux-Arts Ball that is a tradition in architecture schools and groups. In 1993 NOMA's event was held in New York City at the United Nations Building and in 1994 at Chicago's Harold Washington Library.[20]

NOMA's leaders have urged its members to have a strong social conscience by empowering people in marginalized communities to shape their environment. The architect and politician Harvey Gantt pleaded with NOMA members at their 1991 conference banquet: "There's a fire burning out of control in our communities everyday . . . and the answers are not always going to come from more money. We cannot be spiritually and physically removed from that population. We've got to get our hands dirty. What's our responsibility as well-educated architects and engineers?"[21]

On a similar note, in the wake of the 1992 South Central Los Angeles riots, Robert Easter, then president of NOMA, addressed the organization's Los Angeles chapter: "We can no longer embrace individual achievement that is absent of any community concern or contribution to social justice and order."[22] Easter also pointed to individuals of color, especially in the entertainment and sports industries, with financial handlers who have no interest in supporting their clients' home communities. In effect, Easter said, those advisors build a "white picket fence" around these celebrities. According to Easter, the same trend is true of many black lawyers, doctors, and community leaders as well as black institutions and churches who believe that employing white architects to design their offices helps define their position in society. He called upon NOMA members to become "fence painters, adding some color to the fences surrounding our most prominent and prosperous celebrities and community leaders."[23] In response to the L.A. riots following the controversial Rodney King verdict, local NOMA members joined the Coalition of Neighborhood Developers to help restore the city's South Central neighborhoods that had been devastated.[24]

NOMA's Los Angeles chapter has also worked to educate its constituent community both about the availability of African-American architects and about the need for architecture. According to Roland A. Wiley, the lack of a major automatic client base within the African-American community is a great concern. Wiley observed, "People in Watts don't just naturally call a black architect."[25]

In March 1993, Easter met at the White House with administration officials of President Bill Clinton, along with representatives of major African-American organizations such as the National Conference of Black Colleges, the United Negro College Fund, the National Medical Association, and the National Bar Association. At that meeting Easter highlighted the benefits of involving African-American architects in urban planning and development. Later that year, NOMA representatives joined members of other professional organizations representing people of color who gathered at the White House to show their support for the North American Free Trade Agreement.[26]

NOMA's twenty-fifth annual convention, held in 1996 in Los Angeles, was marked by a somber mood set by the recent unraveling of affirmative action programs across the nation. If preferential college admission policies and set-aside programs for architects of color were abolished, the group asked, what would be the consequences for NOMA members? For years, many architects of color have depended upon majority teams to include them in bidding for public work. In addition, most of their firms are small, billing well under $1 million annually. The loss of set-aside programs could be devastating.[27]

NOMA members have also called for reforms in architectural education. In 1991 William J. Stanley III, president of NOMA, wrote in a letter to the organization's members, "Our students, educators, interns and practitioners are very concerned about declining enrollments, lack of adequate minority faculty members, isolation, and racism on campus."[28] Promoting architecture as a career to students of color in elementary and high schools has long been another NOMA goal. In this regard, NOMA initiated an architectural design competition for these students. NOMA presented the awards at its "Big Fellows and Little Fellows" reception. Members of the AIA College of Fellows serve as jurors for the competition.[29]

As of 2000, membership in NOMA totaled approximately seven hundred, drawing together a diverse group of practitioners, educators, and students. Paid members numbered about two hundred. Regional professional chapters of

NOMA have formed in Atlanta, Boston, Dallas, Detroit, Illinois, Los Angeles, New York, North Carolina, Philadelphia, Washington, D.C., and elsewhere. Student chapters of NOMA–the National Organization of Minority Architectural Students (NOMAS)–have formed in schools across the United States.

In addition to NOMA, other organizations that serve African-American architects in the United States have included the New York Coalition of Black Architects and the Congress of African American Architects. The International Union of Architects is the counterpart of NOMA abroad. Other international organizations include the South African Union of Architects.

The Organization of Black Designers (OBD) was founded in 1990 by David Rice.[30] It includes not only architects, but also graphic designers, advertising designers, product designers, interior designers, fashion designers, and transportation designers. It currently lists over 3,500 members. Through its education programs and award competitions, OBD endeavors to strengthen and better recognize the quality of work of each of its members, as well as the profession as a whole.

There are also organizations for architects in other ethnic groups. The Asian American Architects and Engineers Association (AAAE), headquartered in San Francisco, was established in 1978 and is now part of a statewide organization, the Council of Asian American Business Associations. Frank Fung was AAAE's first president, succeeded in 1980 by Gordon Chong. The organization now has a Southern California chapter as well. AAAE's mission includes eliminating prejudice and discrimination, economic and otherwise, and providing equal opportunities for its constituency; serving as a clearinghouse and information center; cooperating with public bodies and other organizations on matters of civil rights; and advising on enactment of local, regional, state, and national legislation that affects the civil rights of its members. During the late 1970s, President Jimmy Carter's administration invited AAAE to participate in discussions about increasing business opportunities for persons of color in federal contracting. In 1983, AAAE led the campaign to draft legislation in San Francisco calling for goals of 30% for Minority-Owned Business Enterprises (MBEs) and 10% for Women-Owned Business Enterprises (WBEs) in all city procurements. Once the ordinance was adopted, large architecture and engineering firms established partnerships with smaller MBEs/WBEs, allowing many Asian-owned firms to prosper. In the early 1990s, AAAE organized and conducted workshops to assist residents of Oakland in rebuilding their homes after the devastating fires.[31]

In Chicago, a group of Latino and Latina architects and architectural students belong to an organization called Arquitectos.

ORGANIZATIONS FOR LESBIAN
AND GAY ARCHITECTS

Only relatively recently have lesbian and gay architects "come out of the closet" in the architectural work environment. In 1995, Stephen Glassman, a gay member of the American Institute of Architects' Diversity Task Force, argued for equal civil rights for gay and lesbian designers:

> As an architect, my personal struggle for equality in the profession emerged when I realized that lesbian and gay design professionals were being marginalized, passed over in hiring and promotions, and emotionally traumatized by hostile or insensitive working environments. Daily remarks diminish one's self esteem and affect one's ability to fully contribute. It hurt me to see that the vast majority of gay architects, inhibited from feeling free enough to "come out" in the workplace, were suffering in ways that could not easily be addressed because of their invisibility. My fight to add sexual orientation protections to the AIA's Code of Ethics heightened my awareness of the profession's general lack of diversity and its insensitivity to multicultural and minority concerns.[32]

The Organization of Lesbian and Gay Architects and Designers (OLGAD) is a national organization whose work has focused on three key issues: (1) reclaiming lost history, identifying lesbian and gay architects throughout history and recognizing their contributions to architectural design; (2) identifying spaces and places that have played a significant role in the history of the lesbian and gay movements; and (3) analyzing a unique aesthetic of what gay and lesbian designers refer to as "queer design."

Regarding efforts to reclaim lost history, Jonathan Boorstein's presentation at the 1995 American Institute of Architects' National Diversity Conference recalled his experiences opening up the gay, lesbian, and bisexual caucus at a previous conference session. At that time, he had asked participants to name their favorite gay or lesbian designers or architects and to cite their own gayest or most lesbian designs. When they could name hardly any, he was shocked. He criticized the absence of this topic from architectural history courses.[33] In this respect, according to Boorstein, architecture stands apart from other fields such as literature, where the sexual proclivities of writers are often part and parcel of the educational experience.

A number of regional organizations have formed as well, some affiliated with and others independent of OLGAD. Camille Victour provides an inspiring account of her role in establishing the Boston Gay and Lesbian Architects and Designers (BGLAD), which began in 1991 as a committee of the Boston Society of Architects.[34] In Chicago, the Gay and Lesbian Building and Trade Professionals (GLBTP) issued a directory in order to advertise their collective services to the vast local lesbian, bisexual, and gay communities. The organization includes architects, contractors, home inspectors, interior designers, and others in the building industry.

In the Bay Area, the group Castro Planning + Action (CAPA) was formed in 1995. Formerly known as Eureka Valley, the Castro is the cultural hub of San Francisco's gay and lesbian community, and it serves as a mecca nationwide. As its reputation began to spread, the Castro rapidly became a major tourist attraction. Traffic congestion, increased housing costs, and other urban problems soon followed. Homelessness there reached crisis proportions in the 1990s.[35] CAPA has tried to shape the future of the Castro neighborhood through planning, action, and building relationships with other neighborhoods and city government. The organization includes over one hundred members who address community issues such as housing, economic development, safety, gay and lesbian visibility, transportation, traffic and parking, neighborhood institutions, services, and general planning. CAPA holds neighborhood workshops with the assistance of volunteer planners, architects, and landscape architects. Together they work with local government agencies and neighborhood representatives on proposed changes to the Castro's built environment.[36]

BUILDING BRIDGES:
JOINING FORCES FOR DIVERSITY

In 1991, the AIA revised its public policy on civil rights, stating, "The American Institute of Architects strongly supports equality of rights under the law and opposes any denial or abridgment of equal rights by the United States or by any state on account of gender, race, creed, ethnic origin, age, disability, or sexual orientation."[37] The extant human rights rule in the AIA code of ethics was amended accordingly. In 1992, under the leadership of W. Cecil Steward as AIA president, the AIA formed the President's Task Force on Equal Rights and Proactive Action. Its charge was to present to the AIA board a comprehensive strategic plan to implement the 1991 civil rights policy. It soon became known as the Diversity Task Force and included members from the AIA Minority Resources Committee, AIA Women in Architecture Committee, NOMA, and OLGAD. Later the AIA Diversity Task Force was renamed the Diversity Committee. Its "definition of diversity refers to anyone who has experienced a sense of disenfranchisement in the architectural profession, including but not limited to those people diverse by gender, race, creed, ethnic origin, age, disability, or sexual orientation."[38] In 1992, the Diversity Task Force prepared a "Declaration of Intention to the AIA Board of Directors" outlining several areas needing attention, including AIA leadership, publications, policies, mentorship, education, and employment practices. It received an overwhelming endorsement.

This was the start of AIA's National Diversity Program. It aims to provide all women and underrepresented members with equal access and influence in all levels of the AIA and the profession; to increase visibility and promote public awareness of the contributions that underrepresented architects make to the field; to foster role models and mentors; and to serve as a "gateway" for underrepresented members as they become involved in AIA's professional interest areas and other institute activities. In a typical year, activities have included the AIA National Diversity Conference and two events at the national AIA convention–the Women in Architecture No-Host Dinner and the Minority Fellows Reception–as well as coordinating links with related organizations and AIA component chapters to establish local diversity programs.

In 1994, the American Institute of Architects held its first National Diversity Conference, in Washington, D.C. As I sat in the keynote session and looked around the room, my first reaction was that this was "the photographic negative" of my typical architectural experience. For the first time, women and persons of color were in the majority, rather than the minority. Harvey Gantt was a special guest at the conference. The conference generated an abundance of energy and enthusiasm.

The 1996 AIA diversity conference in Boston featured a tribute to Julia Morgan, Frank Israel, Paul Williams, and Ronald Mace. Their pioneering work has advanced the status of women, lesbians and gays, racial and ethnic minorities, and people with disabilities, respectively. Students from local colleges and universities presented the tribute. The conference's first book signing was held, commemorating the fact that a mass of critical writings on diversity issues was now available. Andrew Young, former mayor of Atlanta, was one of the keynote speakers at the 1998 AIA diversity conference, held in that Georgia city. Attendees participated in a walking tour along Atlanta's historic Auburn Avenue and its Sweet Auburn district. They visited the boyhood home of Dr. Martin Luther King Jr. and the Ebenezer Baptist Church, where King preached.[39]

The National Diversity Conference united architects, designers, students, teachers, AIA leaders, and allied professionals. Conference events encouraged mutual understanding and explored cultural issues in architecture and education. They covered a range of topics, including small-business issues, encountering the glass ceiling, visibility, grassroots advocacy, political activism, education, and design aesthetics. Caucus sessions addressed special needs of women, persons of color, people with physical disabilities, and gays and lesbians.

In 2000, the AIA National Diversity Conference, "D2K: Connecting the Dots," was to be held in Chicago, but the event was canceled due to an insufficient number of conference registrants. However, three local organizations in Chicago—Arquitectos, Chicago Women in Architecture, and the Illinois Chapter of the National Organization of Minority Architects—cosponsored a one-day series of diversity workshops. Patricia Saldaña Natke led a charette to develop a new community center in the heart of the predominantly Hispanic Little Village area of Chicago. Honorary Chair Wendell Campbell, FAIA, one of the founders of NOMA, spoke about his experiences as one of the first African-American architects to establish his practice in Chicago.[40]

Walter Blackburn was appointed to chair the AIA Diversity Task Force in 1992, and he served in a leadership capacity there for six years. He was elected AIA vice president in 1994. During this period he twice sought election as AIA president, but his candidacy was unsuccessful. Had he succeeded, he would have been the AIA's first African-American president. Blackburn died of cancer in 2000 at age sixty-two. The National Underground Railroad Freedom Center, to be built in Cincinnati, soon to be the world's largest African-American cultural facility, will stand as a tribute to Blackburn, its designer.[41]

SPEAKING OUT WITH ART: EXHIBITING DIVERSITY

Several exhibits sponsored by organizations of underrepresented architects have offered unique venues in which to speak out. Their combined influence has been powerful. In fact, exhibits are some of the most effective ways of making diverse designers visible to the public.

An international exhibition of women's architectural work has been displayed at all conferences of the Union Internationale des Femmes Architectes (UIFA). As noted earlier, these events, held once every three years, have rotated to sites around the globe, from France to Scandinavia, Eastern Europe, and South Africa. Exhibits have included those by the German Federal Republic Section of UIFA, the Austrian Cultural Institute, and the Museum of Finnish Architecture.[42]

The major exhibits "That Exceptional One: Women in American Architecture, 1888–1988" and "Many More: Women in American Architecture, 1978–1988," organized by AIA's Women in Architecture Committee and opened at the 1991 AIA national convention, spread the word about the accomplishments of women in architecture when they toured fourteen cities over a three-year period. They are now housed in the International Archive of Women in Architecture in Blacksburg, Virginia.[43] In part, the exhibits marked the one hundredth anniversary of Louise Blanchard Bethune's election to membership in the AIA.

"That Exceptional One" and "Many More" inspired several local exhibits around the United States including: "In Harmony with the Land," organized by San Diego Women in Architecture and the San Diego Historical Society; "Women's Choices, Women's Voices in Architecture," mounted by Chicago Women in Architecture and the Chicago Chapter of the AIA; "Women's Work: Architecture and Design," put on by California Women in Environmental Design and the Organization of Women Architects; "Women Architects of Puerto Rico, the Caribbean, and Florida: Their Work," planned by the Puerto Rico chapter of the AIA and its Women in Architecture Committee; and "Matri/Archs: Pioneering Women Architects of Oregon," organized by the Women in Architecture Committee of the Portland, Oregon, AIA.[44]

Three Chicago architects, Carol Crandall, Kay Janis, and Sally Levine, co-designed "More Than the Sum of Our Body Parts," a 1993 exhibit held at Chicago's Randolph Street Gallery. The trio, along with sixty other architects involved in the exhibit, called themselves CARY, an acronym derived from "Chicks in Architecture Refuse to Yield to Atavistic Thinking in Design and Society." Their name was inspired by the caryatid, a structural column in the shape of a woman that was used widely in the architecture of ancient Greece. Because they shoulder the structural burden of the architecture, caryatids have come to signify the oppression of women. Carol Crandall conveyed the flavor of the exhibit, "We started out with a handful of ideas, many of them sparked by the recession, since we know so many women who have lost their jobs. We began to question how far women have come to be so disposable in the lean times. It was a rude awakening. . . . We wanted the vignettes to be garish and funny and funky at first glance, but on closer examination, to reveal something else, something double-edged."[45]

Much as the Guerrilla Girls aimed to expose the lack of diversity in the art world, the women of CARY, through their multimedia display, sought to expose the exclusion of women in the architectural world. Their message is powerful. Some of CARY's attention-grabbing vignettes are shown in figures 9 and 10.

Chicks in Architecture Refuse to Yield (CARY) to Atavistic Thinking in Design and Society, a group of women architects, staged an exhibit at Chicago's Randolph Street Gallery in 1993. This vignette, "The Glass Block Ceilng," was co-designed by architects Carol Crandall, Kay Janis, and Sally Levine. Photograph courtesy Carol Crandall and Sally Levine.

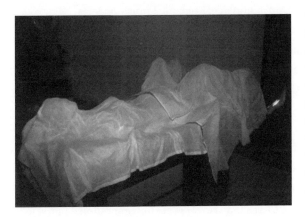

"Just Relax, You May Feel Some Discomfort," another of CARY's vignettes for its 1993 exhibit, depicts a woman awaiting a gyneco-logical exam. It was co-designed by architects Carol Crandall, Kay Janis, and Sally Levine. Photograph courtesy Carol Crandall and Sally Levine.

One of CARY's designers, Sally Levine, followed up two years later with an exhibit entitled "ALICE (Architecture Lets in Chicks, Except . . .) THROUGH THE GLASS CEILING" displayed at San Francisco's New Langton Arts Gallery. Her exhibit sparked much discussion in the media. Like the CARY exhibit, its message was serious but accented with dashes of humor. It included such installations as "The Glass Slipper," which showed the footsteps of the tango painted on the gallery floor, the woman's footprints moving backward and the man's going forward. Another installation, "Shining Armor," addressed the ambiguity of affirmative action and whether or not women need knights in shining armor to help them struggle through the system. A third installation, "Smoke and Mirrors: Now You See Her, Now You Don't," depicted the frustration felt by women who do not receive proper credit for their work, when they are made to feel demeaned and invisible.[46]

In 1998–99, "Women in Chicago Architecture" was exhibited at the Art Institute of Chicago in conjunction with the twenty-fifth anniversary of CWA. This marked one of the first times that the work of women architects was displayed in a major urban museum. About 120 women were represented and projects from twelve firms owned totally or in part by women were highlighted: Bauer-Latoza Studio; DLK Architects; Langdon Associates; Eva Maddox Associates; Mayer Jeffers Gillespie Architects; Maureen Reagan Architects, Ltd.; Roula Associates Architects; Ross Barney and Jankowski; Searl and Associates; Rubio/Durham Architects; Tigerman McCurry Architects; and Urban Works, Ltd.[47]

A 1993 exhibit held at the Chicago Athenaeum Museum of Architecture and Design, "Design Diaspora: Black Architects and International Architecture 1970–1990," featured one hundred built projects designed by fifty black architects from the United States, Canada, Brazil, Jamaica, England, France, Nigeria, Cameroon, Senegal, South Africa, and the Netherlands. A 1994 exhibit, "Design Legacies: A Tribute to Architects and Designers Who Have Died of Aids," was sponsored by Design Pride '94, the first International Lesbian and Gay Design Conference, a special project of OLGAD; Design Industries Foundation Fighting AIDS (DIFFA); and the Elsie de Wolfe Foundation. It commemorated the twenty-fifth anniversary of the Stonewall Rebellion, the New York City uprising that sparked the modern gay and lesbian civil rights movements. It was the first exhibition of its kind and held at Gallery 91 in New York City. As Jonathan Boorstein noted, "Not only has the industry lost many of its brightest talents at their creative peak, but the effects of those losses may reverberate for generations: in the loss of teachers and mentors, and in a collective blunting of the cutting and competitive edge, especially among the avant-garde."[48] Among those designers celebrated were Mark Kaminski, Robin Jacobsen, Michael Taylor, and Robert Currie.

DIVERSE DESIGNERS SPEAK OUT— BUT WHO IS LISTENING?

What have these organizations accomplished? Which of their goals have been achieved? Which have not, and why? To date, such groups have been most successful at providing opportunities for employment, networking, communication, and fellowship for their members. Affinity groups have served as effective sounding boards for those who feel uncomfortable or are being treated unfairly in the workplace. Learning how others have survived and moved beyond their own struggles can be comforting to those who feel frustrated and isolated, especially those working in small firms. Camille Victour describes the benefits of BGLAD to lesbian and gay architects, "For all of us, but especially for me, getting to know one another and hearing other people's stories has helped tremendously. We have given each other the support we need to come out at work. We have found a sense of community, solidarity, and visibility within the profession that was sorely lacking before."[49]

Organizations have provided mentoring opportunities to young people, a key ingredient to diversifying design. Students are welcome as members and encouraged to participate in meetings, conferences, and other activities; those who do take part gain much from their new professional contacts. Many students attend national NOMA conferences, and they bring back to their respective campuses the information gleaned from these events. By mingling with established professionals in the field, they gain familiarity with firms and the path to securing jobs once they graduate.

Another major achievement of affinity groups is increasing visibility, but here the record is mixed. Lectures, conferences, and exhibits have all been highly effective ways of promoting the work of diverse designers. The publication of proceedings such as those of the AIA National Diversity Conferences has ensured that a public record of these activities will be preserved. Yet most publicity has circulated within the profession itself. This is simply part of a wider issue: the popular press has historically given architecture short shrift. It rarely covers architectural events, and when it does, articles are often relegated to the "Entertainment," "Home," or "Real Estate" sections of newspapers.[50] As a result, the public rarely learns about diversity issues in architecture–or about architecture at all.

The record is also mixed regarding the goal of promoting equality within the profession. Although affinity groups have made valiant efforts, they have not achieved improved work conditions in the field. In this respect, they have been far less successful than their counterparts in the legal profession who have changed policies and practices nationwide. But such groups can not effect change singlehandedly. They need the backing of the mainstream organization. What more needs to be done?

1. *Even greater visibility is needed.* When NOMA is next held in Los Angeles, the event could be featured in the *Los Angeles Times.* Or whenever the AIA National Diversity Conference is next held, coverage on national television would garner wide attention. The AIA could assist smaller groups–whether they

be AIA-affiliated or not–by providing press releases to the media. Perhaps architects must invite civil rights leaders such as Jesse Jackson to their events so that journalists will take note.

2. *The history of affinity groups should be carefully preserved.* Right now, such efforts are much too tenuous. Officers of women's organizations must donate copies of their minutes, newsletters, and other archival materials to the International Archive of Women in Architecture (IAWA) at Virginia Polytechnic Institute and State University. In this regard, some organizations have been more successful than others. While some routinely publish newsletters, others have not adequately recorded their own history. Almost all are run on a volunteer basis and on a shoestring budget. As a result, when officers rotate from year to year, materials are often lost. Some groups do house their archives permanently at a central location; for example, CWA records are deposited at the Chicago Historical Society. Other groups store their historical documentation in boxes that move from one person's house to another, making them all too perishable.

3. *Each organization must establish and maintain a presence on the World Wide Web.* Many have already done so. The Internet provides an excellent venue for publishing organizational histories, opening them up for research. Web sites should be updated regularly to include current activities and other pertinent information. Each group should establish a permanent e-mail address, no matter who the current officers are. This allows new members to find the organization easily and sends an image of stability to the outside world.

4. *Officers must be rotated and new members must be encouraged to assume leadership roles.* These are key principles in determining which groups succeed in the long run and which groups fail. This is especially important in all-volunteer organizations with no paid staff and where burnout is likely. In this respect, CWA's policy appears to be a success. Other organizations are in a fragile state, and some, such as San Diego Women in Architecture, have folded altogether. According to one former leader of that organization, the group simply burned out; when it came time for officers to retire, no one was willing to take their place. This scenario is all too common in volunteer organizations whose members have demanding full-time jobs by day and must eke out precious hours during evenings and weekends to run the organization. For those with parental responsibilities at home, the problem is simply compounded.

5. *Age diversity within these organizations must be maintained.* Some groups, such as CWA, have been more successful than others in retaining their older, more accomplished members. If older members feel that they are no longer needed, they are likely to bow out. Yet these senior professionals are key to

maintaining a successful organization. Older members can be featured as guest speakers and their work exhibited at important events. Field trips can be arranged for younger members to visit offices of their older counterparts. Simply highlighting their recent accomplishments in a newsletter is another way to ensure that members of all ages feel valued.

6. *Even greater interaction between "mainstream" and underrepresented architects is needed.* Inviting white males–especially those in professional and community leadership roles–to participate in conferences, exhibits, and other key events sponsored by affinity organizations helps them acquire greater sensitivity to the needs of their less powerful counterparts. Follow-up after the event is essential. For example, white male principals from top firms in Atlanta attending the AIA diversity conference can follow up by inviting underrepresented architects to present their work at AIA local chapter events or at in-house presentations at their firms. Such presentations can ultimately lead to opportunities that are mutually beneficial.

■

Organizations such as CWA, NOMA, OLGAD, the AIA Diversity Committee, and other affinity groups have made substantial contributions to the architectural profession. Their record of achievement during the last part of the twentieth century set the stage for even greater accomplishments in the twenty-first. Just as the new breed of scholars has brought refreshing ideas to the academy, so have these organizations shed new light upon the architectural profession.

Chapter 5

GATEWAYS AND ROADBLOCKS
TO ARCHITECTURAL PRACTICE

> I basically begged for my first job . . . "I'll scrub the
> toilets. I don't care. I just want to work here. . . .
> PLEASE!"
>
> —#110, Asian-American female, age 31

WHILE SOME PARTICIPANTS in my research about the glass ceiling in architecture were members of organizations such as Chicago Women in Architecture and the National Organization of Minority Architects, others chose to fend for themselves. It is often during critical stages in their careers, however, that many architects begin to realize the value of such networks. As a student, a young African-American woman may have experienced no race- or gender-related problems whatsoever. Once she graduates, she may be thrilled to be out of school and competing on the job market. But only when things begin to go awry, through no fault of her own, may she feel the need to turn to others like herself for help.

Architects' professional experiences during critical rites of passage can have long-lasting impacts, coloring their perceptions of the field and their future prospects in it. This is especially true for underrepresented designers whose status in the profession is fragile to begin with. Interviews, internships, the Architect Registration Examination (ARE), and the first job serve as milestones. But are they gateways or roadblocks? My survey and interview respondents shed light on this question. This chapter also examines architects' reflections on their careers. How satisfied are they with their current positions, and with their careers overall?

INTERVIEWING

> My first real interview experience was with a firm in Washington who will remain nameless, because I have zero respect for them, and they do still exist. I walked into the interview and was prepared to talk to the gentleman about the project architect position. And the first question he asked me was, where are my drawings? . . . And basically what he said to me was that I was not qualified to be a draftsman in his firm. And he made that statement without ever having seen anything that I had ever done. And I was very offended by that. That was the worst experience. That was deflating . . . embarrassing . . . upsetting.
>
> And what made it worse is I had another interview [for the same kind of position] . . . two hours after that. And my whole frame of mind was, [I was] not ready to talk to anybody about anything. And when I left that interview, I was told I was *overqualified* for the job. Something didn't click there. So at that point I just decided that I probably was not made for the corporate world. (I-#10, African-American male, age 39)

The interview process is prerequisite to any career. How architects handle interviews affects their willingness to change jobs. For both the potential employee as well as the employer, interviews can be anxiety provoking. For some they can be a pleasant experience, for others an adventure, and for still others a dreaded ordeal that one is forced to endure.

In my survey, architects were asked at how many offices they interviewed before they found their current position. The average was 3.4. Men interviewed at an average of 3.3 offices, while women interviewed at an average of 3.4; and whites interviewed at an average of 3.8 offices, compared to people of color, who had interviewed at an average of 2.6 places of employment. However, these gender and racial differences were *not* statistically significant. I also asked architects how easy or difficult it was for them to find their current position. Over half of those responding (55%) found it easy, while just under a quarter (22%) found it difficult. Again, *no* significant gender or racial differences were found.

Four out of ten (42%) sampled agreed that race, ethnicity, and gender are significant factors when interviewing for architectural positions; however, no significant gender or racial differences were found. Slightly more (45%) agreed that gender is significant; and here significant gender differences were found. As one might expect, compared to their male counterparts, women were much *more likely* to agree that gender is a significant factor when interviewing for architectural jobs. Slightly over half the women sampled (54%) and just over a quarter of the men (28%) agreed with this statement. Even more striking is the fact that over eight out of ten architects (82%) agreed that physical appearance is a significant factor in the architectural interview process. Both men and women strongly agreed on this issue, as did whites and persons of color.

My survey asked respondents how often they had been asked inappropriate questions during an interview for an architectural position, such as inquiries about their marital status or intentions to have children. Although questions like these are technically not illegal, they open a Pandora's box: among other things, they can be used as evidence of discrimination in a court of law should prospective employees claim that they were treated unfairly during the hiring process.[1] Although three-quarters of my respondents answered near the "never" end of the scale, 9% near the "always" end of the scale, and the rest in between, statistically significant gender and racial differences were found. White women and women of color were *more likely* to have been asked inappropriate questions. The architect Sally Levine was quoted in a 1996 article about problems women encounter in architecture:

> "Too often, during an interview, women are told, 'Okay, now I'm going to ask you some illegal questions,' which generally deal with her age, marital status, whether she has young children, how she deals with day care, etc.
>
> "Your choices then become standing up and walking out of the room (but you really need a job), suing somebody (but there are only two people present so it becomes your word against his), or sitting there and taking it (and getting a job where no one respects you). . . . So each woman sits there and has to make her own decisions. Again, that's a no-win situation because none of those are reasonable options."[2]

How did architects in my study react to job interviews? Some respondents reveal a double standard; they were rejected for reasons they could not understand. While some prospective employers told them that they were underqualified, others told them they were overqualified. This mixed message signals possible racism or sexism at work.

Several architects in their thirties and forties cited frustrating interviews. One might expect more negativity to be reported by older architects, who were com-

peting for jobs in less socially liberated times. The fact that some of these relatively young, underrepresented architects experience problems even today is
revealing.

The vast majority of men found interviews to be a positive experience. Some
admitted that the more interviews they had, the more adept they became at
negotiating them. One white male (#92, age 41), comparing his early interviews
with later ones, put it succinctly, "Then: 'Can you use me?' Now: 'Here's what I
can do for you.'" Another white male (#22, age 36) explained that it was a natural process because he had confidence in his abilities. Yet another (#120, age
38) found it a challenge at first but later thought it was routine. For men of col-
or, the experiences were mixed. One African-American male (#160, age 38)
claimed his experiences were "always good."

How did women view job interviews? Their responses were mixed. A few
claimed never to have had trouble. One believed that interviewing for design
jobs may be easier than in other fields because applicants have visual aids to
show. But overall, more women than men reported negative experiences. Among
the words women used to describe their adventures—and misadventures—with
job interviews: nerve-wracking, tough, terrifying, awful, demeaning, unnatu-
ral, horrible, desperate, frustrating, uncomfortable, terrifying, and disappoint-
ing. Here is a sample of responses:

> [It's] tough. Trying to be professional and still present a female pres-
> ence is not easy. It is too easy to project wrong and inappropriate to be
> friendly—there is very little safe ground. (#84, white female, age 39)

> For instance, one interviewer asked me to name the last five books I'd
> read, and then criticized me for reading the autobiography of a woman
> artist instead of Frank Lloyd Wright's. All this [for] a $3/hour tracing
> job. When I commented that the pay was very low, he said that a pro-
> fessor's wife (a non-professional) had the job before and had never
> complained of even lower pay. I gathered that he felt that he didn't need
> to take a woman's career and survival needs very seriously. (#143,
> white female, age 41)

> I really hate interviewing. From the first time to now, it's usually the
> same. I deal with more racism and sexism than anything else. So every
> time I interview I just prepare myself for such immature behavior. I am
> tired of being denied jobs because of the color of my skin or my gender.
> Given a chance, and if they could get past my color and gender, I be-

lieve they will find that I have a lot of talent I could offer them. (#203, African-American female, age 29)

What was funny is that they always asked me what my husband did and where he worked. And they actually did that when I interviewed in 1990, too. (I-#1, African-American female, age 40)

INTERNSHIP

I realized that if two white males were talking, that no one would notice it. But if one of them was talking to me, that it would be noticed and that the assumption would be that I was not doing my work and that I was keeping him from doing his. So I refrained from any social conversations. And I just kept my nose to the drafting board. And as a result I accomplished a lot more than my coworkers. (I-#27, African-American female, age 66)

Internship is a critical period in the development of an architectural career. It is here that, after graduating from architectural school, young architects are first exposed to the professional work environment. The nature of this early experience can shape the future of their careers—possibly making or breaking them as architects. A 1996 study reported that approximately 4,500 architectural graduates entered the work force as interns each year.[3]

For years most architectural interns were trained by mentors. The daily interactions between mentor and pupil allowed young architects to learn the craft on the job. Nonetheless, research on mentoring indicates that senior members of almost any field are most likely to foster especially close relationships with those who are mirror images of themselves. Those who are not mirror images often get left behind. This pattern creates acute problems in a profession such as architecture which is homogeneous in terms of gender, race, and sexual orientation. From a historical perspective, one can only speculate about the kinds of internship experiences offered to those already underrepresented in the architectural profession: Were women interns truly given opportunities equal to those of their male counterparts? Were the doors of practice open as wide to interns of color as they were to whites?

As architectural practice became more complex, the need for architects to make a more structured transition from formal education to architectural registration became paramount. The internship required was generally three years long, and for many it was simply a "hit-and-miss approach to practical training in the field."[4] For some architects, the three-year internship could be rewarding, providing exposure to a broad range of responsibilities in the profession. Yet for others it could be a stifling experience, offering nothing more than assignments such as incessantly drawing the infamous toilet partitions or stairway details. It was largely a matter of luck.

In 1979, the Intern Development Program (IDP) was instituted by the National Council of Architectural Registration Boards (NCARB), along with the American Institute of Architects. It sought to address glaring deficiencies during this transition period and to make the internship a standardized, systematic process nationwide. The program gradually has been adopted on a state-by-state basis. While some states' architectural registration boards require IDP training for initial registration, other states accept IDP training as equivalent to their training standard for initial registration. As of late 2000, forty-four states required IDP. By 2002, forty-seven states will require IDP.[5] An IDP Coordinating Committee, including representatives from the American Institute of Architects, the American Institute of Architecture Students, the Association of Collegiate Schools of Architecture, and the National Council of Architectural Registration Boards, establishes the IDP's policies. Each of these organizations regards the internship as a crucial stage in the career of a young architect, as stated in the *Intern Development Program Guidelines:* "Internship is, in many ways, the most significant developmental period in your career as an architect. It's a time when you: apply your formal education to the daily realities of architectural practice; acquire comprehensive experience in basic practice areas; explore specialized areas of practice; develop professional judgment; continue your formal education in architecture; and refine your career goals."[6]

The IDP dictates specific requirements that interns must meet while under the direct supervision of a registered architect, and it also specifies a detailed recording system to ensure that these requirements are met. Each intern must work together with a sponsor at the firm where he or she is employed, as well as an advisor, an architect generally outside the firm of employment. Both the sponsor and the advisor oversee the intern's professional development. Specific objectives of the IDP are to: (1) define areas of architectural practice in which interns should acquire basic knowledge and skills; (2) encourage additional training in the broad aspects of architectural practice; (3) provide the highest quality information and advice about educational, internship, and professional issues and opportunities; (4) provide a uniform system for documentation and periodic assessment of internship activity; and (5) provide greater access to educational opportunities designed to enrich training.

Specific periods of training are required in four major categories: design and construction documents; construction administration; management; and related activities, which includes professional and community service.[7] Interns must acquire a total of 700 training units, wherein one training unit equals eight hours of activity, for a total of 5,600 hours of training. If a graduate enters the internship program with a professional degree in architecture from an accredited program, the total time required to complete the internship is three years. If a graduate enters the IDP with a professional degree in architecture from a nonaccredited institution, the time span to complete the internship rises to five years. Entering the IDP with other types of degree requires that the internship will last anywhere from seven to thirteen years. Interns are given credit proportionally for both part-time and full-time employment. Once the IDP requirements are met, the intern is eligible to sit for the ARE.

In addition to the lengthy process required to serve as an architectural intern, young architects must also make significant financial investments. As of 2000, the record compilation fee was $265 to establish a National Council of Architectural Registration Boards Council Record, an individual's entry in the official record-keeping system to be used during the IDP. This cost applies when a transmittal is made twelve or more months following receipt of the application. And if a transmittal is made within twelve months of the application, the fee rises. An annual maintenance fee is also charged for record keeping.

The systematic approach offered by the IDP, in contrast to the informal ways of mentoring that historically took place in the profession, stands to benefit greatly those who are underrepresented in the field. By offering participants a broad spectrum of experiences, it is much more likely today than ever before that women, persons of color, and gays and lesbians will receive fair treatment at this critical entry point in their careers. Nonetheless, fairness is never a guarantee, and the program is not without flaws. In 1999, Pamela Hill and Beth Quinn from Montana State University coauthored a study sponsored by the National Council of Architectural Registration Boards. They surveyed one thousand current and former interns to find out their perceptions of the internship experience. Their research was described by Lee Mitgang in an article in *Architectural Record*, who said that it

> yielded unsolicited comments from about a dozen interns who attested to the prevalence of IDP cheating. . . . Perhaps the most common falsification takes the form of what some call a "liberal interpretation" of IDP record-keeping rules by both interns and their bosses to fit their office's

circumstances. . . . Most agree that widespread cheating will likely persist until the more deep-seated problems of ignorance about IDP on the part of interns and employers, the inflexibility of some of the program's requirements, and the near absence of intern mentoring in many architecture offices are meaningfully addressed by the profession as a whole.[8]

Despite recent improvements in the IDP, the internship process remains the focus of sharp criticism. For instance, in 1996, Deborah K. Dietsch, then editor-in-chief of *Architecture*, acknowledged that "the present system of internship is broken, and no one seems prepared to fix it." While the IDP is supposed to teach architects the practicalities of the field and prepare them to take the registration exam, passage rates from the June 1995 exam show that over 60% of interns who took the test failed its design problem, even after three years of office experience. As Dietsch aptly remarks, "If medical interns failed at the same rate, it would cause an uproar." Dietsch also admits that interns are often ripe for professional exploitation, many of them grossly underpaid, and others not paid at all.[9]

Difficult as it may be for nonarchitects to believe, it has long been common practice for some stellar architects to "hire" young graduates for free, offering them the so-called privilege of working in a big-name firm and thus enhancing their resumes. For decades, budding young architects fresh out of school were elated to work gratis for Le Corbusier or Frank Lloyd Wright. As some observers have argued, this practice recalls the profession's aristocratic roots, wherein architects–who after all, didn't really need the money–viewed their work as a labor of love.

Even today, some architects routinely make promises to vulnerable young interns and fail to deliver. For example, upon graduation, one of my former students was thrilled to land a job at the office of a well-known West Coast architect, where he was hired freelance to build models. Yet months later, after the young man had completed the models and despite his constant prodding, the architect failed to pay him. Although he finally was issued a paycheck, the event left him frustrated and disillusioned–and rightfully so. In a scathing critique of the internship process published in *Progressive Architecture*, Thomas Fisher argued, "Probably everyone in this profession has–or knows someone who has–worked without compensation or worked long hours as an intern without overtime pay. It's tradition, we're told, all part of paying our dues to the profession. But it is also illegal, and it's scandalous that the architectural community has looked the other way for so long."[10]

Fisher's article was based on a response to a solicitation of information run in the March 1994 issue of *P/A*. Among the various types of exploitation that readers described were the failure to give young employees credit for their work, the reneging on promises of advancement, and the luring away of interns from other firms, only to lay them off a few months later. Fisher admitted that while he initially believed that abuses in the profession were few and far between, his readers' responses proved otherwise. He concluded that "non-compliance with the law, especially regarding interns' overtime pay and consultant status, is widespread."[11]

As a result of numerous tales of exploitation, the American Institute of Architecture Students (AIAS) and the Association of Collegiate Schools of Architecture (ACSA) fought back against the system. They recently adopted much-needed policies to curb abuses: principals of firms who do not pay their interns are not invited to speak at national and regional conferences, attend juries, receive awards, or hold an ACSA office. Nonetheless, as many young interns dread the consequences of blowing the whistle on their older colleagues, it is likely that such exploitation in the architectural profession continues to this day.

What are the implications of such abuses for underrepresented architects? Here the complex issues of gender, race, and class come into play. It is possible that many of these architects may be totally unaffected, since they simply cannot afford to donate their services for free. Most architects need a salary and cannot count on a wealthy relative to pay their bills. Yet as a result, their resumes may not catch the attention of potential employers who would recognize their experience at these star firms. Ironically, some are caught in a double bind and penalized in the profession for failing to play this unfair game.

Boyer and Mitgang report that despite IDP's accomplishments, the program has not solved the problems of internship. While they found many mutually satisfying IDPs at numerous firms around the country, they also heard many stories about internships that were grossly inadequate. They raise a valid point:

> The truth is that architecture has serious, unsolved problems compared with other fields when it comes to supplying on-the-job learning experiences to induct students into the profession on a massive scale. Medicine has teaching hospitals. Beginning teachers work in actual classrooms, supported by school taxes. Law offices are, for the most part, in a better financial position to support young lawyers and pay them living wages. The architecture profession, by contrast, must support a required system of internship prior to licensure in an industry that has neither the financial resources of law or medicine, the stability and

public support of teaching, nor a network of locations like hospitals or schools where education and practice can be seamlessly connected. And many employers acknowledged those problems.[12]

Given that the percentage of women graduating from architectural programs across the United States is on the rise, while the percentage of women who are registered members of the American Institute of Architects remains relatively low, we must examine the nature of the internship experience—especially for underrepresented architects. What happens to those women who graduate from architectural school but fail to become registered and/or join the AIA? Where else are they going? The internship can help provide the key to this mystery.

As Boyer and Mitgang report, one intern told them that she had been stuck for months doing relatively menial tasks such as toilet elevations. Another intern at a New York City firm expressed her frustration, "Honestly, I've thought of getting out of the business so many times. I think this is a good firm. The people are wonderful. But I do feel that through school I've built some knowledge and talent and now it's like I'm just feeding them to someone without getting anything back."[13]

Another intern, who had been routinely working sixty to seventy hours a week for a year and a half, apparently "slacked off" to fifty hours a week after his wife had a baby. As he told the research team, "The partner called me in and I got called on the carpet for not working hard enough."[14] This last case points out that at least at that office, as is so often true elsewhere, the internship process is far from family-friendly—a serious problem that affects both men and women in the field. The internship usually coincides with women's childbearing years. If a couple in their mid-twenties to early thirties decides to have children, and one of them is an architectural intern, chances are that the frequent expectation of marathon working hours, which conflict with the twenty-four-hour job of caring for a newborn, will have a negative impact on them, both personally and professionally. More often than not, it is the woman who will end up giving up her career or at least temporarily putting it on hold.

Young women architectural graduates accustomed to a critical mass of females in their academic design studios often face a rude awakening: they suddenly discover that they are the only professional woman in the office. Many architects are employed in small firms where it is likely that the only woman in the office is a secretary. Because a large percentage of African-American and Latino students studied at historically black colleges and universities, their adjustment to professional practice may be even more burdensome.

Most architects in my study had served as interns before the Internship Development Program was instituted. And because the IDP is relatively new, it is too soon to compare the experiences of those in traditional internships with those who participated in the IDP. Thirteen percent of those responding to my survey were currently interns on track toward registration. Hence, most of the sample spoke of the internship process in the past tense.

When asked about the extent to which problems in the internship process presented glass-ceiling barriers, along with a host of other potential barriers, six in ten architects responded "not at all" or "almost not at all." Nonetheless, a quarter of the architects responded on the other side of the scale, with 13% of the total indicating "very much."

How did architects in my study perceive the internship experience? What kinds of relationships did they have with coworkers at this critical juncture? To what extent did they feel that coworkers were willing to share information with them?

My results indicate that for the most part, men's internships were positive. In an open-ended question about the internship, just about all the white males who responded reflected upon it *favorably*. So did most male architects of color. Here is one example: "as far as the coworkers sharing information, I learned a lot in the bigger office. I learned a lot in the small office because I just had to do it, but . . . I didn't have a recipe that I could look at. I was preparing the recipes, if you will" (I-#15, Native American male, age 53).

One notable exception was the following:

> My internships were a patchwork quilt of experiences. In general, most white coworkers were unwilling to share information, and this unwillingness to share was definitely due to racism. . . . I think many white coworkers were intuitively aware that working with me would not advance their careers. Most stayed a bit distant from me, but a few whites became friends [who] helped me, or at least informed me about what was happening to me.
>
> Let me relate one incident. At a large corporate firm, a senior partner was selecting the staff for a team. A mid-level executive specifically asked the senior partner about me, and the senior guy said not to place me on the team. This mid-level person told me about the incident. At that point I decided to plan to leave. I was the only black person at the firm at that time. (#190, African-American male, age 43)

Women's experiences with the internship process were mixed. For many it was an exciting opportunity to learn more about the profession. Yet for others it was highly problematic. Several women expressed concern that their internships were fragile periods in their careers. Compared to long-term employees, interns are especially vulnerable to the whims of changing management, and often they were the first ones to be fired or laid off. Being terminated from a job can be devastating to anyone, but to underrepresented architects who may feel less confident about their abilities, it is an added blow. At the internship stage, as they make their debuts in the profession, negative experiences are even further magnified.

Here are some of their comments.

> Sometimes women feel that they are being kept out of the information loop. . . . I do recognize that I am usually not invited to the client meetings. (I-#28, white female, age 42)

> Significantly lacking in site visits. (#135, Latina/white female, age 28)

> I received many praises from project managers with whom I worked at the beginning of my tenure. I found that most of my coworkers were very willing to share information with me. I was the only woman in the architectural area of the office. . . . I received only one formal evaluation which I asked for after 1 1/2 years of employment. I was rated at that time quite highly and given a raise.

> After three years of employment and many personnel changes[,] I requested an evaluation on several occasions[,] which I never received. At my four year mark, I was fired by a relatively new principal in charge of personnel and told that my work was deficient[,] citing work for which I had only had minimal involvement. This was my first professional job. . . . I found the firing to be devastating. (#289, Native American/white female, age 47)

REGISTRATION

> I had to take the Design Exam three times. The first two times . . . there were bungles which made conditions very uncomfortable. The exam was given in a windowless room in a hotel in a city that was [a] one and one-half hour drive away. We had to bring all of our equipment. The test started very early in the morning. One time the hotel did not honor their room reservation, and I ended up sharing a room with a male acquaintance from whom I had accepted a ride; not a very com-

fortable preparation for the next day. Another time the hotel did not have enough tables, and I worked for twelve hours with my board balanced precariously upon three ballroom chairs. The whole experience seemed intended to make one feel as wretched and as demoralized as possible. (#43, white female, age 41)

The Architect Registration Examination (ARE) is the major hurdle that every architect must confront between internship and professional licensing. The successful completion of the exam turns an intern into an architect. The ARE covers pre-design; general structures; lateral forces; mechanical and electrical systems; materials and methods; construction documents and services, as well as site planning, building planning, and building technology.[15]

Historically, the exam was offered only twice a year, in June and December, and in a limited number of locations. Some sections required candidates to answer questions on a multiple-choice format, much like college entrance exams. But two other sections, Site Design-Graphic (Division B) and Building Design (Division C), were tested graphically, requiring candidates to sit hunched over their drawing boards for twelve hours. Candidates were given an entire building to design and were required to show floor plans, building sections, structural plans, elevations, and many life-safety compliance factors. As the architectural journalist Michael Crosbie has written, "For most candidates (myself included) Division C was a nightmare. You had to juggle and satisfy dozens of program and code requirements, integrating them into a solution that was sensible and not a death trap."[16] Critics called it a "grueling, macho rite of passage." In fact, it is only one of a long line of such rites in architecture, beginning with design juries in school.

The rates for passing the graphic sections of the exam have historically been substantially lower than those for the remainder of the exam. Statistics show that between 1989 and 1993, the passage rates for Division C ranged from a low of 24% to a high of 45%. In 1994, NCARB overhauled the dreaded Division C. Rather than requiring candidates to design a single building, a format that remained virtually unchanged for more than seventy years, the revised version asked candidates to solve six vignette problems in twelve continuous hours: Block Diagram, Schematic Design (floor plans), Building Section, Structural Plan, Mechanical and Electrical Plan, and Accessibility. A discrete problem was presented in each vignette. As a result of this dramatic change in the exam's format in 1994, passage rates for Division C soared to 53%.

A few states require that candidates take an oral exam before they are granted a license. In California, for example, which registers between 20% and 25% of all architects in the United States, candidates are required to answer orally some questions about the state's stringent seismic codes and other issues. The rationale for the oral exam, in addition to the traditional written and graphic exams, is that calling upon candidates to analyze and integrate knowledge in practice scenarios offers extra protection for the public. A typical oral-exam team consisted of three white males in a small hotel room. As one examiner acknowledged, this experience may have been especially intimidating to women and to candidates of color.

In addition to the substantial time commitment needed to prepare for and take the ARE, architects must make a significant financial investment. As of late 2000, the minimum cost for taking the entire exam was $981, and it could go higher depending upon the registration board administering the test.[17] Also as of 2000, approximately 310 test centers were set up around the country to administer the ARE.[18] Each state has its own registration board, as does Washington, D.C.; Puerto Rico; Guam; the Virgin Islands; and the Northern Mariana Islands. Some states may require additional fees. But the fee only gets architects in the door. In addition, they must pay for study guides and seminars to help prepare for the exam, and these can cost several hundred dollars. In addition, some may need time off to take the exam, resulting in loss of pay. In sum, the exam is an expensive undertaking, especially for those who are already the lowest-paid members of the profession.

The ARE traditionally put a special strain on architects with small children at home, on single parents, and on countless others who either could not afford it or were simply unable to get away for an extended period. More often than not, many of these were women. For those working far away from the testing sites, this often meant lengthy travel arrangements and an overnight stay. The exam also created special challenges for architects with physical disabilities who were forced to endure the twelve-hour marathon Division C.

In February 1997, the ARE underwent a dramatic transformation. NCARB worked with the world renowned Educational Testing Service of Princeton, New Jersey, the organization that develops the Scholastic Aptitude Tests (SAT), Graduate Record Examinations (GRE), and others, to develop a reliable, computerized exam. As a result, the ARE is now offered at a network of computer-based test centers; approximately 210 sites are available nationally, and the list is growing. Multiple-choice test questions are presented one at a time on a computer screen, with answer choices presented on the computer as well. The graphic portions are presented in a series of vignettes. Candidates are required to draw a solution using a mouse that meets the scenario and program requirements for each vignette. Tutorials are provided before each division in order to assist candidates with using the computer-based tools.

Another major change is that the ARE is now administered throughout the year, and candidates are able to take the exam whenever convenient. Candidates can choose to take all of the divisions of the exam at once, a few at a time, or just one at a time; however, if they fail a division, they must wait six months to retake it. They may spread their payments over several months and charge exam fees to a credit card. At first glance, these changes appear to be major improvements that will benefit those traditionally underrepresented in the profession. No doubt many of the problems described above will be remedied by the high-tech, computerized version of the ARE.

Because the computerized testing system was instituted only in 1997, all the architects who participated in my study had taken the ARE "the old fashioned way." The vast majority of architects (79%) surveyed had taken and passed the ARE. My average respondent had passed the ARE eleven years prior to the survey. The number of times it took to pass the exam varied widely, with an average response of 2.3. However, one individual reported taking the ARE fourteen times before achieving a passing score.

The passage rates of men and women architects were about the same. Men took the ARE an average of 2.5 times and women an average of 2.3 times; however, this difference is *not* statistically significant.

How, if at all, did the passage rates differ by race? Whites sat for the exam an average of 2.1 times compared to persons of color, who took it 2.8 times; and this racial difference *is* statistically significant. Further analysis reveals a statistically significant difference between men of color, who passed the exam after an average of 3.2 attempts, and the other three demographic groups: white men took the ARE an average of 2 times, white women 2.2 times, and women of color 2.4 times before they passed.

Architects' descriptions of the exam ranged from mild praise to sharp criticism. As one might expect, those who passed it in its entirety the first time were more likely to have fond memories of it. By contrast, others spoke bitterly about the exam, calling it excruciating, emotionally draining, a frustrating waste of time, an extreme horror, a source of great anger and frustration, grueling, horrible, brutal, harrowing, and, in one person's words, a "dreadful ordeal–just a rip-off of people in every way." Most of these negative remarks came from women.

My results reveal that for those architects with family responsibilities, taking this lengthy exam produced additional strain. Pregnant women had a tough time sitting still for so long. People with young children needed to make special child-care arrangements. Dilemmas like these may partially explain the substantial drop in the percentages of women architects who become registered compared with those who graduate from architectural school. It is possible that for some women, the exam itself may have posed an insurmountable obstacle, so much so that they avoided even taking it at all.

One can only speculate what impacts the new computerized ARE will have on the profession, and on women and persons of color in particular. While the high-tech ARE appears to remedy many deficiencies of the past, perhaps new, unforeseen problems will arise. How will underrepresented groups, compared to the traditional white, male architects, fare under the new ARE? That remains to be seen.

Here are a few reactions to taking the ARE from my research participants:

> The usual: intense, bleeding ulcer, exhaustion. (#130, white male, age 50)

> Intense—a table of women telling each other how they'd awoken at 4 A.M. to feed kids. During the design exam, my ex-husband, a registered architect, brought me [our] most difficult child to care for. [My ex-husband] was an instructor at the school where the exam was held. Others, men, vomited at the beginning of the exam and left down the fire stairs without being seen. (#200, white female, age 50)

> It was such a milestone to pass; felt like a heavy load was lifted. (#52, Asian-American female, age 34)

FIRST JOB

> My first architectural job was a drafting one held while in high school. A black neighbor, a friend of my father's, told him about an opening at a large, 100-plus-people white firm downtown. My father, who knew I had wanted to work for an architect for years, picked me up at school and drove me straight there. . . . I worked for this company for about five or six summers, both while in high school and during my college years. I rose up the ladder to even supervise people during the latter summers. . . . This was my first real experience at working with non-black people. What I learned was how to get along, how to take orders, and how to manage others. This job gave me the confidence to handle

drawing assignments in college. Also, money made from this job went into a savings account which I still maintain as a "nest egg." I have used that "egg" as collateral for several loans. (#190, African-American male, age 43)

Just like the ARE, the first job is another milestone in one's architectural career. Whether a dream come true or a nightmare, it is rarely forgotten. Newly minted young architects, fresh from their adventures in school, are in a vulnerable state of mind. Whatever transpires in that initial place of employment can color one's perceptions about future prospects in the profession. While early success encourages persistence later on, frustration and failure can have the opposite effect.

What were architects' first jobs like? How did they get that first job? And what did they learn from it? I asked survey participants to respond in an open-ended question.

Most architects found their first positions by responding to job advertisements. Others had help from college professors who offered them a network of professional contacts. Some told of family connections. What were these initial entry positions? Many were draftspersons, others were computer programmers, model makers, code checkers, and space planners. Only a handful were hired as designers from the outset.

Many architects fondly recalled their first job as a unique learning experience. For instance:

[I worked] right out of school as a drafter. [I] advanced steadily and was thrown into a lot of projects. (#160, African-American male, age 38)

I was hired as a student intern during my sophomore year in college—my first exposure to a "real" architecture firm. My boss was just starting out on his own and wanted to help a student out. That's how he started out. (#288, Latina, age 29)

For others, their experiences at the first job were mixed:

[My first job was] drafting bathroom and stair details at a large firm. [I] learned I wanted to work at a small firm to see the whole building! (#173, white female, age 34)

[My first job was] part time with a large firm. . . . [During the interview] the partner "showed" me to the project manager through a glass window. I learned that I didn't want to work for a large firm. (#104, white female, age 47)

Nonetheless, several women—but none of the men—indicated that their first jobs routinely required them to do typing, secretarial work, or run errands. This was a pattern that both older and younger women described. Being treated like a secretary or "Girl Friday" often dimmed their vision of the future. For these women, a significant mismatch occurred between their expectations and what they actually experienced on the job. Considering that large numbers of women appear to be dropping out of the architectural profession, treating women and men equitably in that first place of employment is critical. Here are a few of the women's remarks:

> My first architectural job was after I graduated. . . . I took over another woman's position. . . . I got along great with my coworkers. Looking back, I was not taken seriously. I did not take my job seriously. It was so bad [that] even the secretaries would ask me to do their errands. (#349, white female, age 36)

> As a student in New York City, I typed specifications, answered the telephone, poured drinks, baby-sat the principal's kids, and shopped at Bergdorf Goodman's for clients' dresses. (#200, white female, age 50)

> [My first job was] one month typing. [I] was hired as a secretary/ draftsperson but the day my employer told me he never intended to allow me to draft, I quit! (#185, white female, age 55)

■

These rites of passage—interviewing, internship, registration, and the first job— reveal dramatic gender differences. While many architects have no trouble leaping over each of these hurdles, others do. And most of those who do are underrepresented architects. My research revealed significant gender differences during each of these stages. In every instance, women encountered greater difficulties than their male counterparts. Women's experiences with their first job tended to be more negative than those of men; many struggle to be taken seriously as architects. Significant racial differences were demonstrated in the rates at which people passed the ARE, whereby persons of color had to take the test more often than their white counterparts, perhaps because they had fewer opportunities in architectural internship experiences prior to taking the exam.

In effect, what serves as a gateway for traditional architects often becomes a roadblock for underrepresented architects. Ironically, when taken together, my findings suggest that at critical stages of one's career development, those runners whom the field needs most are most likely to drop out of the race.

Chapter 6

OBSTACLES IN THE
ARCHITECTURAL WORKPLACE

> In the first few offices that I worked in, the only
> females, of course, were the receptionists or the
> secretaries. In fact, at my very first firm, a woman
> came in to apply for a draftsperson's position, and
> she was the talk of the office. No one had ever seen
> this before. And it was a real experience. . . . Even
> though there have been some serious inroads—
> which is good—it's still thought of as a gentleman's
> profession.
>
> —I-#9, African-American male, age 61

MANY UNDERREPRESENTED ARCHITECTS come up against obstructions that prevent them from pursuing their dreams. What special challenges do underrepresented designers encounter? This chapter examines issues such as isolation on the job, sexual and racial discrimination, pay inequity, sexual harassment, the glass ceiling, and the interweaving of personal and professional lives. It also explores how architects handle layoffs, and why some choose to drop out of the field. Although some of these issues have been examined individually in prior studies, this is one of the first times that they are presented in a broader context.

A few words of caution are in order. What follows paints a glaringly negative picture of the architectural profession. Yet my research and analyses provide important insights that suggest strategies to improve opportunities for underrepresented architects and for the profession in general. These will be discussed at length in chapter 8.

Isolation in the work environment is a theme that pervades the experiences of underrepresented architects throughout this study. The majority of architecture firms employ fewer than five workers.[1] As a result, for many architects–

whatever their gender, race, or sexual orientation–the office environment is one of relative isolation, a far cry from the camaraderie of large studios in architectural school.

An underrepresented architect is likely to be a token: the only woman, the only African-American man, or the only lesbian in the office. For example, Bradford Grant and Dennis Mann's research demonstrates that most African-American architects work in firms with only a small number of African-American employees; one out of every five African-American architects is the only black employee in the office. As the researchers recognize, "This could possibly set the stage for an uncomfortable work place environment for the lone black architect."[2]

Serving as an ambassador of your gender or sexual orientation is stressful. The experience of a Latino architect featured in *LA Architect* is a case in point. Gabe Armendariz was raised in East Los Angeles and first studied architecture at East Los Angeles College, where about 80% of the students were Hispanic. He then transferred to California State Polytechnic University, Pomona, where the ethnic proportions were reversed. When he later went on to work for Gensler, a major Los Angeles firm, he recalled, "It was very hard for me . . . to come up the escalators and see that the people working behind the fast food counters, or the maintenance people, were all Hispanic."[3]

Standing out in the crowd can be both a plus and a minus, depending upon the circumstances. Responses to token individuals tend to be magnified. While this means that others can pay more attention to them, it can often lead to false generalizations about others like them. Being "the first" and "the only" often results in undue pressure to succeed or in self-consciousness, low self-esteem, and loneliness. Ellis Cose provides a telling account of how tokenism affects African-American professionals in his book *The Rage of a Privileged Class*.[4]

GENDER OR RACIAL DISCRIMINATION

I almost always found that if you were black, you were in production. You were never, ever in design. It was so rare. I think the first time I met a black person who said he worked in design, I couldn't believe it. . . . I see more discrimination because of race than sex today. And I just think now even when I look at big firms, they usually have one black person. (I-#29, African-American female, age 46)

Is there discrimination in the architectural profession? The answer is a resounding yes. Two-thirds (68%) of my survey respondents had seen or heard about *gender discrimination* in an architectural office, somewhat under half (44%) had personally experienced it, and over a third (36%) had known first hand or heard about a coworker's quitting a job because of it. Four out of ten (42%) had witnessed or heard about *racial discrimination* in an architectural office, and only 18% had either personally experienced it or had first-hand knowledge or heard of a coworker's quitting a job because of it. Just over a quarter of those surveyed (27%) had quit a job in architecture because of unfair treatment, and 12% had been fired as part of unfair treatment. Only 3% had filed or been party to a job discrimination suit against an architectural employer.

Significant gender and racial differences emerged. Table 5 shows that along several lines, women were more likely than men to be treated differently and to experience and perceive gender discrimination. Compared to white architects, architects of color were more likely to have personally experienced or seen or heard about racial discrimination. They were also more likely to have known first hand or heard about a coworker's quitting due to racial discrimination. An even finer analysis by both gender and race revealed that compared to white women, architects of color were significantly *less* likely to have been fired because of unfair treatment.

Just over half the sample (54%) had witnessed or heard about clients engaging in sexual discrimination in awarding projects, while under half (46%) had personally experienced this. Even more–just about two-thirds (65%) of those surveyed–had witnessed or heard about racial discrimination by clients in awarding projects, and about a third (35%) had personally experienced it.

Respondents were asked to indicate how much discrimination or preferen-

TABLE 5. Have You Ever . . . ?

	Male	Female
Experienced gender discrimination? (n = 399)***	2.0	1.3
Seen/heard about gender discrimination? (n = 400)***	1.5	1.2
Quit because of unfair treatment? (n = 399)***	1.8	1.7
Seen/heard about a co-worker quitting due to gender discrimination? (n = 400)***	1.8	1.6
Changed your appearance to be taken more seriously? (n = 400)***	1.7	1.4
Changed your name to be taken more seriously? (n = 403)**	2.0	1.9

Note: Average response given where 1 = yes; 2 = no; $*p < .05$; $**p < .01$; $***p < .001$

tial treatment, if any, they believed each group generally encounters in architectural practice. Most believed that underrepresented architects experienced some form of discrimination by coworkers, subordinates, superiors, and others. They believed women of color suffered the most discrimination from construction workers and contractors but somewhat better (although far from preferential) treatment from coworkers, subordinates, superiors, and consultants.

Most felt that men of color experienced some discrimination from coworkers, subordinates, and consultants and more discrimination from construction workers. Most believed that white women experienced neither discrimination nor preferential treatment from coworkers, but that they experienced some discrimination (from less to more) from consultants, clients, subordinates, superiors, contractors, and construction workers.

By contrast, the average responses about white men leaned toward preferential treatment. Most believed that these men received the greatest preferential treatment from contractors, superiors, and clients.

One of my interviewees made some disturbing comments about sexual discrimination in the job market: "I know specifically in Chicago that there are offices that simply don't hire women. They just don't do it. The guys at the top of the ladder are, simply, point-blank, uncomfortable hiring women. . . . And they point-blank practice discrimination. . . . My husband is a senior associate there [at a Chicago firm], the one and only there. And I know exactly what happens in that office. Every time he tries to get a woman in there—even if the only appropriate, qualified candidate is a woman—the principals will choose not to hire [at all] rather than hire her" (I-#7, white female, age 35).

Yet another white female spoke about routinely seeing her employers dismiss those job applicants with "weird names" (according to her, a Spanish surname, or an otherwise "foreign-sounding" name). Rather than even being brought in for a job interview, these applicants were simply knocked out of the running altogether. Although this smacks of xenophobia, some other architects believed that the opposite trend occurs, that is, that those designers born abroad, whether they be men or women, are at an advantage in the field.

PAY INEQUITY

I had experience with one particular firm where the guys got paid more than the women. For example, I had a friend there after I left who was very competent, had her license, was nice, and she was training people. She was going beyond the call of duty. And she trained this wonderful

new intern, and he moved in from another state, and she found out–
well, she did his payroll–that he was making $3,000 or $4,000 more
than her. He didn't have any experience. She had five years. Very odd.
Very odd. And this happened quite a lot. Things like that . . . make me
cynical. (I-#21, white female, age 33)

Architects are paid notoriously low salaries, especially in light of the rigorous education and training required to become licensed and the extremely long
hours required on the job. For years, women in architecture have been grossly
underpaid and exploited, to the point of absurdity. Two outrageous examples
come to mind. Sophia Hayden, architect of the Woman's Building at the 1893
World's Columbian Exposition in Chicago, earned a meager one-tenth of what
her male counterparts were paid for designing other buildings at the fair. She
received an honorarium of a thousand dollars plus expenses. Apparently, her
difficult experiences in designing the Woman's Building and seeing it built broke
her heart and she never built again.[5]

Perhaps even more bizarre is the case of Lisl Close, a longtime Minneapolis
architect who graduated from MIT in the 1930s. At that time, Richard Neutra's
office in California suggested that she pay twenty dollars a month for the privilege of working there. William Lescaze in New York City said he couldn't take
her on because it "'would disrupt the drawing room,'" she recalled.[6]

Starting salaries for architects are far lower than those in comparable professions. In the mid-1990s the Center for the Study of Practice at the University
of Cincinnati reported that the average annual starting salary for architects was
only $22,125. At the same time engineers could expect a starting salary of
$35,530.[7] According to the AIA, the median salary for intern architects at that
time was $24,700; licensed architects with eight to ten years of experience but
who were not managers or principals of a firm earned a median salary of
$38,900, while principals or partners earned a median of $50,000. By contrast,
partners in some large practices earned over $110,000.[8] Grant and Mann's sur-
vey revealed that the average salary for African-American partners in architectural firms was $66,413; for private-sector employees, $47,846; and for public-
sector employees, $64,746.[9]

Dissatisfaction with low pay was common among all architects in my research. Nonetheless, my survey revealed significant gender differences. Compared to men, women were much more likely to cite "pay inequities for work
of equal or comparable value" as a glass-ceiling barrier in their architectural
careers. No significant racial differences were found.

The average salary of architects in my survey sample was approximately $43,440, but earnings ranged widely from $0, for those who were temporarily unemployed, to $160,000. A concurrent salary survey of 3,300 architects conducted by the AIA showed that the average salary for a principal in private practice was $44,800, a figure fairly close to my average.[10] Average salaries for various demographic groups in my study varied greatly. Of those architects working full time, white men earned the most ($54,990), followed by men of color ($49,430), women of color ($40,350), and, at the bottom of the list, white women ($38,980).[11]

How do these figures compare with national labor statistics at about the same time? For every dollar earned by white men, African-American men earned 75 cents; white women, 72 cents; Hispanic men, 64 cents; African-American women, 63 cents; and Hispanic women, only 56 cents.[12] My research demonstrated that for every dollar made by a full-time white male architect, full-time men architects of color earned 89 cents; full-time women architects of color, 73 cents; and full-time white women architects, 71 cents. There is no doubt that white male architects are at a distinct financial advantage.

According to the Equal Employment Opportunity Commission, in the mid-1990s college-educated women earned 29% less than college-educated men.[13] All practicing architects are college educated, and my study reveals that white women earned 29% less than white men, and women of color earned 27% less. Salary discrepancies in the profession are on par with those nationwide.

My analysis revealed that women consistently earn less than their male counterparts, regardless of their years of full-time, professional experience as paid registered architects. Gender differences are even more pronounced when one examines salaries of full-time architects who work for others, that is, architects who are neither the principals nor owners of their firms and who are not sole

Average Salaries for Full-Time Architects (those who work for others)

My survey revealed significant pay gaps between men and women architects. The gap widens the more experience architects have in the field. Graph by the author.

practitioners. The gender gap in pay is evident at the outset of architects' careers (there is a difference of about $8,000 between men's and women's salaries), narrows midstream (a difference of about $1,000), and widens the longer they are in the profession. For those with ten to fourteen years of experience and for those with the most professional experience (fifteen or more years, full time), the gap is about $13,000; women earn only 80% of their male counterparts' salaries. When we break down the data by both gender and race, other disturbing differences appear. (See table 6.) While women of color who work for others actually earn higher average salaries than each of the other three demographic groups when starting their architectural careers, the picture soon becomes more complex. Once they have obtained fifteen or more years of experience, the pattern reverses; they earn only 70% of the salaries of their male counterparts (both white men and men of color); white women earn 76% of their male counterparts' salaries.

TABLE 6. Average Salary for Full-Time Paid Registered Architects Working for Others

Years of Experience	White Men	White Women	Men of Color	Women of Color
1–4	$21,333	$20,745	$22,000	$26,467
5–9	34,200	35,571	26,750	33,444
10–14	45,550	37,300	39,333	47,507
15 or more	60,857	46,000	60,650	42,583

These figures provide resounding evidence of pay discrimination against women architects. Compared to men with similar levels of professional experience, women are paid substantially less. In fact, little has changed since the 1983 American Institute of Architects survey of women architects and the 1983 survey of Detroit architects.[14] This blatant gender bias, especially when women work for others, helps explain why so many frustrated female architects flee traditional practice to open their own firms.

How does the discrepancy in architects' salaries compare with conditions in other fields? A 1991 study published in *Planning* revealed that females and planners who were persons of color are docked almost $2,000–and females of color $4,000–for no other reason than their gender or race. A large survey conducted by the Society of Women Engineers documented that women engineers who are managers maintain salary parity with men throughout their thirties; however, once they enter their forties, a salary gap begins to open. For engineering managers over fifty, the gap typically widens, with men earning almost $10,000 more per year than their female counterparts.[15]

How do the gender differences in architects' salaries revealed by my own research compare with more recent findings? Statistics in table 7, based on figures from the U.S. Department of Labor, Bureau of Labor Statistics, show gender differences in average annual salaries for full-time architects. While in 1995, the difference was $3,720, in 1999 the gap totaled $20,764. In fact, the situation for women architects may well have gotten even worse.[16] Note, however, that these figures, unlike my own, do not match men and women with comparable experience.

TABLE 7. Average Annual Salary for
Full-Time Architects

Year	Men	Women	Difference
1995	$38,532	$34,812	$ 3,720
1996	41,548	31,070	10,478
1997	46,384	26,602	19,782
1998	46,436	39,010	7,426
1999	51,116	30,352	20,764

Architects were asked if they believed they had ever been denied or granted a salary increase or job promotion because of their gender, race or ethnic background, physical impairment or disability, age, or sexual orientation. On each of these items, the average responses fell just about in the middle, indicating that none of these variables was significant. The responses about gender, age, and race or ethnic background leaned slightly toward the "denied" side of the scale. However, the average responses for women of color and white women were significantly lower (i.e., they were *more* likely to say "denied") than those for white men and men of color. Similarly, men and women of color were significantly *more* likely to indicate race as a factor in being denied a salary increase or job promotion. Women of color were *more* likely than both groups of men to say they were denied an increase due to age, and white women were *more* likely to say the same compared to white men. These findings suggest that age seems to be more disadvantageous to women's career advancement than to men's.[17] Here is what some architects had to say:

> [I was in a] situation where the guys were making more money than the women. . . . This other woman and I started at $16,000. That was

low at that time. Other people were getting between $18,000 and $20,000. . . .

This is a real problem because [my husband, also an architect] and I have exactly the same number of years of schooling, we have exactly the same degrees, we have been working in practice for exactly the same number of years. And yet he has been able to attain a level of pay and a level of exposure and experience only because he's a man in that office. And no woman would have ever been given the opportunity to do that there. (I-#7, white female, age 35)

I was hired because they felt that since I was married and had a husband who could support me, that if they had to let me go because there wasn't any additional work, they wouldn't feel so bad. Plus they didn't have to pay me such a high salary because my husband was also working. But the thing that really freaked us out: my husband was told the same thing. He didn't need as high a salary because, after all, his wife was working, which we thought was really a crock. So it works both ways. (I-#26, foreign-born white female, age 51)

There was blatant pay discrimination in that office, and we all knew about it because one day the secretary became very upset and she kind of told. (I-#14, African-American female, age 36)

The issue of benefits is also a concern among architects. Nationally, the percentage of firms providing benefits increases as the firm size grows. Solo practitioners are much less likely than employees in larger firms to receive benefits through their firm. For example, while over half (58%) of all architectural firms provide medical insurance, almost all (97%) of those with twenty or more employees do so. Yet only about a quarter (27%) of those with one sole practitioner do. While 12% of all architectural firms offer dental insurance, only 2% of those with sole practitioners offer it, compared to 46% of those with twenty or more employees.[18] Furthermore, the 1993 AIA survey of architects concluded that architects in underrepresented careers, such as corporate architects, government architects, developers, contractors/builders, and architects in colleges and universities, enjoy higher pay and better benefits than their counterparts in private practice.[19]

My survey asked architects what kinds of benefits their firms provide. (See table 8.) Health benefits topped the list, but almost one-quarter of the respondents worked at offices that did not have any. Just over one-quarter were enti-

TABLE 8. What Benefits Does Your
Firm Provide for Architects?

Benefit	Percentage
Health insurance	77
Bonuses	50
Dental insurance	41
Flex-time	39
401K plan	36
Long-term disability	29
Unpaid parental leave	28
Profit sharing	27
Other pension plan	26
Overtime pay	25
Paid parental leave	8
Day-care facilities	3

Note: Multiple responses are possible; *n* = 404

tled to unpaid parental leave. Recall that the Family and Medical Leave Act, which provides an individual with unpaid leave to care for a newborn child or a sick family member, does not apply to architects in firms with fewer than fifty employees. Statistically significant gender differences were found for health insurance, profit sharing, and bonuses. Male architects were more likely to receive each of these benefits.

How do my figures compare with some national trends for women workers? The U.S. Department of Labor's Women's Bureau conducted its "Working Women Count!" survey in 1994 and found that 23% had no pension, 14% had no sick leave, 56% with children age five and under reported having trouble finding affordable childcare, and 43% of the part-time workers lacked health benefits.[20] By comparison, in my survey, of those women architects currently employed full-time, almost all (96%) worked in offices with no day-care facilities; three-quarters (74%) worked in offices without pension plans, although some had a 401K plan; and one in five (21%) lacked health insurance.

SEXUAL HARASSMENT

> It got so bad that even after I put in my resignation, the project architect put up one of those stupid girlie calendars. I asked him not to, and he did nothing. (#349, white female, age 36)

Who can ever forget the confirmation hearings of U.S. Supreme Court Justice Clarence Thomas in 1991, when Professor Anita Hill charged him with sexual harassment? Time stood still as Americans sat by their televisions, riveted by the case. It was a critical point in the history of men and women in the workplace. Sexual harassment has long been present in the working world, but these hearings launched the issue into national prominence. How visible–or invisible–is sexual harassment in the architectural profession?

Architects endure harassment not just from coworkers or employers but from clients as well. Just over half my sample (53%) claimed to have witnessed or heard about sexual harassment from clients during their architectural careers, and just under half (47%) had personally experienced sexual harassment from clients. Not surprisingly, most of these responses were from women.

Almost two-thirds (62%) had personally been the target of clients who engaged in verbal abuse of a sexist nature (including sexist remarks and jokes), and more than a third (38%) had witnessed or heard about such incidents. Regarding verbal abuse of a racist nature, including racist remarks and jokes by clients, over half (57%) had witnessed or heard about it, and under half (43%) had experienced it.

Eleven measures of sexual harassment were analyzed, items that had been used repeatedly in other studies.[21] Respondents were asked if in any architectural work environment, excluding school, they had ever been in a situation where any of their coworkers or supervisors engaged in a certain type of behavior. They rated each of these along a five-point scale ranging from "never" to "once or twice," "sometimes," "often," and "most of the time." The average responses for each of these eleven items fell somewhat below the middle of the scale; none of these mean responses fell into the "often" or "most of the time" categories, thus indicating that the profession appears at least to be aware of these issues.

The *top* three items that the architects reported were coworkers or supervisors telling suggestive stories or offensive jokes (47% reporting "sometimes"; 15%, "often," and 24%, "once or twice"); making crude and offensive sexual remarks, either publicly or privately (37% reporting "sometimes"; 33%, "often," and 7%, "once or twice"); and putting them down or being condescending because of their gender (20% reporting "sometimes"; 8%, "often"; and 22%, "once or twice"). The *least* frequent behavior reported was "treating you badly for refusing to have sex" (98% reporting "never"); "implying faster promotions or better treatment if you were sexually cooperative" (97% reporting "never"); and "continuing to ask you for dates, drinks, or dinner, even though you refused" (86% reporting "never"). When asked if they had ever been in a situation where any of their coworkers or supervisors displayed, used, or distributed sexist or suggestive materials, such as pictures, stories, pornography, or lingerie, about a quarter (24%) reported "once or twice" and 15% reported "sometimes." Asked if they had ever been given unwanted sexual attention by coworkers or supervisors in the office, 21% responded "once or twice" and 9% reported "sometimes."

Statistically significant gender differences were found on several items. Compared to men, women were more likely to report that their coworkers or supervisors were condescending to them because of their gender; made unwanted attempts to draw them into discussions of personal or sexual matters; continued to ask them for dates even though they refused; touched them; and implied faster promotions or better treatment would occur if they were sexually cooperative. In fact, white women experienced forms of harassment slightly more often than did women of color.

Further analysis breaking the data down by each of the four demographic groups revealed statistically significant gender differences as well as racial differences. White males, compared to the other three groups, were more likely to have been in a situation where crude and offensive sexual remarks were made. Both white women and women of color were *more* likely to experience condescending behavior because of their gender (and white women were *more* likely to experience this behavior than were women of color), continuing to be asked for dates even though they refused, and being touched in a way that made them uncomfortable (again, white women were *more* likely to endure this behavior than were women of color). White women were significantly *more* likely than the men to encounter unwanted discussions of personal or sexual matters.

One case in point illustrates how sexual harassment affected a participant in my study:

> I graduated from architecture school in 1975, during a recession that made jobs scarce. I took a hospital facilities job for two years, until I got my first full-time work for an architect. The architect was a sole practitioner with about 5–8 persons in the office. The man was technically competent, and I learned a lot from him. He was a very difficult man to work for, however. Although he understood the value of many things, including my abilities, a profound sense of insecurity and inferiority— and a desperation to make the business succeed—meant that he promised anything to clients.
>
> Although on some levels this architect tried to treat his employees fairly, in compensation and benefits, for instance, many days in the office were emotionally very taxing. He would yell and scream fre-

quently. In trying to elevate his own self-image he would make fun of other people. He would tell crass racial and sexual jokes. I did not object forcefully. Given my own sense of inadequacy, I was convinced that I could not get another job, and adopted camouflage behavior, trying to cope and fit in as best as I could. His behavior eventually progressed to what we now identify as sexual harassment: unwanted hugs, attempted kisses, and suggestions about trips together.

The man spoke of a future business partnership with me. I never felt that the future of my job with him was dependent on sexual cooperation, but rather that his behavior combined a fondness for me, personally, and a wish to capitalize on my assets for his business. Nonetheless the situation was extremely uncomfortable, and after five years of coping, I finally refused to appease one of his temper tantrums, thereby allowing a "frightening first." He fired me.

This was a phenomenally "dark hour" for me, but it also led eventually to a very "bright hour." Although this architect invited me back to work immediately, I felt the need to take advantage of the situation, and extracted time off to prepare a portfolio for graduate school. I was prepared to chuck architecture as a career altogether. I chose to change my field of study and move to a different city for my graduate work.

Eventually my new-found confidence and new location led to many wonderful things. To make money and continue my graduate courses, I began part-time work for an architectural firm. The firm turned out to be an excellent match for my interests and ideas about architectural design and practice, and I have found professional opportunities within it. I am one of ten associates (the only female associate). I am very proud that our firm is the recipient of the [year] AIA Architecture Firm Award. I have also found personal happiness here; I married one of its members, who is now a principal. (#143, white female, age 41)

But harassment is not only sexual. Some women endure agonizing verbal abuse from male colleagues. For example, one woman recounted, "At a Christmas party a drunk white male architect (very successful and someone I didn't know) started screaming at me, 'You aren't a real architect!' (This was in 1993.)" (#102, white female, age 47).

My results demonstrate that harassment in the architectural profession is widespread. The experience is especially painful for women who must confront it while working in small offices. Many feel trapped, unable to escape. The consequences of whistle-blowing in a small firm can be horrendous, as the basic trust that underlies the working relationship of all architects is undermined.

Yet in today's world, where the public is well aware of sexual harassment in the workplace, women in architecture are more likely to face subtler forms of abuse. Some male colleagues routinely question women's credentials, knowledge, expertise, and ability to make decisions; fail to accept directives from women superiors; and attempt to undermine the success of women on the job. Or men may sabotage a woman's efforts. Recall the events noted in chapter 1: the harassment of women architecture students, which rocked the U.C. Berkeley campus in 1992, as well as the issuing of the AIA's Advisory Opinion in connection with its Rule of Conduct 1.401, entitled "Discrimination Against Employees Based on Gender."[22] For all too many women in architecture–whether they be practitioners, students, or faculty–harassment is a familiar experience.

HITTING THE GLASS CEILING

> I was a specifications writer for a firm of about thirty. I could not get clerical assistance or a salary increase, so I left. I was replaced by a white male at twice the salary with a secretary to assist [him]. (#176, white female, age 42)

"Women don't make it in the big architectural firms because of the glass ceiling which exists," says Emma Macari, 1992 chair of the AIA Women in Architecture Committee. "So in order to have some control, they open their own firm. Of course, they open their own firm at a much lower level, so the projects that they go after are not as prominent as the ones the big firms get. It's a self-feeding cycle."[23]

In its article entitled "The Twenty-five Hottest Careers of 1986," *Working Woman* listed architecture as one of the "Ten Worst Careers for Women." It cited insufficient salary, intense competition, and lack of advancement as negative aspects of an architectural career. According to this magazine, "Only 27% of the women in architecture reach upper management, compared to 57% of their male colleagues." However, women who specialize in the financial side of building excel in real-estate development, property management, property appraisal, and market studies.[24] Are the findings from *Working Woman* still true today–or has the situation improved?

Few women or persons of color reach the top echelons of the architectural profession and become partners in major firms.[25] Many sidestep this problem by opening their own firms. In fact, while an average of about one out of every three architects in the American Institute of Architects owns his or her own firm, one out of every two (56%) African-American architects is a firm owner. According to Grant and Mann, "The higher percentage of ownership among African American architects might hint at the existence of a glass ceiling in majority owned firms where the route to ownership or partnership might be less possible for the African American architect."[26]

Moreover, Grant and Mann's survey of 382 African-American architects reveals that an overwhelming majority (86%) of African-American firms are 100% African-American owned. Very few African Americans act in an ownership capacity in either joint-owned (African-American/white or other combination) or majority owned firms. Grant and Mann point out, "While anecdotal information over the past six years has suggested to us that the architecture profession was very segregated, these results seem to confirm that segregation in ownership is a fact."

Grant and Mann's research on African-American architects identified another disturbing trend. They speculate that many African-American owners of firms fled other offices in order to have more control over what they perceived as a racially biased professional environment. In fact, they could cite only ten senior partners in majority-owned firms.

My survey participants were asked the following question: "The U.S. Department of Labor defines the 'glass ceiling' as artificial barriers, based on attitudinal or organizational bias, that prevent qualified individuals from advancing within their organization and reaching their full potential. Have you ever seen a 'glass ceiling' in any architectural firm where you have worked?" Over half the sample (56%) said yes. Of those who had seen it, three-quarters (75%) were women, and over a third (39%) were persons of color.

This issue struck a chord with several white male architects who admitted that underrepresented architects have difficulty rising to the top of larger firms. Yet white male architects also cited problems of their own: the limitations of working in a family-run firm, when they were not family members; age, with fewer opportunities for young persons to succeed; ability to go only so far if you are not a "local boy" (one architect–#153, white male age 28–found this to be particularly the case in the South and in the rural West); and an inflexible office structure where too many principals and project directors crowd out others who excel.

What forms of glass ceilings did men of color encounter in architectural practice? A few Asian-American males cited ethnic stereotyping and being pigeonholed in a position while the firm's owner ignored their requests for promotion. Some Latinos admitted the "good old boy" syndrome still persists. African-American males referred to limited or nonexistent client contact; discrepancies in salaries; "homogenism," when only ex-military white males age fifty-five and up make it to the top; failure to be given an opportunity to go beyond what they were specifically hired for (i.e., drafter, designers developing contract documents); situations whereby older members of the firm hand-picked and advanced project architects while leaving others behind; inability to be admitted to design roles, what one respondent referred to as "the most exclusive club"; and failure to provide opportunities for partnership. Some African-American men noted that women's opportunities are often restricted to interiors or marketing.

Several white women cited the persistence of the "good old boys' club," which excludes women from being "one of the guys." As one woman (#223, white female, age 33) put it, "Opportunities to network in-house are offered to men only." Several pointed to the frequent "pigeonholing" of women into programming, interiors, or other parts of the office—with limited opportunities to branch out of these roles.

White women noted the following: lower starting salaries; inability to be offered raises and positions of manager, partner, and associate; being offered responsibility but not receiving the appropriate position, salary, or credit for it; not being allowed to engage in client contact, field experience, or construction supervision; ageism, regarding their youth; no women predecessors in their firm to use as a measure of success; exclusion of one female officer at vice-president meetings; management exploiting the contributions of female employees; firm's inability to accommodate employees unwilling to work long hours and overtime; and perceptions that women can not be in charge of big jobs. One woman was even denied the opportunity to attend the groundbreaking of one of her projects. Some other accounts:

> [Women] could only advance so high, while men had no limits. (#308, white female, age 33)

> It's the horrible realization that no matter how intelligent, talented, or competent you are, it doesn't or won't make a difference to some people who only see "a girl." (#392, white female, age 33)

> Small firm didn't recognize completion of architectural exam for a woman [by raise, promotion, etc.] but did for a man. (#207, white female, age 42)

After "across the board" salary increases (which were confidential), I discovered [that] the secretary and I were making the same salary. I confronted the senior partner and was told that was all I was worth. (#369, white female, age 45)

Women of color echoed many of the same themes. Among the remarks from African-American women:

If you weren't one of the original (founding) employees, you didn't go far. (#58, African-American woman, age 37)

Women could only do certain jobs and never alone. (#136, African-American female, age 31)

I work for two partners. My advancing is limited because most of the designing and administration is done by the partners. I basically do whatever they don't want to do (mostly drafting). (#203, African-American female, age 29)

Most of the women in my firm hold very subordinate positions. All [are] qualified for higher positions. (#364, African-American female, age 25)

People with technical expertise [are] not given the same kudos as designers. Older women with more experience than men are in lesser positions. (#376, African-American female, age 31)

Latinas addressed issues such as pay inequities; being "artificially" promoted to named positions with little decision-making responsibilities; and geographic biases, not being a native of a particular region, which could be even more limiting than being female or a person of color. As two Latinas put it:

If I were to draw a diagram of it, it wouldn't be a horizontal glass ceiling. It would be a ceiling that stepped up like a ziggurat but each horizontal tier which represents the level you're at gets longer and longer. . . . You reach these plateaus where it takes more time, the horizontal part of the ceiling is longer, and maybe the vertical step up is smaller. (I-#22, Latina/Asian-American female, age 31)

[I see the glass ceiling] everywhere, especially now. There's only so much room at the top of a pyramid and the men (especially white and Asian) are not going to let a woman be their equal. (#325, Latina, age 45)

Some Asian-American women noted that while women managers routinely work overtime to obtain or maintain their office positions, men rarely did so, and that pregnancy limits one's opportunities to advance in the field.

A handful of respondents cited what I call "lookism"—a preoccupation with physical appearance as an organizational bias. One white male believed that at his firm, appearance was prized above all else. Another white female (#184, age 47) stated that at her firm, "No woman became an associate or partner. [The] attitude was that secretaries needed to be beautiful." I have witnessed the latter at more than a few architectural offices, especially at large firms whose secretaries look like they just stepped out of *Glamour* magazine.

In this regard, the experiences of my former architectural students are revealing. In fact, I am not the only architecture professor to have noticed this disturbing trend. Some of us have observed a striking correlation—especially during recessions when jobs are scarce—between the physical appearance of young women architectural graduates and their ability to land their first jobs. More often than not, alumni who are attractive and flaunt their bodies in high-fashion attire (slinky black dresses have often been the rage) are hired just weeks after graduation. By contrast, for more ordinary-looking but equally qualified women, the first job hunt can be excruciating. Several have taken almost a year to find a position. It may be that our profession of design—with its fixation on aesthetics—has taken this obsession much too far. Ironically, some male architects are engaging in subtle forms of discrimination against women whose physical appearance, in their opinion, is not award-winning.

The top three glass-ceiling barriers that surfaced in my study were: (1) management's lack of commitment to establish systems, policies, and practices to achieve upward mobility; (2) pay inequities for work of equal or comparable value; and (3) limited opportunities for advancement to decision-making positions. Compared to men, women found each of the glass-ceiling barriers I asked about more problematic. (See table 9.) The gender gap was widest about sex-based stereotyping and pay inequities. Compared to white architects, persons of color found several glass-ceiling barriers more troublesome. (See table 10.) Racial gaps were widest about both racial and ethnic stereotyping.[27]

When asked "What barriers have [you] found the most difficult to overcome," several architects cited pay inequities. As one white woman (#175, age 29) put it, "The assumption that I am going to have a child and not be as committed combined with the assumption that my husband is the 'breadwinner' and that my need for income and position is secondary." Another white woman (#204, age 55) referred to this phenomenon as "the patriarchal paradigm." This theme

TABLE 9. To What Extent Have You Encountered the Following Glass-Ceiling Barriers?

	Male	Female
Pay inequities (n = 317)***	2.6	3.7
Sex-based stereotyping (n = 319)***	2.0	3.4
Lack of family-friendly workplace policies (n = 295)***	2.0	2.9
Sexual harassment (n = 302)**	1.6	2.1
Age (n = 329)*	2.2	2.5
Limited opportunities for advancement (n = 320)*	2.9	3.4
Lack of management commitment to upward mobility (n = 312)*	3.2	3.6
Lack of management commitment to workplace diversity (n = 303)*	2.9	3.3

Note: 1 = not at all; 3 = somewhat; 5 = very much
*$p < .05$; **$p < .01$; ***$p < .001$

TABLE 10. To What Extent Have You Encountered the Following Glass-Ceiling Barriers?

	White	Persons of Color
Racially based stereotyping (n = 267)***	1.9	2.8
Ethnically based stereotyping (n = 275)***	1.9	2.7
Racial harassment (n = 258)**	1.6	2.0
Racial abuse (n = 262)**	1.5	1.9
Lack of management commitment to workplace diversity (n = 303)**	3.0	3.5
Limited opportunities for advancement (n = 298)*	3.5	3.1
Lack of management commitment to upward mobility (n = 312)*	3.3	3.7

Note: 1 = not at all; 3 = somewhat; 5 = very much
*$p < .05$; **$p < .01$; ***$p < .001$

is echoed countless times in my research, and it continues to be true for young architects. Mothers are forced to confront the glass ceiling if they opt for part-time work, thus impeding their opportunities for career advancement.

Several architects, both young and old, complained of continually being asked to do their own secretarial work. As one white woman (#199, age 37) put it, she had to fight the "perception that all women are born secretaries." Ditto with the notorious "Girl Friday" role. Others complained of religious (a non-Mormon practicing in Utah) and regional biases (working with male clients from the South).

Other problems included:

> The perception that a client will not respond positively to a female. (#71, white male, age 53)

> Convincing bosses women can get dirty or wear jeans on a job site and be respected by construction crews. (#172, white female, age 30)

> Being considered aggressive or authoritative, not bitchy or a pushy broad. (#201, white female, age 37)

> Women's contributions are devalued whereas men's are over-advertised. (#317, foreign-born white female, age 49)

Architects were asked, "What problems or obstacles do you perceive as unique to architects of color?" While one white male responded with an emphatic "NONE!!" several other white males acknowledged serious problems in the field for their nonwhite counterparts. One man recognized that members of under-represented groups face "many obstacles. It is a white male club and the clients are also typically white male" (#131, white male, age 36). Among the obstacles cited by architects of color themselves were bias and discrimination on projects; lack of nongovernment projects, that is, those in the private or commercial sector; and subtle forms of racism. Here are some of the architects' remarks:

> We are not taken seriously. We are not trusted. What I mean by "trusted" is that clients, coworkers, etc., must be sure of one's ability, taste, and training in order to entrust [an architect] with the money for the construction of something permanent like a building. Unfortunately, often our own people do not trust architects of color. (#190, African-American male, age 43)

> The obstacles I perceive as unique to architects of color is "color." I've been denied jobs on several occasions because of my color. I am usually mistaken for "white" on the telephone–almost guaranteed a job until I arrive at the firm–only to see blank faces! . . . Once denied a job because of my color, I realize that there are usually [no persons of color] working there, and [just] one or two white females. (#203, African-American female, age 29)

Dealing with others' perceptions that only architects of color can design for people of color. (#224, African-American female, age 30)

One woman summed up the ideal situation many underrepresented architects hope for: "Having people stop and sit to listen to what you can do, not how you look" (#339, Asian-American female, age 36).

When asked, "What problems or obstacles do you perceive as unique to female architects?" the issues overlapped somewhat, yet others were different altogether. Motherhood was one of the more common themes, although respondents also raised other issues. Here are some responses from men:

Traditional barriers . . . but I see them diminishing. (#98, white male, age 36)

In general, women are more emotional than men. (#197, white male, age 36)

Here are some of the women's remarks:

I found it difficult to be taken seriously when I was pregnant. (#127, white female, age 40)

White males think they are protecting you from the harsh contractor by not letting you go into the field. Instead they are prohibiting growth in your career. (#136, African-American female, age 31)

In assuming the role of architect, women redefine–both for themselves and for the men around them–what it means to be female. Essentially, they have to adapt to the male values of competition, aggression, and individualism to succeed. Even if some men intellectually support women's inclusion in the field, they are often emotionally uncomfortable with them. Whether consciously or not, they tend to blame their discomfort on the women, who then face criticism and ostracism. If women retain their more traditional female trait of cooperation, they are not seen as authoritative enough to handle additional responsibility. This is sexism, whether intentional or not. As one Latina put it (#147, age 41), "I believe that most men do not have confidence in their female colleagues, and that this and fear of criticism by the male establishment prevents them from promoting women in traditional offices. . . . Together with the crisis mentality that pervades most architectural offices (the wolf is often at the door), these factors prevent women from achieving high levels of management in offices."

> I have sacrificed income, labor, sleep, respect from peers. You name it—
> architecture has required it. (#367, white male, age 34)

How have architects been able to combine both their personal and professional lives? In a profession with such demanding hours, is this possible to achieve?
As Jane Darke, of the British feminist collective Matrix, has argued:

> If they [women architects] wish to combine a career with marriage and
> parenthood, they are liable to experience strain in the combination of
> architect, mother and wife which is not usually present for architects
> who are also husbands and fathers. . . . It is also more difficult for a
> woman to become a partner in a practice, since the ideal new partner is
> in his or her thirties, with a wide network of contacts with potential
> clients and a willingness to put in considerable unpaid overtime. This
> is the time when many women take a break to have children, with con-
> sequent loss of professional contacts and reduced capacity to work long
> hours.[28]

Recall that in the United States, the Family and Medical Leave Act (FMLA)
affects only a minuscule number of architects since most work in small firms.
In the United Kingdom, Statutory Maternity Pay, a provision of the state, fails to
affect most British architects. It, too, applies only to firms with five or more
people, and two thousand of the five thousand architectural practices in the U.K.
do not qualify.[29]

But laws like the FMLA cover only part of family life. Such measures do assist families in coping with some major life events such as the birth or adoption of a child, or caring for a sick relative. But what about the rest of the time,
for example, while children are growing up? Preschool children present the
greatest challenge to working parents. But even later on, school hours and work
schedules of full-time architects rarely coincide. What if school begins at 8:30
A.M., but Mom or Dad architect needs to be at the office at 8:00 A.M.? What if
elementary school lets out at 3:00 P.M., but Mom or Dad architect isn't out of
the office until 5:00 P.M. and still needs to commute home? Not to mention the
meetings, overtime, and deadlines that, for many architects, make the typical
eight-to-five workday unrealistic. What if a child is sick and has to stay home
from school, or has an appointment with the doctor or dentist? What happens

during summer vacation? What about children who need their parents to drive them to and from baseball practice or ballet lessons? Such dilemmas are not just women's issues. They are human issues that concern all working parents. Architectural employers can no longer afford to ignore them.[30]

I asked architects several open-ended questions to explore these concerns. Just over half (54%) of my sample had children under eighteen years old; four out of ten (44%) had children under twelve; and just under a quarter (23%) had children under five. Just over a quarter (29%) of the sample were women with children, and 19% were women with children under twelve.

Just over half the women (54%) but only about a quarter of the men (26%) surveyed did *not* have children. In other words, my data show that female architects are twice as likely as male architects to forgo having children. This raises a host of questions: Of those architects with children, is it easier for men than women to survive and thrive in the profession? Should they decide to pursue an architectural career, must women give up having children? Why do more men than women architects have children?

I asked architects, "What kinds of personal sacrifices have you made to get where you are today?" The typical response was that they gave up valuable family time in order to pursue and maintain their careers. Every demographic group in the study made comments to this effect, often with regret. Several respondents pointed to marriages and relationships that had dissolved because they were too wrapped up in their work. Others lacked time for a social life. Some spoke of monetary sacrifices, and for many, the first years of practice were losing financial operations. Many women delayed having children in order to pursue their careers, and several gave up the idea altogether. While some expressed regret, others referred to these as "conscious decisions" rather than "sacrifices." Other women spoke of the opposite scenario, putting their architectural careers on the back burner in order to devote time to their families. Here are some of the architects' comments:

> Another great sacrifice made when teaching at a black college . . . was my social life. I decided to focus squarely on being a good teacher. This required quality time, and thus I cut back on going to nightclubs, etc. However the payoff was improved rapport with my students, and my courses were well organized and well attended. (#190, African-American male, age 43)

> I started architecture school when I was 29 years old with a husband, two daughters age 9 and 7, and was rather poor financially. I never sac-

rificed cooking a good meal from scratch and being home with my children, except for the hours that I had a class. But I sacrificed many, many hours of sleep, lived like a pauper, didn't buy a house or even own a car, and gave up any social life (no movies, etc.). (#304, white female, age 44)

I didn't have a "real" relationship during college. I was "married to school." But it was worth the wait. I'm happily married now! (#288, Latina, age 29)

Another question asked, "Have any experiences outside of your work significantly impacted your career? In general, what part have events in your personal life played in your career growth?" Several architects mentioned that marriage had a significant impact, and that being wed to another architect helped their careers. Others pointed to divorce as a critical turning point. Still others spoke of having children and putting their architectural work in a different perspective. Several cited moving to a different city as a pivotal point in their careers. A few pointed to important political events—for men, the Vietnam War, and for women, the women's movement. Here are some of the personal situations cited:

AIDS [acquired immune deficiency syndrome]—I am HIV [human immunodeficiency virus] positive and have been very active in HIV-related activities. This has had both a positive and negative impact. (#391, mixed-race female, age 39)

My children—or my boss's perception of them—have slowed my advancement down, I believe. (#195, white female, age 44)

As a girl, I was taught not to stand up before people and tell them I was great. I was not taught to brag. Little girls of my generation, particularly, were taught to be modest, demure; and having to learn to stand up before a reviewing group of people and tell them I'm great and my firm is the best, that was very hard for me. (I-#16, white female, age 54)

My involvement in the Latin American community and the women's liberation movement has impacted my career such that I'm now actively involved in the local AIA Minority Professional Interest Area and the local Association for Women in Architecture. These efforts at building the community of architects are rooted in personal experience. (#147, Latina, age 41)

THE PART-TIME ARCHITECT:
A VANISHING SPECIES?

Last fall during a local breakfast for "mothers in architecture," I discovered there are many women facing the same challenges that I am. We discussed at length parental leave and its unspoken impact on one's career. Many felt that the written policy was not always supported[,] in an unspoken way, especially at the larger firms.

Most mothers at the breakfast preferred a part-time schedule [in order] to juggle all of their responsibilities. It was surprising to me how many women said they could not work part-time because their employers felt it was incompatible with our profession. If they did work part-time, they were expected to receive a lower hourly wage, for their flexible schedule. It baffles me why employers in professions such as architecture . . . do not see the value in part-time employment. Most women I know who work part-time get almost as much accomplished as those who work full time. (#139, white female, age 37)

A key question is, Can architects–be they mothers or fathers–work part-time without damaging their careers? Jane Darke believes not. Drawing upon results of a study of women in architectural practice in the United Kingdom, she argues: "Architecture is not an ideal occupation for part-time work. If women want to work part-time they may be confined to helping out on other people's schemes rather than designing and supervising schemes of their own, since the latter requires the designer to be constantly available to answer queries and clear up problems."[31]

This issue surfaced repeatedly in my research. My results provide strong evidence that, more often than not, the field is unfriendly–and in some cases, downright hostile–toward those unable to commit themselves to a full-time position. In fact, only 7% of those surveyed were currently working part-time. Full-time work in architecture usually exceeds the 40-hour work week. Survey respondents worked an average 46.7 hours per week and reported that in a typical work week, they are expected to work an average of 5.6 hours overtime. The highest number of hours worked in one week was an average of 66.7, with one person reporting a grueling 140-hour work week.

Here statistically significant gender and racial differences were found. Men's highest work week was an average of 70.5 hours, compared to women's, at 64.2 hours. And whites' highest work week was an average of 68.2 hours compared to persons of color at 64.6 hours. Could this pattern relate to the disturbing pay discrepancies? Does clocking in a few extra hours advantage white male architects and their pay scales?

The all-nighter syndrome of the academic design studio is often carried into professional practice as well. Such marathon hours make it exceedingly difficult to maintain any semblance of a regular home life.

Half those architects surveyed (50%) agreed that "A female architect who takes maternity leave probably will damage her career." While almost two-thirds (63%) agreed that "A female architect can have preschool children and work full-time," a significant gender difference was found; women were *less* likely to agree. Nonetheless, three-quarters (74%) agreed that "A female architect can have school-age children and work full-time"; no significant gender differences were found.

Just how receptive is the profession to part-time work? A few firms go out of their way to accommodate part-timers, and a few architects have had successful careers while employed part-time, but they are the exceptions rather than the rule. Two women advanced to unusually high positions after having worked for several years in a major architectural firm in Chicago. Later, when they began raising children, they were able to negotiate part-time schedules. However, stories like theirs are rare.

Several women who advanced in mainstream architectural firms believe that the only way women—or men, for that matter—can work part-time while still establishing their architectural careers is to work for themselves. That way, they can set their own schedule and work when they want. In their view, the need to work part-time also explains why so many women flee traditional practice to work for the government, where hours are less erratic and less demanding. Traditional architectural firms can rarely accommodate their family needs.

As one woman at a large Chicago architectural firm put it, "So often we have architects who are applying for part-time work, but the work that needs to be done requires full-time effort. Our bosses simply are not interested in hiring new part-time workers. Why should they hire one person part-time when ten architects willing to work full-time are lining up at our doors? We have reached a point where we who now work part-time actually end up working a full load in any case, so our employers are getting more for their money. We have learned to be much more efficient on the job than we would have been otherwise."

One woman dramatically underscored the problem: "About the time that men are making the biggest strides—really in the critical years of carving out their places in their careers—is just about the time that women have to fish or cut bait on the issue of children. And, if they choose the mommy side of things . . . [they] feel quite compromised in actually maintaining their full-time [work] obligations with the care and attention to their kids. . . . I find that many of them choose, then, to work part-time, which is *the kiss of death.* You cannot do it" (I-#7, white female, age 35).

Is working part-time in traditional architectural practice truly "the kiss of death?" If it is—or even if it is perceived to be—this must account for the large numbers of women who disappear from the field. The profession appears to be far from family-friendly.

LAYOFFS

My darkest hour came with my second firing. I had worked overtime and was in the office at 7:30 on a Friday night building a model—when my boss and his dog walked through. I had been asked to come in on Saturday morning to discuss something (unspecified) and I asked if we could discuss it at this time. "No," he wanted to do it on Saturday. So I drove in to the office Saturday and was terminated—told to get out after making prints of anything I wanted for my portfolio—but he ("my boss") did not want me ever to return.

He said that I had misrepresented myself at my interview sixteen months before and that he couldn't believe how little I knew.

Note: This is the man [who] said I could not call him by his first name. I had also found out that someone who had quit one month prior to this point in time (a man, of course) had been getting over a dollar an hour more than me and had less experience and [fewer] abilities. He just had an Ivy League education (five-year) vs. my graduate degree from a midwestern university.

Two weeks after being fired, I received a phone call from the bookkeeper at 10:30 one night—telling me that my former boss wanted his tuxedo vests that I had been altering for him (to get extra money) back so that he could use them—it now being opera season in Dallas. They were exchanged for a cashier's check at a neutral location (I could not return to the office), and that ended all relations.

Until a few years ago, I was seeking my NCARB certificate and had to contact this man for a reference—no response. NCARB finally called the man (whose business was defunct by this time) and he told them that I was unprofessional. Even years following my separation from his company, he was haunting me. I received my NCARB certificate but not without having to explain some of the sexual harassment I endured just to keep a job that I had hated (and didn't even pay health insurance). (#84, white female, age 39)

Perhaps more than most other professions, architecture is subject to the ebb and flow of the economy. Many architects are hired to work on a project-by-project basis, and once the project is over, and if no new projects are in the works, they are laid off. Others are fired with little or no explanation at all. But who gets laid off–and for how long? How do architects deal with this uncertainty?

Since they began their careers in architecture, those in my survey had been unemployed an average of 1.2 times; however, the range was great–from zero to twenty times. I found a statistically significant gender difference: women were *more* likely to have been unemployed *more often* than men; men had been unemployed an average of 0.9 times, compared to women at 1.3. No significant racial differences were found on this issue.

One might speculate that compared to men, women are more likely to take time off to have children and hence be temporarily unemployed. But recall that compared to their male counterparts, the women architects I surveyed are twice as likely *not* to have children. In fact, over half the women in my study did not even have children–which throws the maternity-leave theory out the window. Instead, my data confirm what many women have long suspected: when it comes to deciding which architects get laid off, women are the likely candidates.

The average length of the first unemployment period was 6.5 months, with a range of 0–10 years. On this item, no significant gender or racial differences were found. The average length of the second unemployment was 8.3 months, with a range of 0 to almost 10 years. Here, while no statistically significant gender differences were found, I did find a statistically significant racial difference. White architects' second period of unemployment lasted an average of 5.4 months, compared to 13.6 months for architects of color. Hence architects of color were unemployed for a significantly longer period of time, the second time around, than were white architects. Note that some but not all of these periods of unemployment were due to layoffs.

Are underrepresented architects often the last ones hired and the first ones fired? The evidence suggests that this is true. As an article in *Designer/Builder* confirms, "Women are often the last hired and the first fired, denying them the opportunities to build up a long enough tenure to actually move through the ranks."[52] Once laid off or fired, those already disadvantaged may find it even harder to land another job. When this situation is repeated, it is not surprising that they decide they are simply better off somewhere else. Nonetheless, getting fired is traumatic for all architects. Among the situations they cited:

> Being cold-heartedly laid off by the man I most admired, and feeling I had no foot-hold in the profession, no support. I developed a negative view of the professional establishment that has persisted for eleven years. (#132, white male, age 43)

> Fired for "lifestyle." [Later,] as a corporate architect, I denied the firm any work! (#130, white male, age 50)

> Getting fired (for the last time) at Christmas. (#383, African-American male, age 43)

> Getting fired when asking for [my] yearly review—[I later] started my own business. (#323, white female, age 43)

> An economic recession caused the firm to "downsize." Layoffs seemed arbitrary except that several of the professional women were let go, while men of similar position were retained. (#99, white female, age 43)

DROPOUTS

> All people of color continue to be subject to discrimination to a much greater extent than do women. (#152, African-American female, age 38)

In 1989 the AIA hosted a "Large Firm Roundtable" with Cynthia Woodward, a specialist in human resources management for design professionals, as its featured speaker. She asserted: "There seem to be some disturbing patterns in work histories of women that negatively affect both their careers and our firms. We have finally succeeded in attracting a substantial percentage of women to the profession but we seem to be losing them just at the point in time when their training makes them valuable contributors."[33]

That same year, the AIA's Women in Architecture Committee hired a consultant, Roberta Feldman, to design a research study about attrition rates of women in the profession and in school. She proposed to examine the following issues: Is the dropout rate in architecture schools higher for women than it is for men? Compared to their male counterparts, do fewer women graduates eventually become registered? Have men's and women's attrition rates in architecture school and in the profession changed over time? What policy changes are needed? The research plan called for a comprehensive set of surveys and interviews culminating in three reports to be presented to the AIA. The research would have cost $32,000 to complete. Unfortunately, the AIA chose not to fund it.[34]

With this in mind, I asked two open-ended questions on my survey to address these issues. One was: "Do you know of anyone who has had a particularly negative experience in architectural practice—and dropped out of the field as a result? Please explain." Almost fifty architects answered "yes" to this question. According to their reports, several of their colleagues had exited the field, largely due to low pay and long hours. For many architects, that sharp imbalance is the straw that breaks the camel's back. Several former architects retooled themselves with business or law degrees, which offered them much higher starting salaries.

An inability to find work, especially during economic recessions, was another reason for quitting the field. While architects moved onto related fields, such as interiors, construction, or real estate development, others left altogether. One woman told of a friend who had started her own architectural practice but soon became overextended financially. Although still licensed as an architect, she was currently applying to become a letter carrier. Other respondents described friends and acquaintances who found their college professors too rough and who were "turned off" from the profession as a result of unpleasant experiences in school.

Here are some of the responses concerning layoffs:

> Yes—She was laid off from several firms . . . never got a sense of job security and could not develop fully as a professional because she did construction documents but never saw the rest of the business. . . . [She was] "pigeonholed" into one technical level. (#88, white female, age 35)

> They get sick of it. Of not getting the recognition or not getting the next opportunity or being the one that gets laid off all the time and therefore is on the constant looking-for-a-new-job treadmill. It becomes emotionally exhausting, and so there's only so much you can do of that. (I-#20, white female, age 41)

> I had to stick with it because I knew other young women who were in my age group . . . who had graduated around the same time I did and

who dropped out of architecture. And I think it's because they had other options. I didn't have any other option. I had nobody to support me, so I had to work, and I had to stick with it. So that kind of perseverance was what did it. The perseverance was because I had to. (I-#27, African-American female, age 66)

I know of many people who are considering changing fields, none who have actually done so. Most often they slide off into tangential fields such as architectural administration, become owners' representatives, etc. Architecture is never easy, and during times of economic recession, people face negative experiences every day. (#147, Latina, age 41)

A second question asked specifically about women who fled the field: "What do you think is responsible for the relatively high percentage of female architects who drop out of the profession?" Over fifty architects responded. A few who answered this question—men and women alike—were unaware of the problem. Yet, on the other hand, a number of white male architects acknowledged that sexist practices were to blame. Long hours, low pay, inability of the profession to accommodate architects who are mothers, and a high degree of frustration with stifling working conditions were among the most common reasons suggested. Several people believed that women simply got tired of constantly having to prove themselves and concluded that they would be better off elsewhere. Among their remarks:

The image of architecture is much more glamorous than the reality. It is actually a high stress, low paying profession. (#174, white female, age 37)

If they get hired, they're given dog work and never promoted, never sent out in the field, never consulted in meetings. Patronized if they voice an opinion. (#199, white female, age 37)

I think that motherhood is the single biggest deterrent or the single reason for the relatively high percentage of dropouts.... You weigh your options and there are only twenty-four hours in a day, and there's only so much of you. Where do you give it? And to many of us [women architects], the children come first. (I-#16, white female, age 54)

The job is too hard for the rare rewards. Many women harbor a great deal of hopelessness which comes from seeing themselves and their female colleagues face continual disappointment from lack of promotion, lack of pay equity, sexist comments from male colleagues, difficulty in getting responsibility, and unexplainable lack of professional success when they know they are bright and talented. (#147, Latina, age 41)

A few individuals in my sample actually did drop out of the profession. Here is what two of them had to say:

> When I finally quit I had achieved a level of success that was recognized by my clients. I was running the space planning and interiors department with a reasonable level of success. Which my boss recognized only when clients called him and praised my work. . . . I love the inner workings of architecture—It is just the old-fashioned mindset of the heads of offices that I have had trouble with throughout my career. As one of my third-year professors put it, "A woman has no place in architecture and if you were smart you would get out." I survived three more years of school and then entered the profession [only] to discover that a female who speaks her mind is sanctioned as an outcast, whereas a male who speaks his mind is recognized as a forward thinker and praised. The "politics of architecture" is a subject that all schools should teach—It would soften the blow for people like me who were brought up to believe that men and women were equal. (#84, white female, age 39)

> I have personally "dropped out" of the architectural field. I cannot pinpoint exactly one event that triggered my decision. Some of the contributing factors were:
>
> – lack of challenge in my career and the inability to find a position that suited my objectives
> – low compensation
> – the tendency in the profession towards CAD (Computer Aided Design), and feeling "pigeonholed" because of my knowledge and abilities in this area
> – the inability to find someone who could become a mentor
> – feeling the general attitude that I should be an interior designer, or that I wasn't as capable as a male with the same experience
>
> In general, I must say that I didn't enjoy my experience in the practice of architecture. . . . I think most of the art has disappeared from the field, and I personally felt creatively stifled. (#91, foreign-born female, age 27)

Many architects face turmoil in their profession. Low pay, grueling hours, and relatively few rewards eat away at even the most dedicated designer's desire to remain in the field. Yet for underrepresented architects, the situation is even more of a challenge. My research demonstrates that discrimination runs rampant and that inequities in salaries and benefits are widespread. In fact, the longer women remain in the profession, the wider the pay gap with their male counterparts. Ironically, they are penalized rather than rewarded for their loyalty to the profession.

Although sexual harassment is no longer as common as in the past, it still exists. Sexual harassment and discrimination touch some architects deeply, but others are unaware of their existence. Women face more subtle forms of harassment on the job and they confront more glass-ceiling barriers than do their majority counterparts. For many women, integrating personal and professional lives, while continuing to work full time, is near impossible. While many prefer to work part-time, circumstances often prohibit their doing so. In all too many cases, underrepresented architects are indeed the last hired and the first fired. It isn't surprising that so many choose to drop out of the field.

No doubt that the picture painted by this chapter is bleak. Yet despite this devastating critique, many architects cling to this profession. The next chapter explores how some have transformed personal turmoil into triumph.

Chapter 7

SUCCEEDING IN THE ARCHITECTURAL WORKPLACE

> There are many layers of glass ceilings, not just one:
> I have [broken] through several of them only to find
> another. White males may have one or two layers
> which may include youth and inexperience. Once
> they break those two ceilings, it's pretty clear sailing.
> Women and minorities of course have those two
> layers, but after breaking through, they have many
> more to go.
>
> —#226, Asian-American female, age 45

WHY DO SOME UNDERREPRESENTED ARCHITECTS triumph in the field while others don't? How have certain architects managed to pierce that glass ceiling? Several factors come into play: those who succeed often identify mentors who take an interest in their careers, find a hospitable work environment that allows them to grow professionally, and, in the case of those who have family responsibilities at home, work flexible hours. This chapter explores these possibilities.

PEOPLE HELPING PEOPLE

> [My mentor] took me aside after the . . . initial meetings and would critique the way I handled myself with clients–how I spoke, how I presented. . . . He was very instructive, and he did it in a very nice manner. He did it only to help. . . . He was relatively young, so I think he could empathize with my situation of being new. (#I-5, Latina, age 35)

In many fields, including architecture, mentoring has proven to be an effective way of helping younger professionals learn the ways of the profession and climb the career ladder. When asked, "Throughout your career in architecture, how often have you had a mentor–a person who 'showed you the ropes'?" about a third of my respondents (34%) answered "always" or "almost always." About the same percentage (37%) answered "never" or "almost never." The topic of mentorship engendered much discussion. Some who lacked a mentor replied with cynicism, often regretting that they missed this opportunity. For example:

> I had two or three instructors who encouraged me, and later occasional kindness from colleagues, but this has been more of a "sink or swim" process–I've done some dog paddling. (#99, white female, age 43)

> This is depressing–I never had any. (#326, Latina, age 45)

For those who did have someone who "showed them the ropes," the gender or race of the mentor was immaterial; the key is that the mentor served as a valuable resource. In a few cases, the relationship with the mentor appeared to have a parent-child quality. In others, it was more of a relationship between peers. Some argued that rather than having only one mentor, it was more important to have a number of people upon whom they could rely for advice. Here is what some respondents had to say:

> They showed me that art, creativity, construction, and business could be combined as an enjoyable way to spend one's life. (#124, white male, age 48)

> By luck, I have almost always had a mentor. Now, I make it a priority to find someone in a level above me who can provide mentorship to me no matter what job situation I go into. And in turn, I have expressly become a mentor to several young men over the years. (#190, African-American male, age 43)

> My first boss was terrific. He showed me the ropes and included me in client meetings, construction site visits, etc. I was involved in all phases of a project from beginning to end. (#288, Latina, age 29)

FINDING THE RIGHT FIRM

> My firm has sponsored my membership in the AIA, sent me to computer classes on company time, and sent me to professional development seminars. They also pay me salaried days for the days I spend taking

the Architecture Registration Exam. Considering our size, it's generous. (#110, Asian-American female, age 31)

A key factor in architects' career success is their ability to find their niche—a work environment where they not only feel comfortable, but where their talents and abilities are recognized. In addition to finding a supportive work environment, survey participants reported that being active in professional organizations like the AIA, women-in-architecture groups, and the National Organization of Minority Architects (NOMA) contributed to their professional success. Others credited continuing education and professional development courses and networking outside their own firm.

Management practices can either make or break employees. While true for all architects, this is especially the case for those underrepresented in the field. Supervisors who take an interest in their personnel, continually offering them more challenging assignments and encouraging their professional development, are essential for success. By contrast, bosses with a passive "sink or swim" attitude watch on the shoreline as their underrepresented architects drown. Too many near-death experiences lead one to stay out of the water altogether.

Respondents were asked to rate where they believed women and people of color have the greatest and least chances for career advancement, and they were to select from a list of fifteen work situations. Most architects surveyed believe that women (both women of color and whites) have the *greatest* chance for career advancement in interiors, government work, and running a husband-wife firm; and that women's *lowest* chances for success were in a large firm, working for a male boss, and in an architectural firm. In other words, they perceive women to be best off when they are somewhat out of the mainstream of architectural practice.

Respondents agree that women's chances for career advancement are *best* in a small firm, somewhat less so in a mid-sized firm, and worst in a large firm. They believe that women's chances for climbing the ladder are, *in order from best to worst option,* in interiors, government work, marketing, computer work, corporate firm, real estate development, and an architectural firm. Respondents believe that women's best chances for advancement are in running a husband-wife firm and running their own firm, and their lowest chances for success are in working for a male boss.

Most of those surveyed believe that architects of color have the *highest* chances for career advancement in government work, working for a person of color, and running their own firm, and their *lowest* chances in marketing, real estate development, and interiors. The issue of firm size revealed no real differences; that is, architects of color are perceived to be just as well off whether they are in a large, mid-sized, or small firm. Regarding the type of firm, respondents believe architects of color are most likely to succeed, *from best to worst option,* in government work, computer work, a corporate firm, architectural firm, interiors, and marketing. Most believe that architects of color are best off working for a person of color or running their own firm. Compared to how my respondents perceive women's chances for success in the field, the picture for architects of color is somewhat brighter. Nonetheless, respondents still do not believe underrepresented architects are as likely to succeed as whites in some of the more traditional areas of the profession.

These perceptions underscore the fact that most of those surveyed believe that underrepresented architects are advantaged when they escape the confines of traditional architectural practice. These views also reinforce gender and racial stereotypes, for instance, that women are best off in interiors and minorities best off in government.

Several common themes underlie the success stories of underrepresented architects in my research. The successful individuals generally fall into two camps: those who had become corporate architects—an avenue that they wished they had learned more about in school—or those who had opened up their own architectural practice and became their own bosses. *In general, the corporate architects' experience was much more positive than the experiences of architects in traditional practice.* Corporate architects were generally offered greater visibility, more responsibility, more contact with clients, continuing education, and substantially more pay. Here is one example:

> Every time I was feeling as though I was getting bored with my assignment, I have always had decent managers who realized that if they were really to keep me within the company that they had to provide more challenging environments or experiences. . . . [My corporation] puts a fair amount of emphasis on continuing education, a very strong relationship with a manager. . . . If you are a good performer, they make sure that your manager . . . knows about it. . . . There's . . . the understanding that you have to do professional development. . . . They encourage you to have a network outside of the company . . . whereas I know a lot of other companies would fight against that. (I-#12, Latina, age 35)

From what I could ascertain from my data, what matters most in finding the right firm is the perception of a unique chemistry between employer and employee. In fact, no single prescription applies. However, certain company characteristics foster success. I asked architects, "Is there something your firm did to help you succeed?" For some, accommodating a part-time schedule for working parents was a major factor. For others, having an employer that allowed them to prove themselves initially and develop special areas of expertise was key. A common theme was that their bosses trusted them enough to provide them with the chance to grow and flourish beyond their job descriptions. Here are some of the responses:

> They have always promoted me as a team member of the firm. My presence at all meetings and presentations helps to give me more credibility. (#228, white female, age 35)

> There was a case where I was doing some construction management and one of the contractors tried to go over my head because he didn't like the answer he was given. And my boss stood up for me and told him that I was the one in charge of the project and I had instructed him what to do. (I-#14, African-American female, age 36)

> In the beginning I would be given menial tasks, and I didn't refuse to do them, but then I let the firm know that I was capable of much more and wanted much more, and they gave me more challenging assignments. And if you don't do that, they'll have you doing menial tasks continuously. There is a difference between ten years' experience and one year's experience repeated ten times. (I-#27, African-American female, age 66)

SHATTERING THE GLASS CEILING

> Every time you prove competency in any role (as a minority) it's something nobody expected of you, so it is important that you get the chances to display your talents. However, even though I broke the glass ceiling, that hole closes for the next person–they have to fight and prove themselves again. Ideally, the holes should remain. (#355, African-American male, age 39)

According to the AIA Firm Survey 2000–2002, 12% of the principals and partners at firms are women, while 6% are persons of color. The percentage of women-owned business enterprises (WBEs) increased to almost 9% in 1999 from just over 7% in 1996. By contrast, the percentage of minority-owned business enterprises (MBEs) remained steady at 7% over the same three-year period. The average size of a WBE is about 5 people, while that of an MBE is just over 7 people. WBEs shared a growth in the percentage of firms in all size categories except for sole practitioners, which dropped to 35% in 1999 from 52% in 1996. The percentage of larger WBEs (20 or more employees) doubled from 2% in 1996 to 4% in 1999, while large MBEs grew from 4% in 1996 to 9% in 1999. In 1999, 9.9% of firms that qualified for municipal, state, or federal set-aside programs reported no billings from set-asides. A higher percentage of MBEs (30%) than WBEs (5%) reported any billings from set-asides in 1999.[1]

How did architects shatter the glass ceilings they encountered? About 40% of my survey respondents believed they had done so. Of this 40%, three out of four were women, and one out of three were persons of color. I asked a number of questions to find out how they had broken through. By far the most frequently cited means is to open one's own firm. In fact, about one-fifth (17%) of my respondents were solo practitioners; nationally about one-third of all architectural firms fell into this category at the time I conducted my survey.[2] As one white woman (#285, age 71) put it, "Breaking through isn't possible. I circumvented being employed by becoming an employer."

Several fled a hopelessly restrictive situation and moved onto another job. Others routinely sought out management positions, while maintaining a record of excellent work. A number pointed to major breakthroughs such as winning major design competitions or design awards or having their work published. Others cited their election to prominent positions in local or national professional organizations such as the American Institute of Architects.

Some called attention to specific turning points in their careers. As one white woman (#96, age 27) recounted, "When asked to clean someone's pens, I explained that you have to tie your own shoes and clean your own pens. I received respect thereafter." Here are other watershed events that were mentioned:

> When I became more valuable to my firm because of what I knew—not because I was black or because they needed me to achieve an Equal Employment Opportunity (EEO) rating. (#320, African-American male, age 36)

> I have been successful in doing the kind of work I have wanted to do (design, client contact, salary increases, etc.) but have often had to initiate these incremental raises and promotions—or insist on them! (#232, Asian-American/white female, age 41)

In order to pierce the glass ceiling, architects must overcome many challenges. I asked interviewees, "What is the biggest challenge you have ever faced?" Here is what they had to say:

> I was really relegated to the office and didn't get out much to interact with contractors or clients. And then all of a sudden, I had the opportunity to move from one city to the next, and I took a completely different type of job. From working for architects, I started working for the city as a construction project manager. And so it was a great challenge to me . . . I had worked for architects for almost seven or eight years. And none of them that I had worked for had ever let me even attend a job meeting before. And here it was: I went from private to public practice where I was running job meetings. (I-#1, African-American female, age 40)

> Early in my career, I was faced with a lot of hostility and objections from other employees who were white male employees. And it was a challenge to overcome this and to turn them around so that maybe we didn't become friends, but at least the overt hostility decreased, diminished. (I-#27, African-American female, age 66)

> The biggest challenge was being handed a project, what I had always wanted, a whole project from start to finish, from planning, design, construction, without really having had any of that experience. I didn't know if I should laugh or cry. That was the biggest challenge, knowing where to start and to admit what I knew and didn't know. (I-#8, Latina, age 40)

THE PROMOTION

How and why did architects receive promotions? It is not enough for architects to simply toil away for hours on end. At the end of the day, what matters is what architects have to show for their efforts. Architects who have excelled on the job made sure that their superiors recognized their accomplishments.

Successful architects stressed that their supervisors needed to be aware of their economic value to the firm. As one associate principal in a major Chicago architectural firm put it, "You want to make sure that your boss realizes how much money s/he would lose if you quit."

They also carved out a particular niche, a unique technical expertise that made them critical to the firm's success. One woman spelled out her winning combination: constantly striving to "push the threshold" in her work while designing a building that is still functional. Another woman stated, "I always remember that I love this profession. I decided what my best attributes were, and used them to the best of my ability."

Women architects who took time out to raise families were most likely to be promoted if they had established themselves professionally early on in their careers. Passing the ARE and becoming licensed as soon as possible seemed to be a prerequisite. These architects distinguished themselves while working full-time, reaching that benchmark where they became indispensable to the firm. Only after that were they able to negotiate a reduced work schedule. As one woman put it, "We bring in lots of money to the firm, and we have our own clients, so our firm has now allowed us to do our own thing." A number of women who advanced in mainstream architectural offices cautioned that having children first and then becoming professionally licensed is almost impossible. Some notable exceptions were women who were self-employed, often with spouses who were able to support them financially while they become professionally established.

Another trait that allowed underrepresented architects to be promoted was the ability to stand up for their rights and take charge of their careers. At the very outset, they drew clear boundaries about what kinds of work they would or would not do, refusing to be pigeonholed. They made a point of reiterating that they were architects, not secretaries. For example, one architect, now a successful associate principal in a major Chicago architectural firm, recounted her reaction when she was asked to do her own typing: "I explained to my boss that I didn't even know how to type, and that I was sure that someone else would do a much better job at that. And even if I had been a crack typist, I wouldn't let anyone know it." Another architect who was asked to answer the phone simply let it ring. "I simply wouldn't allow it," she stated. She cautioned that that strategy could have cost her job, but even if it had, that job was not for her.

As one of my African-American women interviewees put it, "I decided to make that jump from allowing myself to be kicked around, to taking charge of my career and directing it the way I wanted it to go." As another woman put it, "We need to immediately take charge. Make it known we know what we are doing. Sit at the head of the table and run the meeting: 'Gentlemen . . . ?'"

Another trait integral to a promotion is resilience: the ability to bounce back after defeat. One African-American male partner at a prominent architectural firm attributed this quality to his own success. He began his career in the early 1960s and struggled for two years to land a job at an architectural office in Chicago. He acknowledges, in retrospect, that this was likely due to the fact that he was black. Earlier in his life, as a teenager growing up in the South, he had been harassed routinely by police. Nonetheless, he didn't let these negative experiences overwhelm him. Today he is working on "some of the most exciting architectural projects in the world. I don't focus on the negative," he explained. "Be the best that you are. It's the best way to handle discrimination." His strategy for advancing in his firm: "I was like a quiet pit bull. I told myself, 'I'm going to be a partner here. I'm going to do the best project here. You can not deny me that role.' You've got to outshine the others and make them realize how valuable you are."

CAREER REFLECTIONS

When I first got this elevated position at this very major architectural firm, I found the files where they had been advertising for an architect to fill this position: in the *New York Times,* the *San Francisco Chronicle,* the *San Francisco Bee,* and the *Wall Street Journal.* And when they couldn't find a white male whom they felt was better qualified, they offered it to me. Had I been a white male they wouldn't have looked anywhere else. (I-#27, African-American female, age 66)

The extent to which architects are satisfied with their jobs influences their perceptions of the profession and their willingness to stay in it. Underrepresented architects are especially vulnerable in this regard.

Architects surveyed were generally satisfied with their current jobs. Over three-quarters (79%) of the architects were satisfied with their jobs overall.[3] They were asked to rate their satisfaction with various aspects of their current jobs, including personal challenge, management, salary compensation, employee benefits, office support, advancement, and training opportunities. They were *most* satisfied with personal challenge (78% were satisfied) and *least* satisfied with salary compensation (35% were dissatisfied). Responses did not differ significantly either by gender or race on any of these items, with one exception. Both white men and men of color were significantly *more* satisfied than were white women and women of color with office support at their current jobs. Office support staff can sometimes pose problems for women architects. In a field that men have dominated for so long, support staff are often unaccustomed to working for professional women. As one respondent points out, "The female secretaries in your own office or others don't treat you half as well as they treat men and [they] hinder your performance" (#325, Latina, age 45).

When asked to reflect on their careers overall, most architects report high levels of satisfaction; just under three-quarters (72%) were satisfied.[4] Architects were *most* satisfied with their architectural accomplishments to date, as well as their future career prospects in architecture, and *least* satisfied with their architectural supervisors and employers. Significant gender and racial differences were found on two of these issues. Men of color reported significantly *higher* levels of satisfaction than did the other three groups with their employers. Women of color reported significantly *lower* levels of satisfaction with their future career prospects in architecture. In light of the fact that this demographic group has the *lowest* representation in the profession, this finding is disturbing.

When asked, "How do you rate your current position compared to members of the opposite sex with similar work status—either in your firm or elsewhere?" the typical male response was "about the same." By contrast, female architects rated several aspects significantly *lower* than did male architects, including salary compensation, desirable work assignments, and opportunities for advancement. (See table 11.)

TABLE 11. How Do You Rate Your Current Position Compared to Those of Members of the Opposite Sex?

	Male	Female
Salary compensation (n = 358)***	3.1	2.3
Opportunities for advancement (n = 365)***	3.2	2.6
Desirable work assignments (n = 357)***	3.2	2.7
Participation in management decisions (n = 347)***	3.2	2.7
Amount of respect from superiors (n = 336)***	3.2	2.8
Amount of respect from contractors (n = 355)***	3.3	2.5
Amount of encouragement from superiors (n = 332)**	3.1	2.8
Amount of respect from consultants (n = 370)**	3.2	2.9
Attracting clients/new business (n = 334)**	3.1	2.8
Amount of respect from clients (n = 363)*	3.2	2.9
Amount of respect from subordinates (n = 345)*	3.2	3.0

Note: 1 = much less; 3 = the same; 5 = much more
*$p < .05$; **$p < .01$; ***$p < .001$

I asked architects, "How, if at all, do you think your career would have been different if you were a member of the opposite sex?" While a handful believed that their careers would have been the same, most felt otherwise. Men's opinions are mixed. Here is what some male respondents had to say:

> Never would receive credibility from prospective clients needed to start a firm. (#98, white male, age 36)

> Maybe it's easier now for a black woman because she may pose less of a threat and get more opportunities. . . . I know that women, whether they be black or white, have a difficult time in this profession because there are a lot of things that aren't said–little cliques and groups that exclude women. I know that. (I-#13, African-American male, age 60)

> Not as much respect, even with talent. (#106, Asian-American male, age 57)

However, most women believed that they would be better off professionally as a man, particularly in terms of salary and career advancement. A few women perceive their gender to be a plus and use this to their advantage. Here is a sampling of women's responses:

> I think I'd probably be making $10,000 or $15,000 more. I think that I might have been given more opportunities on really exciting projects. I would have been invited to play golf . . . to go drinking. (I-#21, white female, age 33)

> If I were a black male, I do not think I would have had the opportunities I have been fortunate to have. I think I am less threatening. If I had been a white male, I would probably be a principal in a major firm or would have my own firm by now. Women of my generation were not afforded the opportunity to network, to be involved in the forefront of projects early in our careers, because clients and contractors were not receptive to our presence. (#152, African-American female, age 38)

> Considering how good I am, I probably would be making double my salary and own my own firm for twenty years instead of ten. I would probably be ready to retire. . . . As a man you can go play golf with the guys. You can go out drinking with the buddies. You can get jobs that way. You can hang around with the guys after work. Until more and

more women get into the business, there are so many networking [opportunities] that as a woman, you are kept away from. (I-#25, Asian/Latina, age 54)

■

Many architects manage to triumph in the profession because they are either fortunate enough to land in a supportive work environment early in their careers, or intelligent enough to flee what they perceive to be a dead-end job. When they have mentors to guide them, their journeys are easier. Working for employers who provided opportunities for them to develop professionally—and who recognized their work—are two keys to success. So is developing an indispensable area of expertise.

My research demonstrates that, with a handful of exceptions, underrepresented architects are most likely to flourish beyond the confines of the traditional architectural office. The positive side is that government work, corporate architecture, or opening up one's own office provide favorable alternatives. The downside is that not all underrepresented architects wish to pursue these career paths. Not everyone desires to open up his or her own firm or has the means to do so. Furthermore, the profession is creating a two-tiered system: those who manage to survive carve out careers for themselves in mainstream practice; those who refuse to tolerate unfair working conditions must resort to other options.

It is encouraging to learn that most architects surveyed are satisfied with their careers and that men of color reported significantly higher levels of satisfaction with their employers. But the fact that women of color reported significantly *lower* levels of satisfaction with their future career prospects in architecture signals that something is amiss. Most women surveyed believe that their careers would be much improved had they been members of the opposite sex. Will men and women ever be equals in the architectural profession? The final chapter addresses this question.

Chapter 8

DIVERSIFYING DESIGN

> As our world becomes multicultural and as we
> become more universal in our practice . . . the need
> for multicultural practices is going to be the basis for
> profit. . . . You get all these firms that are run by and
> completely operated by and completely employed by
> white males, [and] they are going to have a difficult
> time working in some international arenas. And that's
> when they're going to understand the need for
> diversity. . . . There has to be pressure from the client
> base that we serve to make the process work.
>
> —I-#10, African-American male, age 39

WHAT DOES MY RESEARCH SHOW about the experiences of contemporary architects? Compared to their white male counterparts, how are underrepresented architects faring? My analysis reveals several themes:

1. *Rites of passage that serve as gateways to the profession often serve as roadblocks to underrepresented architects.* Interviewing, internship, registration, and the first job are major hurdles to all architects. But when these experiences go poorly, and if underrepresented architects perceive that they are treated unfairly, these individuals can be driven right out of the profession.

2. *The fact that the architectural profession depends so strongly on a changing economy makes it difficult for employees to escape from uncomfortable work situations.* When times are tough and jobs are hard to come by, architects are trapped. This is especially true for those underrepresented in the field. When faced with unfair treatment or dead-end jobs that stifle their professional development, they may have nowhere else to turn. Such situations foster a professional climate that is reactive rather than proactive.

3. *Many underrepresented architects are pigeonholed.* Just as many women lawyers have been steered toward family law, and women physicians toward

pediatrics and psychiatry, women architects are often pegged as interior designers, African Americans as government architects, and Asian-American architects as computer-aided designers. Such pigeonholing limits their job mobility
and opportunities for advancement. They become prisoners of stereotypes,
defined by who they are rather than what they can do.

4. *The phenomenon of "leap-frogging" occurs all too often.* Far too many diverse designers, especially women, train less-experienced white male under-
lings who rapidly surpass them. These colleagues quickly climb their own career ladders, leaving their female counterparts behind to watch in disbelief.
Subordinates become superiors almost overnight. Such instances propel many
diverse designers right out of the profession, never wanting to return.

5. *Working conditions in many architectural offices all too often prohibit
those treated unfairly from complaining.* The vast majority of firms have only
a handful of employees, making confidential complaints impossible. The institutional structure of large organizations, universities, and corporations, where
human resource personnel handle complex issues like sexual harassment and
pay discrimination, is absent from the small architectural office. Many underrepresented architects fear a backlash from being labeled whistle blowers.

6. *The profession is not family-friendly.* This sentiment was voiced repeatedly
by my survey participants. While it no doubt affects both genders, it is a special
problem for women. They must announce to their bosses that they are pregnant, request maternity leave, and, if needed, ask for flex-time or part-time work
in order to be home to nurse their newborns. With the exception of those who
are self-employed and a handful of others, it seems that women architects who
work part-time are jeopardizing their careers. In fact, only about half the women
in this research had children, and many admitted trading a family life for a
career. But succeeding as an architect should not force people to choose between
the two.

7. *Many underrepresented architects are unprepared for what awaits them
in the profession.* For women, whose numbers have increased in architectural schools, being the sole person of their sex in the professional design studio
is a startling experience. For many men of color trained in historically black
colleges and universities, the experience of being "the one and only minority" in the office is also a rude awakening. When they make their debut in the
working world, they are often dismayed by the multitude of problems that may
arise.

8. *Even in the new millennium, when strides have been made in other fields,
gender and racial discrimination still run rampant in the architectural profes-*

sion. The percentage of respondents who admit that they had seen or heard of discrimination is much too high; two-thirds of those surveyed had witnessed or heard about gender discrimination and four out of ten had witnessed or heard about racial discrimination in an architectural office.

9. *Significant gender and racial differences are found along several important issues. For the most part, the experiences of underrepresented architects are far more negative than those of their white male counterparts.* Among the most disturbing differences are inequities in salaries and benefits. My research confirms what many have long suspected: that women architects earn significantly less than their male counterparts with comparable levels of professional experience. The pay gap between men and women becomes wider the longer they remain in the architectural field. To make matters worse, the salaries of women of color–the group with the lowest representation in the profession (less than 1%)–lag farthest behind those of their male counterparts (both white and men of color) the longer they have been in the profession. Compared to white men, men of color, and white women, women of color report significantly lower levels of satisfaction about their future career prospects in architecture.

10. *Although many underrepresented architects have shattered the glass ceiling and succeeded in the profession, they must overcome many more obstacles placed in their way.* Architecture is a demanding profession for all, but underrepresented architects must face even greater challenges in an unusually "chilly climate." Those who shattered the glass ceiling often did so by opening their own offices; yet this is an option not open to or desired by all.

11. *Architects who escape the traditional arena of private practice seem to be significantly better off.* Prior research has documented that nearly all architects working beyond the confines of the typical design studio tend to enjoy higher pay and better benefits than their counterparts in more traditional settings.[1] My research confirmed that underrepresented architects who fled traditional practice for government posts, corporate work, and real estate development had much more satisfying experiences. Yet if greater numbers of diverse designers continue to pursue alternative careers, the mainstream of the profession will stagnate.

12. *Finding a supportive work environment is a key factor for those who triumphed in the profession. Knowing when to leave a stifling office setting is essential.* In fact, management practices can either make or break the future of architectural employees. Unenlightened managers with a "sink or swim" attitude are in large part responsible for the high numbers of underrepresented architects who flee mainstream architectural practice.

Ironically, unless drastic changes are made, the profession will likely continue to alienate those diverse members that it needs most. Architecture will remain a bastion of homogeneity. In sum, diversity in design is only in its incipient stages. Although many diverse designers have ridden the wave to success, too many others are struggling to remain afloat.

ARCHITECTURE THROUGH
THE LOOKING GLASS

In my review of the literature I examined hundreds of publications about diversity in the art world,[2] science and engineering,[3] planning,[4] landscape architecture,[5] law,[6] and medicine,[7] fields to which architects often compare their profession. A detailed analysis of each discipline is beyond the scope of this book. However, some conclusions emerge about those fields that shed light upon my research findings.

How do comparisons with other fields help us see and remedy the deficiencies in the architectural profession in terms of fostering and supporting diversity? How does the relative progress of architecture stack up with that in other professions? How have major professional organizations in other fields responded to the need for diversity, and how has this compared with architecture? My examination reveals several themes, but one emerges above all others: *Compared to the pace at which most other fields have responded to diversity, the progress of architecture has been nearly glacial.* Measured against how planning, landscape architecture, law, and medicine have responded to diversity, architecture has lagged substantially. Why has architecture been the last straggler in the race?

First, the entry of underrepresented architects into the profession has been slow. In fact, the entry of diverse constituents into architecture most closely parallels that of physics, astronomy, and engineering. The proportion of underrepresented architects at the turn of the twenty-first century closely resembles that of the sciences and engineering.

Second, the AIA began to collect gender and racial demographic data only in 1983, long after other professions had already begun to do so. At first glance, this may not seem significant, but it is. Only with longitudinal demographic data can a profession monitor its progress. Until such data is recorded and maintained regularly, the history of diversity in any field remains a mystery.

Third, key events in other disciplines marked significant milestones in the history of diversity. In the mid-1980s, the art world received a wakeup call when the Guerrilla Girls–an anonymous group of artists, curators, and art museum administrators–burst into the public arena. Their persistence in speaking out about sexism and racism in the art world alerted artists and the public to the injustices that they and underrepresented artists endured. The National Museum of Women in the Arts in Washington, D.C., as well as other museums around the country featuring the artistic achievements of African Americans, Latinos/Latinas, and Asians have brought the contributions of diverse artists into the limelight. Women's History Month and Black History Month have had similar effects on promoting public awareness of the arts.

In 1991, Dr. Frances Conley's battle with Stanford University's Department of Neurosurgery forced sexism in medicine into the open. That same year, the televised hearings concerning Clarence Thomas and Anita Hill catapulted gender and racial issues in the legal profession to center stage. Almost overnight, the nation was mesmerized by the term "sexual harassment," a previously taboo topic. In 1992, U.S. Representative Constance Morella of Maryland brought gender discrimination in scientific and technical affairs to national attention. Some of these explosive events served as catalysts to bring gender and racial issues in each field to the public eye for the first time. The public spotlight focused much-needed attention on these issues, yet that spotlight has not yet been directed toward the architectural field. The profession remains in the shadows.

Fourth, in undertaking systematic, empirical research to better understand the experiences of underrepresented members, professional organizations in other disciplines have been proactive. Reports such as those issued by the National Science Foundation, the American Astronomical Society, the American Chemical Society, the National Society of Professional Engineers, the American Medical Association, and the American Bar Association's Young Lawyer's Division underscore each profession's commitment to diversity issues such as pay equity, gender and racial discrimination, and sexual harassment. Each of these organizations has been willing to spend significant sums of money routinely to support these studies, and many have been doing so as early as the 1970s. Many of these reports spell out goals and guidelines for remedying gender and racial inequities in their fields. Such recommendations pave the way toward significant progress.

By comparison, what systematic, empirical research on diversity issues has taken place in architecture? Who has been doing it? Once again, architecture has lagged far behind. On occasion, magazines such as the late *Progressive Architecture* have undertaken short reader polls on diversity followed by brief articles describing the results. Important though these have been, these surveys lack the sophistication of those in other fields. Along with a handful of other academicians, I have undertaken significant research efforts. But compared to those in other professions, our studies have been done on a shoestring budget. Our sample sizes have been smaller, and our research has taken much longer to complete.

Years after other professions joined the crusade for significant diversity research, the Association of Collegiate Schools of Architecture (ACSA) commissioned its study of women faculty in architectural schools, certainly a step in the right direction. However, the ACSA represents only the academic branch of the profession, and it is independent of the AIA. Thus a key distinction sets architecture apart from the other professions: any substantial empirical research on diversity has remained independent of the major professional organization.

Over the years, and to its credit, the AIA has sponsored women and minority task forces, committees, newsletters, and diversity conferences. But in terms of systematic empirical research on diversity, what has the AIA done? Not much. In fact, to make matters worse, when researchers have approached the organization for financial assistance to investigate diversity issues, they have been turned away. Roberta Feldman's proposal to the AIA to examine attrition rates of women architects, one of the profession's most perplexing problems, was never funded. My own letters to the then-president of the AIA requesting financial support for my glass-ceiling research were repeatedly left unanswered. Due to the scarcity of research funding in architecture, many worthwhile proposals have never received financial support. Without a doubt, compared to what their counterparts in other fields have already accomplished, the architectural profession and the AIA have lacked the commitment to seriously investigate and remedy diversity problems.

This scenario is merely part of a broader phenomenon that continues to plague the architectural profession: *researchers remain unwelcome guests in the culture of architecture.* While other professional organizations have been actively engaged in systematic research for years, providing a strong funding base for its constituents to examine key issues in their respective fields, this has not been the case in architecture. The field has suffered enormously because of it. Several scholars have cited this in their critiques of both architectural education and practice.[8]

Fifth, several professions have benefited from the attention of major federal funding agencies and politicians who have served as watchdogs and whistle blowers. For example, the series of reports issued by the National Science Foundation presenting information on the participation of women, racial and ethnic minorities, and those with physical disabilities in science and engineering were mandated by law. A congresswoman intervened by proposing legislation designed specifically to address problems women face in scientific and technical fields. These are indeed successful proactive approaches that promote change.

By comparison, architecture fails to measure up. The only federal agency that serves as a watchdog on this field, as well as on all others, is the Equal Employment Opportunity Commission. However, it is by no means proactive; it can be brought in only "after the fact" to investigate alleged cases of discrimination. Many underrepresented professionals avoid contacting the EEOC for fear of being blacklisted. The AIA has its Professional Code of Ethics, as well as its AIA National Ethics Council, but the methods of enforcing alleged violations are vague. Furthermore, the AIA fails to maintain statistics about the number of cases and complaints. An "honor system" appears to be in place, but it is ineffective. As a result, injustices in the architectural profession are allowed to continue.

In sum, when it comes to diversity, the architectural profession is behind the times. In many respects, the profession today is essentially functioning in the year 1975. While the first wave of feminism and civil rights has come and gone in most other fields, and a second wave is now riding through, they have barely touched the contemporary architectural profession.

Because researchers have only recently begun systematically to collect demographic data in the field, the early history of diversity in architecture may be unrecoverable. Without an explosive event to call the public's attention to the need for diversity in architecture, gender and racial discrimination in the profession will remain a secret. By not compiling a solid base of empirical research, any major professional organization remains out of touch with its constituency. The AIA, for example, will continue to look less attractive to women and architects of color, who ask, What's this organization doing for me? Without a proactive watchdog agency to ensure that women and persons of color are truly treated fairly, the architectural profession will allow gender and racial discrimination to persist. Compared to other disciplines, architecture has clearly resisted rather than embraced diversity.

STRATEGIES FOR INDIVIDUALS

What can individual architects do to help promote and achieve diversity? The American Institute for Managing Diversity, based in Atlanta, Georgia, provides a wide array of services and resources to those wishing to diversify their work environment. The Women's Bureau at the U.S. Department of Labor in Washington, D.C., sponsors a toll-free telephone service offering advice and referrals for work and family issues; a pension-education campaign to help women plan for their retirements; and a Fair Pay Clearinghouse providing technical assistance to detect and remedy wage discrimination. It also offers a "Working Women Count!" honor roll to recognize employers, organizations, and others who implement policies and practices that enable greater participation of women in the work force. As each new initiative is publicized, more and more workplaces will be inspired to follow suit.[9]

Women interested in starting their own architectural firms can receive assistance from Women Incorporated, a Los Angeles–based nonprofit organization dedicated to empowering women to found businesses by helping them obtain loans and assisting them with other services. It offers a multi-billion-dollar loan pool set up purposely for women entrepreneurs by the Money Store, the nation's largest Small Business Administration lender, as well as discounts on long-distance phone service, overnight shipping, and group health insurance. Several other organizations can provide assistance to women, whether they have their own firms or not.[10]

Organizations that provide assistance to persons of color include the Department of Civil Rights, AFL-CIO, in Washington, D.C.; International Committee Against Racism, Brooklyn, N.Y.; National Association for the Advancement of Colored People (NAACP) in Baltimore; and Chinese for Affirmative Action, San Francisco. The Gay and Lesbian Advocates and Defenders in Boston provides assistance to gays and lesbians.

If problems cannot be resolved within an architectural workplace, employees can file claims with the Equal Employment Opportunity Commission (EEOC). In 1995, over twenty-six thousand workers filed sexual discrimination or harassment claims with the EEOC, a rise of 47% from the previous five years. The EEOC operates a toll-free line to connect callers with its nearest office. Attorneys typically handle these cases on a contingency basis. If the employee wins, the lawyer collects 30% to 40% of the award. In the case of a loss, the employee must pay out-of-pocket expenses up front, usually in the thousands of dollars. Most cases are actually settled or dismissed before trial.[11]

Underrepresented architects must be astute in selecting their places of employment, especially when the economy is good and it is an employee's market. Job applicants must look beyond the rhetoric to see what employers are really offering to help promote diversity.[12] Are firms truly committed to diversity, or is their commitment only skin deep? What kind of data do offices have to support corporate claims that diversity is valued? Can job applicants speak with other employees like them to find out how comfortable the workplace is and what kinds of opportunities they are offered? What kinds of demographic profiles does a particular firm have to show? Where are the underrepresented employees in the organizational hierarchy? How long have they been at their current positions? What kinds of training and professional development programs are offered? How is work recognized and rewarded? What kinds of opportunities are available for part-time work, or maternity or paternity leave? To what extent are flexible work hours possible? Is telecommuting a possibility?

NEW TOOLS FOR THE SCHOOLS

Many argue, and rightfully so, that the profession will not change until the educational system undergoes a fundamental transformation as well. What can architectural schools do to promote diversity? How can graduates of architectural programs learn to become more sensitive to–and proactive toward–diversity issues in the workplace?

Only when a critical mass of underrepresented faculty is hired will problems begin to be remedied. But it is not enough to simply hire a diverse faculty, heave a sigh of relief, and believe that the problem is now solved. Schools of architecture must also promote and reward greater numbers of underrepresented faculty. Many individuals need special support and networking systems to enable them to excel. They crave friendship and support from among their white male colleagues. Many require career guidance to navigate the precarious route to tenure.

Administrators of architectural schools can exert leadership by showcasing the work of underrepresented faculty and alumni in school lecture series, exhibits, panel discussions, newsletters, Web sites, and other public venues. Columbia University, for instance, has offered a "Women in Architecture" lecture series. New Jersey Institute of Technology has exhibited the work of its women alumni.

It is imperative that incidents of discrimination, harassment, and unfair treatment in architecture schools be dealt with promptly and effectively. Students, faculty, and staff must be made aware of what constitutes appropriate and inappropriate behavior, particularly in design studios after hours. They must also be alerted to mechanisms available for filing complaints; unlike architectural offices, most universities have an extensive procedure already in place.

Teaching assistants play a critical role in this process, as they serve as role models to other students. All too often, I hear of incidents where male teaching assistants make brash statements to women students such as, "Let's face it. Women can't design as well as men, and you know it." Such kinds of behavior must be stopped. Teaching assistants, students, faculty, staff, and administrators all need diversity training.

In *Design Juries on Trial,* I call for a fundamental restructuring of design studios and juries that could ultimately encourage more diverse students to remain in architecture. My alternatives to juries include staging an opening night, where an exhibit of completed student work is held and each project is accompanied by an open folder for comments from faculty, students, and other visitors; a round-robin format that breaks review sessions into highly interactive small groups that meet concurrently; private videotaped reviews with individual students; and a brochure or portfolio presentation that can be easily circulated to students, faculty, and other critics and reviewed privately. These alternatives promote common themes: increased student participation; a focus on the design process as well as the design product; clarifying criteria and demystifying design; reaching a higher level of learning; less tension and no public humiliation; a more efficient use of review time; and introducing a variety of physical environments and presentation media.[15]

Some progress is underway. In fact, some instructors now require students to present their design projects on Web sites on the Internet, making them available to a wide audience and offering less intimidating ways to critique student work. For example, at the University of Illinois, Robert Selby, Brian Orland, and I have routinely required our students to document every phase of their housing design studio on the Web. This includes both the students' interim and final design projects, as well as the entire design process. This allowed our clients, low-income residents of East St. Louis, Illinois, to critique the students' work whether or not they were physically present on our campus. It also provided the opportunity for guest critics to evaluate privately the students' projects both before and after their public design review. Similarly, in another one of my design studios, where every phase of the research and design process has been documented on a Web site, student teams from Urbana-Champaign were linked with practicing architects who reviewed their work from locations such as Chicago, Peoria, and St. Louis.

In a essay that Sherry Ahrentzen and I co-wrote, we identified situations in which gendered practices occur in architectural education, especially in design studios and juries.[14] These include a curriculum of great men and great monuments, that is, male-centered concepts of precedent and mastery; the "mister-mastery-mystery" phenomenon, a highly patriarchal master-apprentice model reinforced in design studio; an examination of whether women design, think, or learn differently; double-speak and cross-cultural communication, an analysis of who talks how much with whom in design studio; and sexual harassment. Based on our analysis, we suggest ways in which educational practices can be restructured to provide enhanced opportunities for both women and men in architecture. We include a series of thought-provoking questions for architectural faculty, including those aimed at teaching practices that promote male-centered ideas of mastery and precedent; teaching practices that devalue diversity or stigmatize difference; the nature of faculty-student communication; and sexual harassment (see tables 12–14). A similar set of questions can increase the sensitivity of architectural faculty to racial issues.

The 1993 issue in the *Journal of Architectural Education* on "Gender and Multi-culturalism in Architectural Education" featured several articles challeng-

TABLE 12. Assessing Teaching Practices That May Devalue Diversity or Stigmatize Difference

---

Do we talk about and judge buildings or actions by referencing masculine and feminine attributes?

Do we explain to our students the meanings behind such attributions?

Do we allow for multiple avenues for learning, knowing, and creating?

Do we provide students the opportunity to choose different instructional and learning modes?

Do we form stereotypes of female students? of male students? of their work?

Do we question the basis for our perceptions of differences between men and women?

TABLE 13. Assessing Teaching Practices That Promote Male-Centered Ideas of Mastery and Precedent

---

Are women's contributions (as individuals, as part of a team, or as an association or group) to the built landscape acknowledged?

In our curriculum, do we reference buildings, parks, places, and so on that are not only designed by women, but also promoted, programmed, financed, or advocated by them?

Do we take into account contributions and achievements of women and men relative to the traditions and genres of the times and cultures in which they lived?

Are examples and anecdotes drawn from the lives of both men and women?

In our curriculum, do we exclude regions, countries, time periods, building types, and settings in which women made significant contributions to the built landscape?

Do we focus too narrowly on the process of creating our built environment? Do we implicitly suggest that clients, epochs, patrons, users, developers, etc. constrain or contribute to the formation of the built environment?

Do we critically assess how gatekeepers (instructors, texts, magazine editors, and so on) label or identify what is considered to be a commendable building, landscape, architect, creator, contributor, or place?

TABLE 14. Assessing the Nature of Faculty-Student Communication

What number of male versus female students do you call on? Which students do you call by name?

With which students (male or female) do you interact in class more frequently? Which students are more likely to ask for a desk crit?

How do you decide which students to visit during each studio session? How do you decide the scheduling of students to present their work before a design jury?

Do interruptions occur while an individual is talking? If so, who does the interrupting? Who is interrupted? At a design jury, which jurors (male or female) generally respond first?

Is your verbal response to students positive? aversive? encouraging? Is it the same for all students? If not, why? Do female students receive as much informal feedback, encouragement, praise, and critical assessment as male students for their design projects?

Do you tend to face or address one section of the studio more than others? Do you establish eye contact with certain students more than others? What gestures, postures, or facial expressions do you use, and are they different for male and female students?

Do you ask male and female students the same kinds of questions? Do you encourage women as much as men to think for themselves?

Do you sometimes assume that female students are uncertain about their design ideas or are not saying much that is worthwhile because women may tend to state their ideas hesitantly or in an "overly polite" fashion?

Do you, guest critics, or guest jurors ever use sexist humor to "spice up" a dull subject? Do you make disparaging comments about women as a group? How does this affect women in the classroom?

When you refer to users, clients, or designers, do you regularly refer to males or use the generic *he*? Or the universal *man*? Or do you refer to both men and women?

Are your patterns of reinforcement different for male and female students?

ing architectural education to become more sensitive to diversity issues.[15] Similarly, the fascinating essays in Thomas Dutton's anthology entitled *Voices in Architectural Education: Cultural Politics and Pedagogy* call for a greatly increased sensitivity to diversity issues.[16] The past decades have seen a flurry of publications on this topic.[17]

Based on their research, Linda Groat and Sherry Ahrentzen conclude that in three areas—social dynamics, pedagogical practices, and curricular emphases—architectural education needs an overhaul:

- A minimal critical mass of female faculty and students—25% of the entire faculty and student body—is needed at all architectural schools. At schools with this ratio, gender bias is lowest. Schools with the greatest proportion of women students and students of color had the most hospitable environments.

- Faculty must find better ways to teach and evaluate architecture, and they must apply methods that are more responsive to different learning styles. Women students and students of color are troubled by traditional modes of teaching architecture, and they find critiques and grading to be highly subjective.

- Women and minority students want a greater emphasis on the human side and social impact of the field. School curricula must place greater emphasis on courses that address social and cultural issues in design and that reflect the career goals of these students.[18]

Along these lines, Harry G. Robinson III, the former dean of the School of Architecture and Planning at Howard University, has argued:

> Architecture in the United States is emerging from a decade of intro- spection during which the social conscience and humanist attitudes of the late sixties and early seventies were essentially abandoned in favor of a search for the ultimate pastiche and constructions isolated from the people who use them. The academic interest in housing innovation to support inner-city, low-income (or no-income) residents and the need to work with "the people" in producing user-based design and planning strategies is minimal. Indeed, some schools of architecture conduct de- sign studios without a real client, even though their backyards are teeming with social problems that beg an architectural response and can inform a new architecture.[19]

Robinson's point is underscored by Boyer and Mitgang as well: the architec- tural curriculum and its design projects must be more reflective of pressing problems in America's diverse communities. Working on socially relevant is- sues will help attract and retain more diverse students and faculty into the field.

Courses such as my own at the University of Illinois, entitled "Gender and Race in Contemporary Architecture," are one way to incorporate diversity into architectural curricula. Unfortunately, most schools of architecture offer no such courses, or if they do, they are only electives, as is the case at Illinois. Yet a hand- ful of schools are beginning to develop them. At a few institutions they have been part of the curriculum for quite some time. For example, the University of Wis- consin–Milwaukee offers a course in "Gender and Diversity Issues in Architec- ture," taught by Sherry Ahrentzen, which began in the mid-1980s. Ahrentzen described the course as both "revolutionary" and "evolutionary." Students' re- search projects analyzed the environment of a local sexual assault treatment center, sex-stereotyping of children's bedrooms and private spaces, implications of the electronic cottage, spaces used by women artists, women and environ- ment issues in Islamic cultures, and other fascinating topics.[20]

Just as underrepresented architects need their own organizations, all architecture students need courses in diversity. Learning about affinity groups such as women-in-architecture organizations, NOMA, and OLGAD is an essential component of students' education.

Ideally, this perspective must infiltrate the mainstream curriculum, and diversity issues ought to be incorporated into required courses. They could easily be included in architectural history courses, exposing students to the past accomplishments of underrepresented architects. They could be components of professional practice and management courses, preparing future architects for a more diverse workplace. Diversity issues must be incorporated into design studios as well. Students should be assigned projects that force them to confront gender and racial issues first-hand. For example, as part of an assignment to design a performing arts center, design instructors could require a post-occupancy evaluation of a local theater, where teams of men and women students must watch the behavior in and around rest rooms at intermission time. Nonetheless, until educators themselves have both the knowledge of and commitment to this perspective and introduce it into the mainstream, the need for special courses on diversity remains paramount.

Because most architectural faculty are unaware of the literature on gender and racial issues in architecture, they must draw upon the expertise of architectural librarians. Librarians can be guest lecturers in architecture classes, arrange class field trips to the library, and provide useful guidance on Internet searches.[21]

It is equally important that students learn about various career paths available to architects. Becoming a designer is but one of many routes that an architect can pursue. As one of my respondents stated, "The schools still prepare students for traditional, design-oriented careers, which lead to expectations which are constantly frustrated. Many go through long struggles to redefine and re-educate themselves so that they have skills more appropriate to the challenging opportunities this world offers to us. Fortunately . . . I had abilities other than those required for a traditional career path, so that I've had essentially four careers: educator, private practice, corporate architect, specialist" (#130, white male, age 50).

What about reaching out even further into the educational system—not just to the university but also to community colleges, high schools, and elementary schools? How can we encourage even greater diversity in our future architectural student body? The Newhouse Foundation Competition offers an admirable example. It involves students from low-income Chicago high schools in a year of site visits, company shows, and marketing in the architectural profession and in the building trades, culminating in a juried design competition. The program offers students "big brothers" and "big sisters" as mentors. During one of my class field trips to Chicago, Robert Wesley, a prominent African-American architect and principal at Skidmore, Owings, and Merrill, suggested initiating programs for gifted low-income students to study architecture during summers. He also calls upon architects to volunteer two hours a week in local grade schools to help make students aware of the profession.

SENSITIZING THE
ARCHITECTURAL WORKPLACE

How can the architectural workplace be made more sensitive to diversity issues? I asked architects an open-ended question in both the surveys and interviews: "If you believe that architectural firms should be committed to gender and racial equality in the profession, what steps do you suggest they take?" In their answers they mentioned treating employees fairly; expecting less overtime work; instituting special hiring policies to attract talented women and people of all races; and having management set positive examples.

Several stressed the need to place underrepresented architects in positions of responsibility, coupled with appropriate training and support programs. One individual suggested that role reversals in the office were needed, that is, placing superiors in the position of inferiors for some time and having them get a sense of what it's like to be in the other person's shoes.

Other research participants emphasized the need for specific, measurable criteria for promotion as well as for salary increases—perhaps reflective of the number of years of experience at the firm—to help rectify the current situation wherein women and people of color, as one African-American woman put it, "magically miss out on pay increases once they are hired." Several called for major reforms to the educational system, at the university, high school, and elementary school levels. Here are some of their comments:

> The smartest thing that they can do is that they can pay equitably. And they can promote equitably. . . . By creating an underclass of architects within the profession who are not white and who are not male, it's only a matter of time before these people see their prospects as being better if they are on their own. (I-#7, white female, age 35)

One of the things I realize now[,] since I worked for a number of firms over the past ten years, [was that] the first firm I worked for [had] our employee handbook [with] an outline of all the job descriptions and different qualifications for advancement. And it pretty much outlined what you need to do if you wanted to get to a certain level in the company. [At] a lot of the companies I've worked for [since], that has not been the case. (I-#14, African-American female, age 36)

I would say being put in positions of responsibility and being made more visible is important. . . . It's less likely, in my experience, to find women and people of color in the most visible and higher-tier positions, as, say, in production. And those are extremely important roles. . . . In promoting someone, you're also saying that you want it to be visible and publicly acknowledged that you're an important part of an office. (I-#22, Asian-Latina, age 31)

STRATEGIES FOR ARCHITECTURAL FIRMS

Earlier I mentioned the importance of managing diversity, as opposed to simply undertaking affirmative action or other piecemeal programs. It is not enough for architectural firms to simply pick and choose which efforts to undertake. *In fact, all these efforts must be undertaken simultaneously as part of an institution-wide, strategic initiative.* Only this will ensure long-term and ongoing change. With that in mind, here are some ideas that—when used in conjunction with one other—can help architectural firms manage diversity.

MENTORING AND CROSS-TRAINING PROGRAMS

In a previous chapter, I described a number of model workplaces from which architects can learn to promote diversity. In addition to diversity training, mentoring and cross-training are two readily available techniques to help promote diversity in the architectural workplace. At mid- to large-size firms, for example, principals can cross-train by rotating staff on international and/or important domestic assignments. This would not only provide employees a more well-rounded set of job experiences, but it would also expose them to diverse cultures. Easier yet, a young intern architect can shadow a superior on the job for one day a month. Just as medical interns follow their supervising doctors throughout the hospital during rounds, intern architects can do the same with project managers or principals of the firm, albeit briefly. This could give them a chance to sit in on a meeting with a client, meet with other principals of the firm, or visit a construction site.

Firm owners can recruit students from low-income areas with large populations of persons of color to assist in the office during the summers. Whether they be college or high school students, this experience can open their eyes to a possible future in architecture. One white woman in my study described an excellent example:

> My first job in school [was] as an intern for a major university hospital. The man who hired me was a friend of my father and obligated himself to showing me as much as he could about the field I had chosen. He spent one day a week with me[,] taking me to various projects and meetings. He'd send me to different places so that I could spend time with a cabinet maker, master carpenter, electrical, and private practice architect. I spent time with the handicapped so I could appreciate and understand the obstacles and special challenges they face. I even got to sit in on an operation so I could appreciate how a team worked. I had projects that I worked on such as office renovations and once even a medical suite. He would send me to spend a couple of days with the group I would be designing for so that I could understand what I was to be designing.

A MORE FLEXIBLE WORK ENVIRONMENT

Many architects prefer to work part-time. Others desire full-time employment, but with "flex-place" or "flex-time" arrangements that allow them to work a few days a week at home. While child care is a motivation for some, for others it may be simply to avoid grueling commutes across congested urban freeways.

With the increasing popularity of the personal computer, electronic mail, the Internet, and fax machines, it is now easier than ever to work at home. Coworkers can stay in touch with their colleagues with one easy connection to the Internet. By sharing electronic files, project teams can collaborate even across many miles. Many organizations that traditionally required employees to sit at their office desks forty hours a week now allow flex-time and flex-place. Even the Internal Revenue Service, one of the most conservative organizations in the nation, is one of them.

Architectural firm owners must be willing to reevaluate their workplaces and offer greater flexibility with time and space in the workplace. By experimenting they can discover which arrangements work best for specific individuals as well as for the entire office. Such a change would work wonders in diversifying the architectural workplace.

A PROACTIVE APPROACH TO AVOIDING DISCRIMINATION CHARGES

Architectural firms can take several proactive steps to promote work environments where all employees are treated fairly, thus avoiding situations that would spark legal charges of sexual or racial discrimination.[22] First, owners of architectural firms should ensure that supervisors are properly trained. They must know about laws prohibiting discrimination against sex, race, color, religion, national origin, age, and persons with disabilities. They must learn how to communicate effectively with their employees, how to reward people who do a good job, and how to counsel and discipline those who do not. They must be aware of the gross pay discrepancies between men and women in the profession and ensure that women are paid fairly throughout their careers.

Second, firm owners must be certain that their firm has clearly enunciated rules and policies that are carefully followed. They should address issues such as: How many days off will employees receive? How many absences are acceptable before the employer issues a warning? How many writeups within a particular time interval before disciplinary action is taken? It is especially important that all employees be held accountable and that policies be applied in a consistent manner. Inconsistency in applying such policies is a red flag for lawyers. As one lawyer noted, "It makes an attorney's job very difficult when you pull out of the policy manual the section on sexual harassment that says in the case of a complaint the company will do this, this, and this. And we discover that the last six complaints have just been brushed off by a supervisor's saying 'boys will be boys.'"[23] Similarly, credibility and evidentiary problems can be particularly troubling in the eyes of the law if firm owners do not apply the same standards to the draftspersons as they would to the principals in charge.

Third, all firms must have some form of confidential internal dispute resolution system. Employees must be able to rely on it without fear of retaliation.

Fourth, and especially important, owners of architectural firms should conduct self-audits and examine their workplaces just as lawyers from the Equal Employment Opportunity Commission would do while investigating a complaint. They must ask themselves questions such as: Who are our employees? How are they classified? What are they getting paid? How do our numbers compare with those in our community? Are we doing enough to recruit in nontraditional areas? Are we placing women and persons of color in management positions? R. Roosevelt Thomas Jr. has developed a comprehensive interview guide that employers and employees can use to determine the extent to which their firms are succeeding at managing diversity.[24]

EXIT INTERVIEWS

One of the most promising sources of information–one rarely used–is the exit interview. This technique can be used to find out specific reasons why architects resign from their jobs. It can help detect perceived incidents of unequal treatment. Specific questions can be asked, such as: How fairly do you believe you were treated on the job? Compared to your peers, do you feel you were given equal opportunities to grow and advance in your position? What more could have been done to provide you with greater opportunities to grow and learn on the job? What efforts should we make in the future to retain employees such as you?

Information from exit interviews should be carefully documented, collected, and analyzed over time. Key management staff should meet periodically to identify problems and trends and produce ways to remedy them. Exit interview information could be shared anonymously with women in architecture groups, the National Organization of Minority Architects, and the American Institute of Architects. These organizations can publicize such information in their newsletters, at chapter meetings, and elsewhere to make both employers and employees more attuned to specific problems that plague underrepresented architects.

STRATEGIES FOR THE ARCHITECTURAL PROFESSION

What can the architectural profession and its governing organization, the American Institute of Architects, do to promote and achieve diversity? Earlier in this book I described the disturbing case drawn from the AIA's "Code of Ethics and Professional Conduct Advisory Opinion No. 4."[25] It involved the woman architect who was repeatedly harassed by her male coworker; who complained repeatedly to her male supervisor, but to no avail; and who was ultimately fired and replaced within days by a man. She was paid less than he, despite her superior qualifications, and she was denied further Computer Aided Design (CAD) training, which her male counterpart received. While the AIA recognizes that such cases clearly constitute gender discrimination, the AIA ethics code offers little recourse. Complainants are simply advised to contact the AIA's staff ethics counsel to learn about the procedures for filing a formal complaint against a member. Violations of rules are grounds for disciplinary action by the institute, but what measures have actually been taken?

In light of my research confirming that gender discrimination cases like this are all too common in the architectural profession, one can not help but wonder: In the long run, how effective are such procedures? What outcomes can result? What are the repercussions for those who complain? A more effective enforcement mechanism is needed.

Similarly, recall the widespread exploitation of architectural interns who are not paid when they work for some so-called "stellar" designers. Employers who engage in such practices are clearly in violation of the law. But what enforcement mechanism does the AIA have? At present, it merely has agreed, along with the AIAS and the ACSA, that it will no longer invite such employers to serve as jurors, speakers, and in other public roles. This is hardly more than a slap on the wrist.

Regarding harassment, the AIA currently refers its members to Equal Employment Opportunity Commission guidelines for employers, suggesting that they develop an explicit policy against harassment and that it is effectively implemented; that they raise the subject with all supervisory and nonsupervisory employees, expressing strong disapproval and explaining sanctions for harassment; and that they develop a procedure for resolving harassment complaints that encourages victims to come forward, protects their confidentiality, and provides effective remedies and protects victims from retaliation. Such guidelines are excellent, and the AIA has done well to include them in its legal documentation.[26]

But architects must also rely on similar guidelines when it comes to discrimination in salary, benefits, and educational opportunities. The AIA advises employers to consult with an attorney or human resource management consultant to audit their employment and promotion practices to ensure that they comply with current legal requirements. This, too, is sound advice.

Yet in order to be truly effective at remedying the many injustices that are rampant in this profession—illegalities, exploitations, and abuses that especially affect underrepresented architects—the AIA must be even more proactive. Its legal documentation is on the right track; however, the reality is that few architects probably take the time to read through Advisory Opinion No. 4, or even know that it exists.

The primary responsibility of the AIA's National Diversity Committee has been to organize the diversity conference. This event is desperately needed, especially when the profession has so much catching up to do. It provides a forum for participants to discuss issues not raised elsewhere, offers a priceless professional network, and publishes conference proceedings that preserve important discussions. Yet the obvious danger of such a conference, as many participants readily admit, is that leaders are simply "preaching to the choir." It has been heartening to see a few dedicated white male architects from mainstream firms attending this conference. But many more are needed. An unintended outcome of the AIA's efforts is that diversity issues have become marginalized, and the mainstream all but ignores them. Since AIA's 2000 National Diversity Conference was canceled, the future of such diversity conferences is unknown.

The National Diversity Committee has suggested excellent measures to begin to address diversity in the profession.[27] The program is well managed, its members are highly committed, and for many years, the director of diversity programs has served as an indispensable resource. The National Diversity Program serves as a clearinghouse of information on minorities and women in the profession by providing membership statistics and rosters; recommendations for speakers and jurors; sample affirmative action plans; sample workplace policies; lists of related organizations; sample diversity programs; and information on exhibits, conferences, educational/mentorship programs, research projects, audio/visual materials, publications, and archives. Along these lines, the AIA has issued a "Diversity Resources" flyer suggesting specific measures that AIA components—over three hundred local and state organizations—can do to address diversity issues: identify and nurture diverse leaders to serve as chairs on committees and on their boards; appoint diverse members to special task forces and committees; choose diverse members to serve as jurors on awards committees; ensure that events include diverse speakers; establish a mentorship program for women and students of color; highlight the accomplishments of women and members of color in newsletters and in the local press; and provide diversity training sessions for staff, leaders, and members. The AIA also recommends participating in the AIA/American Architectural Foundation Minority/Disadvantaged Scholarship Matching Grants Program; developing an exhibition of works by women and/or underrepresented architects; highlighting member firms that promote diverse employees and that feature exemplary workplace policies; setting up a special incentive program for recruiting diverse members; promoting the inclusion of diverse architects and curricula in architectural education; and establishing a local diversity committee.

Still, it is all too easy for leaders of the umbrella organization, the AIA, to believe that when it comes to addressing diversity issues, the diversity conference is sufficient. It is not. As Marilyn Loden, the change management consultant, argues, "When the need to act overwhelms the long-term purpose of a valuing diversity initiative, what often results is a splashy annual event rather than a detailed, multiyear plan. While some would argue that an annual conference focused on valuing diversity is worth doing because it is still better than doing nothing, this is very debatable. For when the annual event displaces a comprehensive, systematic approach to culture change, it becomes an organizational distraction that actually slows adoption."[28]

Loden's comments are addressed primarily to the workplace and not necessarily to professional organizations. But as my literature review has demonstrated, professional organizations can be a driving force for changing their respective fields. The AIA should take heed of Loden's experiences.

Regarding diversity, the AIA—not just its National Diversity Committee and its diversity program—has tremendous potential to lead social change in the profession. The AIA must take a much stronger stance in actively combating exploitation and discrimination in the profession. *In workshops held by AIA's local component chapters, in keynote addresses at its annual national conventions, in its newsletters, and on its Web sites, the institute must drum into every member its commitment to diversity, its refusal to tolerate illegalities, and the consequences of violating the law.* Currently, the only way that the AIA can hold architects accountable for diversifying their firms is through its diversity conferences, its review of progress made on each year's diversity agenda, and an examination of demographics of members in leadership positions.[29] Current measures are well-intended but do not go far enough.

Awards and competitions, which begin in the architectural schools and continue throughout the profession, serve as an effective agent of change in an otherwise incredibly conservative profession. Awards programs could be initiated that take diversity issues into account. They could be created to honor the accomplishments of underrepresented firms of different sizes, and they could be incorporated into mainstream awards programs. Awards could be given for not only design work, but also for progressive management practices that foster diversity in the profession.

To what extent are diversity issues raised at the national convention of the AIA? Very little. A review of recent AIA convention programs reveals that these issues are rarely discussed in mainstream forums. Instead, they have been relegated to the National Diversity Conference. Ultimately, diversity issues must make their way through every channel of the professional organization, to the component chapters around the country, and to the architectural workplace.

The AIA should assume responsibility for collecting and disseminating information on the current costs of *not* valuing diversity. This would provide an important outlet especially for underrepresented employees, but also for mainstream employees. It would provide useful information for the profession at large. The AIA should become a national clearinghouse, collecting data on attrition patterns, exit interviews, employee discrimination complaints, lawsuit settlements, and employee opinion surveys. If the AIA does not collect this information, who else will?

In a profession where so many employees work in small-scale settings, they are often unable to confront their coworkers or supervisors about gender discrimination, sexual or racial harassment, pay inequity, and other issues raised in this book. Feeling trapped, they desperately need to consult with an unbiased source. The AIA is the logical place to turn.

Ironically, despite its outward appearance of being avant-garde, the conservative architectural profession has been stubbornly slow in embracing diversity. To say that the AIA has been reactive is an understatement. My research shows that far too many women flee and far too few African Americans and Latinos are entering the profession. The AIA must offer its members mechanisms for accountability in promoting, achieving, and managing diversity. Otherwise, architectural firms will continue to merely pay lip service to these issues or ignore them completely.

Other professions have been proactive by funding and conducting comprehensive research on diversity issues and, based upon their results, by issuing reports with specific recommendations for change. In this respect, the American Bar Association, the American Medical Association, and others have been light-years ahead of the AIA. For example, the American Bar Association's Commission on Women in the Profession has conducted extensive research and compiled an informative manual entitled *Lawyers and Balanced Lives: A Guide to Drafting and Implementing Workplace Policies for Lawyers.*[30] It explains how to formulate, draft, and implement written policies. It discusses parental leave, alternative work schedules, and sexual harassment. Each section contains sample policies. The commission anticipates adding chapters in future editions to include mentoring, child-care arrangements, and applications in other professional settings.[31]

The American Council on Education's (ACE) Office of Women in Higher Education provides another model for the architectural profession. The ACE National Network for Women Leaders in Higher Education is a state-based national network of administrators and faculty committed to strengthening women's leadership in higher and adult education. Since its inception in 1977, the program's primary commitment has been to identify and promote the advancement of women in higher education, particularly women of color and those who have not participated previously.[32]

I have attended several events sponsored by the Illinois Planning Committee of the ACE National Network for Women Leaders in Higher Education. In 1996, the Illinois committee sponsored a senior seminar for women with potential to assume leadership positions in higher education. The seminar drew upon the expertise of four search consultants to help participants evaluate career goals, discuss strategies for reaching them, and strengthen presentation skills. The seminar also provided participants with an opportunity to expand professional networks by meeting women in academic leadership positions throughout the state.

The AIA should view the ACE National Network for Women Leaders in Higher Education, and other groups like it, as a successful prototype. For example, state and local chapters of the AIA could provide similar continuing education sessions targeted especially to underrepresented members, but open to all. Sessions could address such issues as job searches and interviews, career advancement, and eliminating discrimination in the workplace.

PUBLIC OUTREACH

Above all else, public outreach is a key to designing for diversity. In this regard, architects can learn much from the success of their counterparts in the historic preservation field. As the preservationist Michael Tomlan of Cornell University has written: "Cultural education that recognizes the nation's diversity and special qualities of local history must be undertaken at all levels, broadening awareness and appreciation of the built environment."[33]

An excellent model of how public education and outreach can promote greater awareness of diversity in design is found at Georgia's State Historic Preservation Office, which has worked hard to create a more culturally diverse preservation program and network ever since the late 1970s.[34] That state's large African-American population and strong cultural presence; a history of conflict in race relations, marked especially by slavery and segregation; and the civil rights movement provided the focus of preservationists' efforts. Yet when the program began, few elected officials, community development specialists, local preservationists, or African-American residents fully understood the historical or architectural significance of the nearby churches, schools, shotgun houses, or commercial buildings. All this was compounded by the fact that few African

Americans were present at statewide historic preservation conferences. This situation mirrors the lack of public awareness of and involvement in architecture today.

Elizabeth Lyon, Georgia's state preservation officer, took the lead in 1990 by holding a one-day meeting to ascertain the level of interest in African-American preservation issues in her state. Fifty people participated, resulting in the formation of the Minority Historic Preservation Committee, with fourteen members appointed from communities around the state that were interested in preserving their local African-American heritage. The committee's goals included fostering participation of underrepresented groups and individuals in the statewide historic preservation movement; increasing public awareness of Georgia's African-American history, both statewide and in local communities, and promoting preservation of historic properties; increasing interaction at the local and statewide levels among organizations, institutions, local governments, local preservation organizations, and individuals interested in preservation of sites related to underrepresented groups; and assuring inclusion of African-American resources in the state's coordinated planning efforts.

Many accomplishments soon followed. With support from the Georgia Power Company, the committee produced a series of four posters highlighting African-American churches, houses, community landmarks, and schools listed on the National Register of Historic Places. The governor unveiled the posters at a ceremony at the state capitol during Black History Month in 1991, and thousands were distributed. The committee also produced a statewide tourism brochure featuring fifty-six National Register properties throughout Georgia associated with African-American history. This was presented to the governor at a special ceremony, and the brochure is now available at welcome centers, museums, and convention and visitors bureaus around the state. The brochure has also been used in the school systems to teach heritage education. In 1989 the office staff developed the "Minority Preservation Network," later renamed the "African-American Historic Preservation Network," a list of all those interested in African-American preservation issues, who receive a monthly newsletter and special mailings; as of 1992, the network had grown rapidly to over two hundred members. The committee's time has been devoted to public awareness activities, expanding the network membership, heritage education, and assisting local African-American heritage projects around the state. As a result of this coordinated series of efforts, more National Register sites have been nominated and a greater variety of preservation projects have been undertaken. According to Karen Easter, of Georgia's Historic Preservation Office:

The greatest benefit, however, is the growing cultural pride within the African American population of Georgia because of their awareness of the accomplishments of their ancestors, and their commitment to preserve the physical resources that attest to those achievements, for generations to come.

Georgia's experience proves that it is not enough for preservation organizations to talk about cultural diversity. What is required is to give people of various backgrounds the opportunity to provide leadership in preserving and thereby embracing their own cultural heritage.

How can this historic preservation model be applied to architecture? It is an outgrowth of what Boyer and Mitgang call for in their critique of architectural education: a greater connection between architects and the public.[35] The products of diverse architects—places that can easily be seen and touched—are all out there, but the average person on the street often doesn't realize that they even exist. Herein lies the challenge.

Through local AIA component chapters, local women-in-architecture organizations, or NOMA chapters, architects could collaborate with state and local officials, community groups, and university faculty, students, and alumni to help promote their work. They could develop walking or driving tours of projects designed by underrepresented critics, consumers, and creators of architecture. This could include both historic and contemporary sites. The map of gay and lesbian historic sites in Boston is an excellent prototype.[36]

For instance, I can envision a "Walking Tour of Downtown Chicago" brochure and Web site featuring projects designed by members of Chicago Women in Architecture, a follow-up to the 1998–99 exhibit at the Art Institute of Chicago. These would include projects designed solely by women as well as those where women played a major role. Such a document would enable visitors to see the Chicago skyline through a different lens. Members of CWA could spearhead its development and seek funding to have it published and disseminated, after which it could be distributed at welcome centers, museums, and convention and visitors bureaus around the state. It could also be available at places such as the Prairie Avenue Bookstore, Chicago's premier architectural bookshop, the Archi-Center, the shops of the Art Institute of Chicago, and elsewhere. Its unveiling could be timed to coincide with National Women's History Month in March and celebrated as part of the city's other commemorative events. City leaders would be recruited to promote such efforts, and local journalists should cover them in their newspapers and magazines. Working together with NOMA, another version

Architectural tours of Chicago buildings by women could include projects such as this Oncology Unit at Rush Presbyterian St. Luke's Medical Center, designed by Sheila F. Cahnman, AIA, of Hansen Lind Meyer, Chicago, Ill. It was completed in 1995. Photograph courtesy Hedrich Blessing Photographers.

Chicago architectural tours could also include this Chicago Transit Authority Elevated Harold Washington Library Van Buren Station, completed in 1997. It was designed by Diane Legge Kemp of DLK Architecture in Chicago, Ill. Photograph courtesy Hedrich Blessing Photographers.

The Tassajara Bath House at the Zen Center in Tassajara Springs, Carmel Valley, could be included in an architectural tour of buildings by women of color in Northern California. It was designed by Mui Ho, an Asian-American architect, and completed in 1985. Ms. Ho has designed a variety of buildings in the United States as well as in China. Photograph courtesy Mui Ho, Architect.

of the Chicago walking tour could feature the work of African-American architects and be showcased as part of Black History month in February.

With yet additional funding, traveling exhibits could be developed in conjunction with such walking tours. They could travel on a nationwide circuit to museums, colleges, and universities. They could also be posted as Web sites and linked with those from each respective city's convention and visitors bureaus.

In Los Angeles, I can picture the "Driving Tour of Greater L.A.," featuring the work of Latino/Latina architects. Houston and Miami could host similar tours. In the Bay Area, "A Walking Tour of Downtown San Francisco" could spotlight the work of Asian-American architects or gay and lesbian architects. Driving tours of Northern California could highlight their work as well.

Why not recruit architecture students from the University of Illinois at Chicago or from the Illinois Institute of Technology to work with CWA or NOMA to develop the Chicago brochure and Web site? Or students from the University of California at Los Angeles to prepare the documentation on a Los Angeles brochure? And students from the University of California at Berkeley for the San

Francisco piece? Such research could be undertaken as part of a regular course or as independent study, under the close supervision of a faculty member.

Funding for these projects should cover widespread distribution not only at public sites but also at elementary and high schools with high populations of students of color. Brochures and Web sites would increase public awareness, from the elementary school child—especially young girls and students of color who might not otherwise consider architecture as a profession—to the older adult who is simply curious about what architects do.

Densely populated cities such as Chicago, San Francisco, or Boston readily lend themselves to walking tours. Chicago's tours could be offered through its ArchiCenter, which already has an unusually active outreach program. Others can be arranged through local tourist facilities. Volunteers can lead tour groups through these environments and answer questions. In less densely populated regions, driving tours are more appropriate and could be incorporated as class field trips for elementary and high school students.

Tours, exhibits, and Web sites are examples of collaborative ventures that can be undertaken when architects reach out to the public. Their potential is tremendous, and the possibilities are endless. Such efforts will go a long way toward promoting diversity in design, educating a largely uninformed but often curious public about the value of architecture. The profession at large, and the public, has much to gain. It is a win-win situation.

CONCLUSION

When it comes to diversity, the architectural profession today stands at a crossroads. I have argued not only for the moral rights of all individuals to enter and advance in this field, but for a professional and societal mandate as well. In striking contrast to the other arts, architecture remains all too homogeneous—too male, too pale. Imagine the world of popular music without Louis Armstrong, Michael Jackson, Julio Iglezias, or even Madonna. Imagine the culinary arts without Thai coconut soup, spaghetti a la Bolognese, or enchiladas verdes. By comparison, the architectural world—for the most part—is just a plain old ham sandwich.

When Ginger Rogers danced across movie screens with her partner, Fred Astaire, it was he who most often received credit for being the century's most talented dancer. Yet the fact remains that, as has often been observed, she did everything that he did, only backwards and in high heels. Is the same true for architects? Why must underrepresented designers have such a tough time, having to work twice as hard to get only half as far?

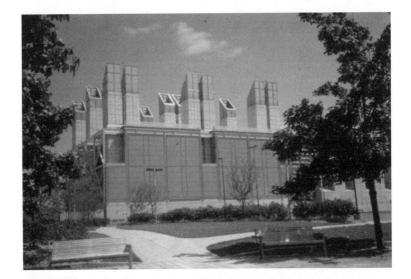

An architectural tour of Boston could include projects by African-American-owned firm Stull and Lee, such as Vent Building No. 7 at Logan Airport, one of several ventilation structures providing fresh air and removing fumes from Boston's Third Harbor tunnel. As part of the Central Artery reconstruction project, known as "The Big Dig," it is one of the largest, most complex building projects in the United States. Completed in 1998, this building received an AIA Honor Award as well as other recognition. Photograph courtesy David Lee.

The architectural profession can remain passive, as it has been for decades, watching silently as underrepresented architects struggle to succeed in an environment that is at best minimally supportive and at worst hostile and unfair. It can continue to ignore those who, in frustration, flee the profession altogether. Unfortunately, as my research has shown, architecture remains a chilly climate for far too many women and persons of color. Yet that need not continue to be the case.

Designing for Diversity must serve as a call for the transformation of this profession, which is long overdue. Recall the potty parity issue, described at the outset of this book. What finally catapulted potty parity into national headlines as a political, gender equity issue was the combined forces of women who were treated unfairly and men who empathized with their concerns—men who were able to see the world through the eyes of their partners, wives, mothers, and daughters. Together they changed laws, improved spaces, and served as powerful advocates for equal access for men and women. Collaboration between those who are adversely affected–whether they be women, persons of color, gays, or lesbians–their supportive counterparts in the architectural mainstream, and a sympathetic public can create a professional climate and in turn a built environment that truly welcomes diversity.

Appendix A

METHODOLOGY

An overview of the methodological approach used in this research was described in the introduction and shown in table 1. A more detailed description is provided here.

DATA COLLECTION

Phase 1 involved interviews with fifty-eight women architects and architects of color, conducted over a ten-year period, approximately 1990–2000. Students from my course on gender and race in architecture conducted these interviews in person, over the telephone, or by e-mail. The interviews generally took from half an hour to an hour to complete. Interviewees were asked to select a minimum of ten interview questions from a list of twenty-one sample questions provided. Students also asked architects to provide any relevant archival information, publications, and visual documentation of their work.

Phase 1 was one of the few research phases for which participants were not anonymous. The following were among the architects interviewed in Phase 1: Ann Beha, Gary Bowden, Denise Scott Brown, Sheila Fogel Cahnman, Susan Campbell, Carol Crandall, Katherine Diamond, Ronald Garner, Ann Hagerty, Mui Ho, Diane Legge Kemp, Tai Soo Kim, Eva Maddox, Julie Marz, Spencer Mason, Margaret McCurry, Patricia Saldana Natke, Ifeanyi "Vop" Osili, Kathryn Tyler Prigmore, Elizabeth Scanlan, Cathy Simon, Norma Sklarek, Jack Travis, Billie Tsien, Robert Wesley, Beverly Willis, and Elizabeth Plater-Zyberk.

Phase 2 relied upon archival data from professional organizations for women in architecture and architects of color. I also solicited information from several professional organizations in other fields, such as law, medicine, and engineering.

Archival data from organizations for underrepresented architects were received from the following:

American Institute of Architects (AIA) Diversity Task Force
AIA Minority Resources Committee

AIA Women in Architecture Committee

Association for Women in Architecture, Los Angeles, Calif.

Austin Women in Architecture, Austin, Tex.

Boston Society of Architects Women in Architecture, Boston, Mass.

Chicago Women in Architecture, Chicago, Ill.

Cincinnati Women in Architecture, Cincinnati, Ohio

Colorado Women in Architecture, Denver, Colo.

Connecticut Society of Architects

Connecticut's Women in Architecture Commission

Kansas City Women in Architecture, Kansas City, Mo.

Maui Chapter Women in Architecture, Maui, Hawaii

Nashville Women in Architecture, Nashville, Tenn.

National Organization of Minority Architects

New Jersey Society Women in Architecture

North Carolina Women and Minorities in Architecture

Northeastern Pennsylvania Women in Architecture

Organization of Women in Architecture, San Francisco, Calif.

Pittsburgh Chapter Women in Architecture, Pittsburgh, Pa.

Portland Chapter Women in Architecture, Portland, Ore.

San Diego Chapter Women in Architecture, San Diego, Calif.

San Francisco Chapter Women in Architecture, San Francisco, Calif.

Archival data in the form of brochures, publications, studies, reports, and surveys were received from the following organizations outside the architectural profession:

American Economic Association

American Institute for Managing Diversity

American Society of Interior Designers

Asian American Arts Alliance

Association for Women Veterinarians

Bar Association of San Francisco

Federation of Organizations for Professional Women

Financial Women's Association of New York

International Black Writers

International League of Women Composers

International Women's Writing Guild

National Association of Women Judges

National Center for State Courts
National Conference of Women's Bar Associations
Quality Education for Minorities
Society of Women Engineers
Women in Communications

Phase 3 consisted of telephone interviews with thirty underrepresented architects. The purpose of these interviews was to explore in greater depth some of the issues that would be raised in phases 4–6 of the survey. Interview questions were identical to the open-ended questions included in the optional portion at the end of the survey. The interview sample included a mixture of volunteers, survey respondents who expressed interest in being interviewed, and people they recommended that I contact. My interview sample included thirteen women of color, eleven white women, and six men of color. Interviews ranged in length from a half hour to 1 ½ hours. All interviews were tape recorded and transcribed. All participants in phases 3–6, a total of over four hundred individuals, remained anonymous.

Phases 4–6 involved surveys completed anonymously by 409 practicing architects nationwide. The survey included two parts. The first part contained eleven pages and almost four hundred items. Most were closed questions with fixed-choice responses, although a few open-ended items were interspersed throughout the survey. Survey questions were grouped around several themes: respondents' current work environments, gender and racial issues in their architectural careers, architectural practice in general, their job histories, and detailed demographic information. In many instances, I purposely selected questions used in surveys of other professions so that previous research results could be compared with my own.

The second part of the survey, which was optional, was comprised of two pages containing thirty-four open-ended questions. Respondents were asked to answer any or all questions that interested them the most. Specific questions addressed four general topics: rites of passage, the role of other people, their "darkest hour" and how they overcame it, and general issues. These questions were identical to those asked in the interviews. Out of 409 respondents, 145 answered some or all of these open-ended questions. Of these 145, the largest group was comprised of white women, followed by women of color, white men, and men of color. A few respondents later sent additional responses to the open-ended questions, and these were also included in the study. Some of these respondents included people who expressed an interest in participating in the study but did so after the data from the survey (i.e., the closed questions) had already been collected and analyzed. These responses were labeled from #410 on.

The survey was administered to three different samples. For *Phase 4*, sample 1 included volunteers responding to an invitation published in 1994 in newsletters of national and local sections of the American Institute of Architects (AIA) Women in Architecture organizations, women-in-architecture organizations that were not AIA-affiliated, and the National Organization of Minority Architects (NOMA). Other volunteers responded to fliers distributed at 1993 AIA and NOMA National Conventions. A total of 128 people volunteered to participate in the study; 94 of these returned my survey, a response rate of 73%.

For *Phase 5*, sample 2 was drawn from a list of randomly selected participants from 1994 national AIA membership rosters. Eight hundred individuals were selected, 200 each from the following groups: white men, white women, men of color, and women of color. Of the 800 surveys, 783 were usable. I received responses from 257 people, a response rate of 33%.

Following the 1994 National Diversity Conference, where I had presented preliminary research results from sample 2, the director of diversity programs at AIA generously volunteered to include my survey as part of a postconference mailing, thus providing the opportunity to expand the research sample. She offered to send it out to both conference participants and AIA board members, thus maintaining the emphasis on a full spectrum of participants, not only women and persons of color. The AIA provided in-kind mailing costs. I had no time to apply for additional funding but viewed this as a unique opportunity that had to be seized.

For *Phase 6*, sample 3, a second set of volunteers was drawn from the 1994 AIA National Diversity Conference. All 220 conference participants were sent surveys, as were 75 AIA board members, in 1995. In contrast to the distribution of samples 1 and 2, staff members at the AIA mailed out this survey directly from their national headquarters, using the list of conference participants as their database. Some of these individuals had already responded to the survey, and hence did not participate a second time. From the new sample I received 58 responses. Coding problems in the AIA mailing process did not enable me to determine exactly which responses came from which of these subsamples, so it is difficult to pinpoint a precise response rate.

DATA ANALYSIS

Students analyzed the information collected in phase 1. While some transcribed the architect interviews verbatim, most simply paraphrased them. Their material was initially presented on exhibit boards and later on a class web site. The issues raised by these architects helped form the basis of my subsequent research.

The archival information from the professional organizations in phase 2 was collected, cataloged, and analyzed. A few of these organizations had conducted surveys and I incorporated some of their questions into my own research instruments. These included surveys from the Association for Women Veterinarians, Federation of Organizations for Professional Women, National Conference of Women's Bar Associations, Society of Women Engineers, and Women in Communications.

Each interview from phase 3 was transcribed in full; some transcriptions took up to eight hours. In all, this process took about two years to complete. A content analysis was performed on all open-ended data.

Quantitative data from the surveys in phases 4–6 were analyzed using the Statistical Package for the Social Sciences. A detailed descriptive analysis of the data and a variety of inferential statistical tests were conducted. Among these were t-tests to distinguish differences between groups, correlations to determine which sets of variables were interrelated, analysis of variance, and others. It took about three years to complete this portion of the data analysis.

All qualitative, open-ended items on the surveys were entered into a database. Every respondent's answer to each open-ended question was recorded and transcribed.

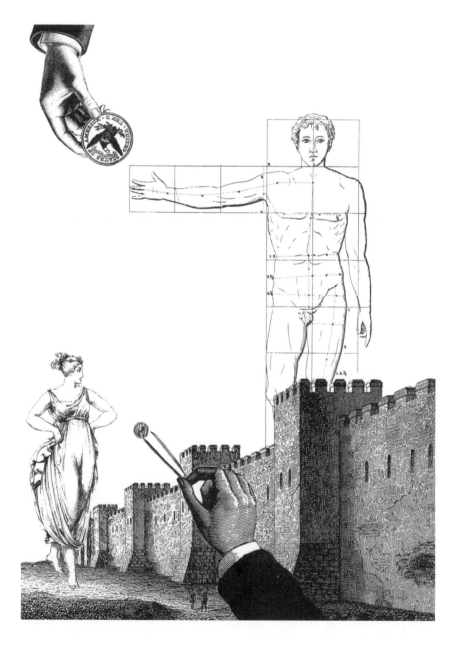

A PORTRAIT OF

SURVEY RESPONDENTS

This appendix provides a demographic portrait of my 409 survey respondents. Almost two-thirds (62%) were female and just over one-third (38%) were male. Racial breakdown included 64% white; 15% Asian American; 9% African American; 9% foreign-born; 7% Latino/Latina; 3% Native American; note that these add up to more than 100% as multiple responses were possible. The largest group of respondents were white women (42%), followed by white men (22%), women of color (20%), and men of color (15%). Regarding sexual orientation, the vast majority (95%) described themselves as straight/heterosexual, 3% as gay, 2% as lesbian, and 1% as bisexual.

Their ages ranged from twenty-four to seventy-five, with an average of forty-one. In terms of physical abilities, the vast majority (95%) reported that they had no disability, whereas 5% indicated that they did.

Regarding marital status, over half (58%) were married for the first time, 17% had never married, 11% were divorced, 11% were remarried, 6% were cohabiting, 2% were widowed, and 1% were separated. Three-quarters (77%) had a spouse who works full-time outside the home, 13% had a spouse who works part-time outside the home, and 11% had a spouse who does not work outside the home. One-fifth (20%) were married to another architect. Over half (56%) had children.

About three-quarters (72%) had a bachelor's degree in architecture, another quarter (27%) had a bachelor's degree in another field, about a third (39%) had a master's degree in architecture, and 8% had a master's in another field; again note that multiple choices were possible.

Regarding their professional status, almost all (93%) worked full-time; this was the case for every demographic group in the sample. Almost 4 out of 5 (79%) had passed the Architect Registration Examination (ARE), 10% had taken it but not passed, and 11% had not yet taken it. The average respondent had 9.3 years of full-time experience as a paid registered architect, with the range being from 0 to 39 years; and 14.9 years of full-time experience as a paid architectural professional, including internships, with a range of 0 to 45 years. Since receiving their architectural degrees, respondents had a range of 0 to 20 employers, an average of 4.4. They had been unemployed an average of 1.2 times, but the figures ranged from 0 to 20.

The vast majority (89%) were members of the American Institute of Architects; 17% were members of local organizations for women in architecture, 8% were members of the National Organization of Minority Architects, and 3% were members of a local organization for minorities in architecture; again note that multiple responses were possible. Of those AIA members, 70% were regular registered architects, 11% were associates, 7% were interns, 3% were fellows, and 1% were emeritus.

Regarding respondents' primary occupation, over two-thirds (69%) were in private architectural practice, 9% were in-house architects in corporate practice, and the rest were government architects, architectural faculty, and in other positions. Concerning the type of work done by respondents' firms, commercial (66%), institutional (56%), residential (56%), and interiors (50%) topped the list, followed by municipal (36%), consulting (30%), development (20%), engineering (17%), and landscape (14%). Regarding their current position—for which multiple responses were possible—about two-thirds (62%) listed themselves as registered architects, 44% as project architect/managers, 28% as designers, and 26% as principals/owners. Other responses included positions in marketing, computer work, and as draftsperson (each 18%), specifications writer and sole practitioners (each 17%), programming (15%), intern (13%), partner, interior designer, consultant, and associate (each 11%), cost estimator (10%), construction manager (9%), job captain (8%), president (7%), plan examiner (4%), real estate development (3%), corporate architect (3%), and nonarchitect (1%).

Most (60%) were paid on a salary, 17% were paid on an hourly basis, and 10% were paid on a contract basis. Annual salaries ranged from 0 to $160,000, with an average of $43,440.

In evaluating the responses to my survey, one must keep in mind that, while they are compelling, they represent just one aspect of the architecture profession. A future study could profitably investigate the viewpoints of employers in the field, as well as those of clients. All of these groups make the practice of architecture what it is: a creative, sometimes frustrating, always challenging pursuit.

Notes

INTRODUCTION

1. The architects for these buildings are as follows: U.S. Embassy in Tokyo, Norma Sklarek; San Francisco Ballet Association, Beverly Willis; Air Traffic Control Tower at Los Angeles International Airport, Katherine Diamond; new Federal Building in Oklahoma City, Carol Ross Barney. Obviously, each worked with architectural colleagues, male and female.

2. Natalie J. Sokoloff, *Black Women and White Women in the Professions: Occupational Segregation by Race and Gender, 1960–1980* (New York: Routledge, 1992), 13.

3. Kathryn H. Anthony, *Design Juries on Trial: The Renaissance of the Design Studio* (New York: Van Nostrand Reinhold, 1991).

4. See Kathryn H. Anthony, Jill Eyres, and Ripal Patel, "Shattering the Glass Ceiling: The Role of Gender and Race in Architecture—A Preliminary Report," in *Breaking the Ice: Building New Leadership, AIA National Diversity Conference Proceedings* (Washington, D.C.: American Institute of Architects, 1994), 6–7, App. A, 1–2; Kathryn H. Anthony, Jami Becker, Tracey Jo Hoekstra, and Melissa Worden with Jill Eyres and Ripal Patel, "An Update on Shattering the Glass Ceiling: The Role of Gender and Race in the Architectural Profession," in *Building Bridges: Diversity Connections* (Washington, D.C.: American Institute of Architects, 1995), App. A, 25–26.

5. John Morris Dixon, "A White Gentleman's Profession," *Progressive Architecture* (Nov. 1994): 55–61 (see discussion of my research on 56, 58, 61). Discussion of my research appeared also in Abby Bussel, "Women in Architecture: Leveling the Playing Field," *Progressive Architecture* (Nov. 1995): 45–49, 86 (see esp. 46, 47, 48); Sheri Olson, "Architecture Doesn't Look Much like America," *Architectural Record* (Nov. 1994): 25; Mubarak S. Dahir, "Why Architecture Still Fails to Attract Minorities," *Architectural Record* (July 1995): 32–33.

CHAPTER 1: DIVERSITY IN DESIGN

The epigraph that opens this chapter is from Ernest L. Boyer and Lee D. Mitgang, *Building Community: A New Future for Architecture Education and Practice* (Princeton, N.J.: Carnegie Foundation for the Advancement of Teaching, 1996), 96–97.

1. Boyer and Mitgang, *Building Community,* xx. Boyer and Mitgang's study was commissioned by five national architectural organizations to analyze the future of architectural education and practice. These were: the American Institute of Architects, the American Institute of Architecture Students, the Association of Collegiate Schools of

Architecture, the National Architectural Accrediting Board, and the National Council of Architectural Registration Boards.

2. Lee D. Mitgang, "Saving the Soul of Architectural Education: Four Critical Challenges Face Today's Architecture Schools," *Architectural Record* (May 1997): 125.

3. *Employment and Earnings* 47, no. 1 (Jan. 2000): 178. Information from the U.S. Department of Labor, Bureau of Labor Statistics.

4. Linda Schmittroth, *Statistical Record of Women Worldwide*, 2d ed. (New York: Gale Research, 1995), 556, 575. Note that the percentages have been rounded.

5. Data in table 2 are drawn from the following sources. Architects: *Employment and Earnings*, 178. AIA members: "AIA Membership Statistics" (Washington, D.C.: American Institute of Architects, Aug. 1999); these figures reflect all categories of AIA membership, and only those who reported their gender and race. Faculty, students, and graduates: "NAAB Statistics Report" (Washington, D.C.: National Architectural Accrediting Board, Nov. 1999). This information includes only those in accredited programs.

6. "AIA Membership Statistics" (Aug. 1999). Exact figures show 1,669 Asians, 1,155 Latinos/Latinas, 563 African Americans, 201 Subcontinent Asians, 92 Native Americans, 78 others, and 40,988 Caucasians. Note that demographic categories are not required for membership.

7. Blair Kamin, "If Women Designed the World It Would Be Kinder and Gentler. Or Would It?" *Chicago Tribune*, Apr. 27, 1997, Sec. 7, 1, 12, 13.

8. Bradford C. Grant and Dennis Alan Mann, eds., *Directory of African American Architects*, 2d ed. (Cincinnati, Ohio: Center for the Study of Practice, School of Architecture and Interior Design, University of Cincinnati, 1996), 169.

9. Robert Traynham Coles, "Editorial," *Progressive Architecture* (July 1989), 7.

10. "NAAB Statistics Report" (Nov. 1999).

11. Heidi Landecker, "Why Aren't More Women Teaching Architecture?" *Architecture* 80, no. 10 (Oct. 1991): 23–25.

12. Michael Kaplan, "Statistics on Tenured Faculty," *Association of Collegiate Schools of Architecture (ACSA) Newsletter*, Sept. 1993, 28. Based on the *1992–93 ACSA Faculty Directory*.

13. See *ACSA Directory 1997–98* (Washington, D.C.: Association of Collegiate Schools of Architecture, 1997).

14. "NAAB Statistics Report."

15. Ibid.; A. Freeman, "Black Architects Termed 'An Endangered Species,'" *Architecture* 78, no. 6 (1989): 28, 30; Bradford C. Grant and Dennis Alan Mann, eds., *The Professional Status of African American Architects* (Cincinnati, Ohio: Center for the Study of Practice, School of Architecture and Interior Design, University of Cincinnati, 1996), 3–4, 11.

16. Margaret Usdansky, "Minorities a Majority in Fifty-one Cities," *USA Today*, Sept. 17, 1991, 1.

17. Richard Conniff, "Chicago: Welcome to the Neighborhood," *National Geographic* 179 (May 1991): 50–77; see map on 57.

18. Michael A. Tomlan, "Who Will Care in the 1990s? Ethnic Diversity Will Play a Greater Role in the Preservation Movement, Particularly in Urban Neighborhoods," *Preservation Forum* 3, no. 4 (Winter 1990): 20–21.

19. Leslie Kanes Weisman, *Discrimination by Design: A Feminist Critique of the Man-Made Environment* (Urbana: University of Illinois Press, 1992), 35.

20. See C. Van Woodward, *The Strange Career of Jim Crow* (New York: Oxford University Press, 1955). This is just one of many sources on this subject. For works on the architecture of the Holocaust, consult Albert Speer, *Inside the Third Reich* (New York: Macmillan, 1970). See also George Mosse, *Nazi Culture* (New York: Grosset and Dunlap, 1966). For a compelling photographic documentation of the World War II internment camps built to house Japanese Americans, see Gary Y. Okihiro (essay) and Joan Myers (photographs), *Whispered Silences: Japanese Americans and World War II* (Seattle: University of Washington Press, 1996).

21. See, for example, Erma Bombeck, "It's a Fact: Women Designed to Spend Time in Rest Rooms," *San Diego Union Tribune*, Mar. 11, 1994, Sec. E, 2; Gail Collins, "Potty Politics: The Gender Gap," *Working Woman* 18 (Mar. 1993): 93; "Inequity in Rest Rooms," *New York Times*, May 10, 1988, Science Sec., 27; T. Mariani, "8,000 Years' Oppression Unrested? Poly Architecture Professor Says Male Designers Have Long Subordinated Women," *San Luis Obispo Telegram-Tribune*, California, Feb. 13, 1996, Sec. A, 1, 5; C. Page, "A Loud Outcry for 'Potty Parity,'" *San Diego Union-Tribune*, Mar. 5, 1994; S. Shafer, "California Takes Major Step towards Public Rest Room 'Equity,'" *Domestic Engineering* (Apr. 1988): 32–33; "Study Confirms Long-held Beliefs on Potty Parity," *Stars and Stripes*, June 17, 1988, 4; J. Woo, "'Potty Parity' Lets Women Wash Hands of Long Loo Lines," *Wall Street Journal*, Feb. 24, 1994, A-1, A-19.

22. John Tierney, "Bathroom Liberationists," *New York Times Magazine*, Sept. 8, 1996, 32 (quote), 34.

23. Collins, "Potty Politics."

24. Woo "'Potty Parity' Lets Women Wash Hands," A-1.

25. Farnsworth quoted in Alice T. Friedman, *Women and the Making of the Modern House: A Social and Architectural History* (New York: Abrams, 1998), 141.

26. See Kurt Andersen, "A Crazy Building in Columbus," *Time*, Nov. 20, 1989, 84, 89; Cathleen McGuigan, "Eisenman's Gridlocked Mind Game," *Newsweek*, Nov. 20, 1989, 74–75.

27. Paul Goldberger, "The Museum That Theory Built," *New York Times*, Nov. 5, 1989, Sec. 2, 1.

28. Jack Nasar, *Design by Competition: Making Design Competition Work* (New York: Cambridge University Press, 1999), esp. 133, 134, 141 on accessibility issues; B. Fisher and Jack Nasar, "Fear of Crime in Relation to Three Exterior Site Features: Prospect, Refuge and Escape," *Environment and Behavior* 24 (1992): 35–56; Jack L. Nasar and B. Fisher, "Design for Vulnerability: Cues and Reactions to Fear of Crime," *Sociology and Social Research* 76 (1992): 48–58; Jack L. Nasar and J. M. Kang, "A Post-Jury Evaluation: The Ohio State University Design Competition for a Center for the Visual Arts," *Environment and Behavior* 21 (1989): 464–84.

29. Andersen, "A Crazy Building in Columbus," 89.

30. Accessibility issues described in Nasar, *Design by Competition*, 133.

31. Chip Johnson, "Tales of Sex Harassment at UC," *Oakland Tribune*, Nov. 17, 1992, A-3–4.

32. Dashka Slater, "Harassment Charges Rock Architecture School," *East Bay Express*, Nov. 27, 1992; Elaine Herscher, "Discord at UC Berkeley Architecture School," *San Francisco Chronicle*, Oct. 29, 1992.

33. Erin McCormick, "Students Urge UC to End Sex Bias," *San Francisco Examiner*, Nov. 17, 1992, A-8; Slater, "Harassment Charges Rock Architecture School."

34. See Amy Saltzman, "Life after the Lawsuit: They Took Their Employers to Court. They Won. But It's Not Over," *US News and World Report,* Aug. 18, 1996, 57–61.

35. See Susanna Torre, *Women in American Architecture: A Historic and Contemporary Perspective* (New York: Whitney Library of Design, 1977); Heidi Landecker, "Why Aren't More Women Teaching Architecture?" *Architecture* 80, no. 10 (Oct. 1991): 23–25; Saltzman, "Life after the Lawsuit," 57–61.

36. See Sherry Ahrentzen and Linda Groat, "Rethinking Architectural Education: Patriarchal Conventions and Alternative Visions from the Perspectives of Women Faculty," *Journal of Architectural and Planning Research* 9, no. 2 (Summer 1992): 95–111; Linda Groat and Sherry Ahrentzen, *Status of Faculty Women in Architecture Schools: Survey Results and Recommendations* (Washington, D.C.: Association of Collegiate Schools of Architecture Press, 1990); Linda Groat and Sherry Ahrentzen, "Reconceptualizing Architectural Education for a More Diverse Future: Perceptions and Visions of Architectural Students," *Journal of Architectural Education* 49, no. 3 (Feb. 1996): 166–83; Linda Groat and Sherry Ahrentzen, "Voices for Change in Architectural Education: Seven Facets of Transformation from the Perspectives of Faculty Women," *Journal of Architectural Education* 50, no. 4 (May 1997): 271–85. At the time of the 1990 study, only 16% of architectural faculty were women, and tenured women faculty represented only 3% of all architecture faculties. In striking contrast to their male counterparts, 81% of women architecture faculty were in either non-tenure-track or non-tenured positions, 18% were tenured, and only 5% were full professors.

37. Groat and Ahrentzen, "Reconceptualizing Architectural Education," 173.

38. Ibid., 172.

39. International students reported the greatest satisfaction with architecture as both a major and a career choice, while Asian-American students were least satisfied, and Caucasians, African Americans, and Latinos/Latinas fell somewhere in between. See Groat and Ahrentzen, "Reconceptualizing Architectural Education," 175.

40. Groat and Ahrentzen, "Reconceptualizing Architectural Education," 177.

41. Mark Paul Frederickson, "Gender and Racial Bias in Design Juries," *Journal of Architectural Education* 47, no. 1 (Sept. 1993): 38–48.

42. Boyer and Mitgang, *Building Community,* 95.

43. John Rossi, "The Jury System in Architectural Education," *AIA Architect* 3 (Dec. 1996): 24.

44. Marilyn Loden, *Implementing Diversity* (Chicago: Irwin Professional Publishing, 1996), 18–19.

45. Ann M. Morrison, *The New Leaders: Guidelines on Leadership Diversity in America* (San Francisco: Jossey-Bass, 1992), 4.

46. "Greenspan Calls Diversity 'Good for Business,'" *San Diego Union-Tribune,* Jan. 17, 1998, C2.

47. Levitt quoted in Charles Gasparino and Joseph N. Boyce, "SEC to Hold Meetings in Effort to Boost Women and Minorities in Corporate US," *Wall Street Journal,* Jan. 19, 1998, A6.

48. "Affirming Diversity: Building a National Community That Works," *Issues Quarterly* 1, no. 4 (1996): 2.

49. This and the next two paragraphs are based on "Points of Law," *Issues Quarterly* 1, no. 4 (1996): 7–8.

50. "Policy in Action: We Are Family," *Issues Quarterly* 1, no. 4 (1996): 16.

51. See Stephen Carter, *Reflections of an Affirmative Action Baby* (New York: Basic Books, 1991).

52. American Institute of Architects, *Architecture Firm Survey Report 97* (Washington, D.C.: American Institute of Architects, 1997), 11.

53. In the United Kingdom as well, Statutory Maternity Pay (SMP) applies only to firms employing five or more people. Firms employing fewer than five are excluded, and this accounts for nearly two thousand of the five thousand architectural firms in the UK. It also applies only to mothers, not to fathers; there is no paid paternity leave. See Ruth Owens, "Holding the Baby: Architects and Childcare," *Architect's Journal* 195, no. 20 (May 20, 1992): 53–55.

54. "Code of Ethics and Professional Conduct," Rule 1.401 (Washington, D.C.: American Institute of Architects) (as of Mar. 21, 1997).

55. "Code of Ethics and Professional Conduct," E.S. 5.1.

56. Unless noted otherwise, this and the next five paragraphs are based on the case described in "Code of Ethics and Professional Conduct Advisory Opinion No. 4: Discrimination against Employees Based on Gender" (Washington, D.C.: American Institute of Architects) in *National Judicial Council* (Jan. 1992).

57. Loden, *Implementing Diversity,* 25.

58. See R. Roosevelt Thomas Jr., *Beyond Race and Gender: Unleashing the Power of Your Total Work Force by Managing Diversity* (New York: AMACOM, a division of American Management Association, 1991).

59. See Teresa Kruzan and John Hutcheson, *The Guide to Culture Audits* (Atlanta, Ga.: American Institute for Managing Diversity, 1998).

60. Unless noted otherwise, this and the next three paragraphs are based on Sondra Thiederman, *Bridging Cultural Barriers for Corporate Success: How to Manage the Multicultural Work Force* (Lexington, Mass.: D. C. Heath, 1991).

61. Marga Rose Hancock, "AIA: Posting No Barriers," *AIA Memo* (Dec. 1992): 3.

62. Michael L. Wheeler, *Diversity: Business Rationale and Strategies: A Research Report* (New York: Conference Board, 1995), 8.

63. "Perspectives," *Issues Quarterly* 1, no. 4 (1996): 10.

64. See Wheeler, *Diversity.* Organizations included in this research on diversity are American Express; Ameritech; Bank of America; Chevron; Du Pont; Eastman Kodak; Ford Motor Company; General Electric Company; Girl Scouts, USA; IBM Corporation; Inland Steel Company; Levi Strauss; Motorola; NASA Lyndon B. Johnson Space Center; National Broadcasting Corporation (NBC); Pacific Bell Pillsbury; Price Waterhouse; Sara Lee Corporation; Silicon Graphics; and the Whirlpool Corporation. Among the more progressive firms were IBM, AT&T, Xerox, and Aetna, who pioneered diversity and work-family programs for their managers and employees as early as the mid-1980s.

65. See general discussion in Thomas, *Beyond Race and Gender.*

66. Unless noted otherwise, this and the next three paragraphs are based on Loden, *Implementing Diversity,* 41–42, 79, 85, 106.

67. To learn more about the nonprofit organization Catalyst, consult the Web site at <http://www.catalystwomen.org/home.html>, accessed Apr. 21, 1998.

68. See *The Catalyst Guide to Best Practices* (New York: Catalyst, 1998).

69. Information is based on a presentation by Etty Padmodipoetro, of the firm Stull and Lee in Boston, at the AIA National Diversity Conference, Boston, Aug. 25, 1996.

70. Information is based on a presentation by Peter Steffian, of the Boston firm Steffian Bradley and Associates, at the AIA National Diversity Conference, Boston, Aug. 25, 1996.

71. Information about Leers, Weinzapfel Associates, Boston, is based on a presentation by Jane Weinzapfel, a principal of the firm, at the AIA National Diversity Conference, Boston, Aug. 25, 1996.

72. Owens, "Holding the Baby," 55.

CHAPTER 2: WOMEN AS CONSUMERS, CREATORS, AND CRITICS OF THE BUILT ENVIRONMENT

The first epigraph that opens this chapter is from Naomi Stungo, "Opportunity Knocked," *RIBA Journal* 101 (June 1994): 20. The second epigraph is from Denise Scott Brown, "Room at the Top? Sexism and the Star System in Architecture," in *Architecture: A Place for Women,* ed. Ellen Perry Berkeley and Matilda McQuaid (Washington, D.C.: Smithsonian Institution Press, 1989), 240.

1. For more on the relationship between Catherine the Great and the architect Charles Cameron, see Dimitri Shvidkovsky, *The Empress and the Architect: British Architecture and the Gardens at the Court of Catherine the Great* (New Haven, Conn.: Yale University Press, 1996).

2. Alison Ravertz, "A View from the Interior," in *A View from the Interior: Feminism, Women and Design,* ed. Judy Attfield and Pat Kirkham (London: Women's Press, 1989), 189–91.

3. For more information consult: Dolores Hayden, *The Grand Domestic Revolution: A History of Feminist Designs for American Homes, Neighborhoods, and Cities* (Cambridge, Mass.: MIT Press, 1981); idem, *Seven American Utopias: The Architecture of Communitarian Socialism, 1790–1975* (Cambridge, Mass.: MIT Press, 1976); Gwendolyn Wright, *Building the Dream: A Social History of Housing in America* (New York: Pantheon, 1981).

4. Unless noted otherwise, this and the next paragraph are based on David Diederich (author and compiler), *Susan: A Susan Lawrence Dana Anthology* (Springfield, Ill.: Dana-Thomas House Historic Site, David Diederich, 1995), 60.

5. Alice T. Friedman, *Women and the Making of the Modern House* (New York: Abrams, 1997); see also Alice T. Friedman, "Not a Muse: The Client's Role at the Rietveld Schroder House," in *The Sex of Architecture,* ed. Diana Agrest, Patricia Conway, and Leslie Kanes Weisman (New York: Abrams, 1996), 217–32.

6. Sara Holmes Boutelle, *Julia Morgan, Architect,* rev. ed. (New York: Abbeville, 1995), 83. The next paragraph is based on pages 169–73 of Boutelle's book.

7. Julia Sommer, "Women Who Built Berkeley," *CalReport* 9, no. 1 (Fall 1992): 11–14.

8. Boutelle, *Julia Morgan, Architect,* 170.

9. Sommer, "Women Who Built Berkeley."

10. "Women's Rights National Historical Park," <http://www.nps.gov/wori/wrnhp.htm>, accessed June 23, 1997.

11. Vernon Mays, "Chapel of Change," *Historic Preservation* 48 (Jan.–Feb. 1996): 34–38. For the design development and construction phases, the two-woman team worked with the Stein Partnership of New York City.

12. "The Memorial Education Center," <http://www.wimsa.org/eductr.html>, accessed Feb. 12, 1998.

13. Abby Bussel, "Challenging Historic 'Truths,'" *Progressive Architecture* 76 (June 1995): 70.

14. This and the next three paragraphs are based on Barbara J. Howe, "Women and Architecture," in *Reclaiming the Past: Landmarks of Women's History,* ed. Page Putnam Miller (Blooomington, Ind.: Indiana University Press, 1992), 27–62.

15. See Kurt Helfrich, "Modernism for Washington? The Kennedys and the Redesign of Lafayette Square," *Washington History* 8, no. 1 (Spring/Summer 1996): 16–37, 91–92; Richard Moe and Leonard Zax, "Jackie's Washington: How She Rescued the City's History," *Historic Preservation News* 34, no. 4 (Aug.–Sept. 1994): 18–19; Richard Moe and Leonard A. Zax, "Jackie's Washington: How She Rescued the City's History," *Washington Post,* May 29, 1994, C3; James A. Abbott and Elaine M. Rice, *Designing Camelot: The Kennedy White House Restoration* (New York: Wiley, 1997).

16. Quoted in Arthur M. Schlesinger Jr., *A Thousand Days: John F. Kennedy in the White House* (1965; rpt., New York: Fawcett Premier, 1992), 676.

17. Jacqueline Kennedy to Bernard L. Boutin, Mar. 6, 1962, personal papers of David E. Finley, Gallery Archives, National Gallery of Art, Washington, D.C.

18. Ibid.

19. "Exhibit B," Commission of Fine Arts Minutes, Oct. 16, 1962, 48, quoted in Helfrich, "Modernism for Washington?" 33.

20. Moe and Zax, "Jackie's Washington," C3. Unless noted otherwise, this and the next paragraph are based on this work.

21. Unless noted otherwise, this and the next three paragraphs are based on Lewis L. Gould, *Lady Bird Johnson and the Environment* (Lawrence, Kan.: University of Kansas Press, 1988), 35–38.

22. Johnson quote, Gould, *Lady Bird Johnson,* 38. For Jacobs's book, see Jane Jacobs, *The Death and Life of Great American Cities* (New York: Random House, 1961).

23. See Beverly Willis, *Invisible Images: The Silent Language of Architecture* (Washington, D.C.: National Building Museum, 1997).

24. See Ivor Powell, *Ndebele: A People and Their Art* (New York: Cross River Press, 1995).

25. See Barbara Oldershaw, "Blackfeet American Indian Women: Builders of the Tribe," *Places* 4, no. 1 (1987): 38–47.

26. See Doris Coles, *From Tipi to Skyscraper: A History of Women in Architecture* (Boston, Mass.: I Press Incorporated, 1973).

27. James Beck, "A 'Female' Architect of Fifteenth-Century Florence," *Source: Notes in the History of Art* 7, no. 1 (1987): 6–8.

28. See Antonio Manetti, *The Life of Brunelleschi,* trans. C. Enggass (University Park, Pa.: Pennsylvania State University Press, 1970); and Antonio Manetti, *Vita di Filippo Brunelleschi: Preceduta da la Novella del Grasso* (Milan: Il Polifilo, 1976), 117.

29. Unless noted otherwise, this and the next two paragraphs are based on Milka Bliznakov, "Woman Architects," *Structurist* 25–26 (1985–86): 121–27.

30. On the Cambridge School, see Dorothy May Anderson, *Women, Design, and the Cambridge School* (West Lafayette, Ind.: PDA Publishers, 1980).

31. *"That Exceptional One": Women in American Architecture, 1888–1988* (Washington, D.C.: American Architectural Foundation, 1988), 11.

32. See M. Weinmann, *The Fair Women: The Story of the Woman's Building, World's Columbian Exposition* (1893; rpt., Chicago: Academy Chicago, 1981).

33. For a comprehensive account of Morgan's life and work, consult Boutelle, *Julia Morgan, Architect.*

34. "Bright Angel Lodge," <http://www.heard.org/edu/harvey/gc/gc8.htm>, accessed Aug. 1, 1997.

35. Arnold Berke, "Drawing from the Desert: Architect Mary Colter Told Stories in Stone," *Preservation* 49, no. 4 (July–Aug. 1997): 34–43; quote from 39. See also Virginia L. Grattan, *Mary Colter: Builder upon the Red Earth* (Flagstaff, Ariz.: Northland Press, 1980).

36. Bliznakov, "Woman Architects," 122.

37. This and the next paragraph are drawn from Lucinda Liggett Eddy, "Lilian Jenette Rice: Search for a Regional Ideal. The Development of Rancho Santa Fe," *Journal of San Diego History* 29, no. 4 (Fall 1983): 262–85.

38. See Elizabeth C. MacPhail, *Kate Sessions: Pioneer Horticulturist* (San Diego: San Diego Historical Society, 1976).

39. Bliznakov, "Woman Architects," 124; unless noted otherwise, this and the next paragraph are based on Bliznakov's article.

40. Betsky, *Building Sex*, 172.

41. Bliznakov, "Woman Architects," 122.

42. Susana Torre, ed., *Women in American Architecture: A Historic and Contemporary Perspective* (New York: Whitney Library of Design, 1977).

43. *Heresies* 11, no. 3 (1981), special issue, "Making Room: Women and Architecture"; Gisela Ecker, ed., *Feminist Aesthetics* (Boston: Beacon Press, 1985); Ellen Perry Berkeley and Matilda McQuaid, eds., *Architecture: A Place for Women* (Washington, D.C.: Smithsonian Institution Press, 1989).

44. Norma Sklarek, "Women in Architecture," in *Encyclopedia of Architecture: Design, Engineering and Construction 5*, ed. Joseph A. Wilkes and Robert T. Packard (New York: Wiley, 1990), 342–55.

45. Clare Lorenz, *Women in Architecture: A Contemporary Perspective* (New York: Rizzoli, 1990); Leslie Kanes Weisman, *Discrimination by Design* (Urbana: University of Illinois Press, 1992); Francesca Hughes, ed., *The Architect: Reconstructing Her Practice* (Cambridge, Mass.: MIT Press, 1996); Debra Coleman, Elizabeth Danze, and Carol Henderson, eds., *Architecture and Feminism* (New York: Princeton Architectural Press, 1996); Agrest et al., *The Sex of Architecture.* Other key sources written in the 1980s and 1990s include: D. Cole and K. C. Taylor, *The Lady Architects: Lois Lilley Howe, Eleanor Manning and Mary Almy, 1893–1937* (New York: Midmarch Arts Press, 1990); Hayden, *The Grand Domestic Revolution;* idem, *Seven American Utopias;* Helen L. Horowitz, *Alma Mater: Design and Experience in the Women's Colleges from their Nineteenth-Century Beginnings to the 1930s* (New York: Knopf, 1984); and B. Marvin, *Berkeley Houses by Julia Morgan* (Berkeley, Calif.: Berkeley Architectural Heritage Association, 1987).

46. "AIA Survey," *Women and Environments* 7, no. 2 (Spring 1985): 20; quoted from *MEMO,* Newsletter of the AIA (Jan. 1984).

47. Rochelle Martin, Wendy Chamberlin, and Sarah Haselschwardt, "Women as Architects: Have We Come a Long Way?" *Women and Environments* 7, no. 2 (Spring 1985): 18–20.

48. Susan Doubilet, "P/A Reader Poll: Women in Architecture," *Progressive Architecture* (Oct. 1989): 15–17; J. Murphy, "Office Politics," *Progressive Architecture* 72, no. 9 (1991): 65, 67; Karen Kingsley and Anne Glynn, "Women in the Architectural Workplace," *Journal of Architectural Education* 46, no. 1 (Sept. 1992): 14–20; Anne McDermott, "Looking through the Glass Ceiling in Architecture" (Master's thesis, School of Architecture, University of Illinois at Urbana-Champaign, 1993).

49. See Blanche L. van Ginkel, "Slowly and Surely (But Somewhat Painfully), More or Less the History of Women in Architecture in Canada: An Account of the Struggles of Women to Find a Way into the Architectural Profession in Canada," *Canadian Architect* 38, no. 11 (Nov. 1993): 15–17.

50. See Lynne Walker, "The Entry of Women into the Architectural Profession in Britain," *Women's Art Journal* 7, no. 1 (Spring–Summer 1986): 13–18; idem, "Women and Architecture," in *A View from the Interior: Feminism, Women and Design,* ed. Judy Attfield and Pat Kirkham (London: Women's Press Limited, 1989), 90–105; see also Stephanie Williams, "Women Architects: Their Work," *RIBA Journal* 91 (Dec. 1984): 39.

51. Walker, "Entry of Women," 15, quoting C. H. Townsend, "Women as Architects," *British Architect* (Dec. 31, 1886): 26, vii.

52. Ibid.

53. Martin Pawley, "PS: Martin Pawley Has Dangerous Thoughts about Women in Architecture," *RIBA Journal* 98, no. 5 (May 1991): 103.

54. Walker, "Women and Architecture."

55. Japanese statistics are drawn from Sklarek, "Women in Architecture," 353; Nicola Turner, "Women and Children First," *World Architecture* 38 (1995): 84–87.

56. Chinese statistics are drawn from Sklarek, "Women in Architecture," 351.

57. Indian statistics are drawn from Sklarek, "Women in Architecture," 353.

58. Scandinavian statistics are drawn from Sklarek, "Women in Architecture," 352, and from "Fourteen Finnish Women Architects," *RIBA Journal* 96, no. 9 (Sept. 1989): 11.

59. Russian statistics are drawn from Sklarek, "Women in Architecture," 355.

60. Information about Russia comes from interviews with Dimitri Shvidkovsky and Katia Shorban, two architects from Moscow, conducted by the author, Champaign, Ill., Mar. 1997.

61. Statistics about Argentina are drawn from Bliznakov, "Woman Architects," 122.

62. See Martin Filler, "Husbands and Wives," *Architecture* 85 (June 1996): 89–124.

63. "Natalie de Blois to Speak at February Brunch," *Chicago Women in Architecture Newsletter* (Jan. 1987): 1.

64. For more information about Mackintosh and his wife and collaborator, Margaret Macdonald, see Janice Helland, "Collaboration among the Four," in *Charles Rennie Mackintosh,* exh. cat., ed. Wendy Kaplan (New York: Abbeville Press, 1996); and Timothy Neat, *Part Seen, Part Imagined: Meaning and Symbolism in the Work of Charles Rennie Mackintosh and Margaret Macdonald* (Edinburgh: Canongate Press, 1994). For information about Macdonald herself, see Janice Helland, *The Studios of Frances and Margaret Macdonald* (New York: Manchester University Press, 1996). For information about the Griffins, see Thomas S. Hines, "Portrait: Marion Mahony Griffin, Drafting a Role for Women in Architecture," *Architectural Digest* 52 (Mar. 1995): 28, 32, 36, 38, 40; Paul Kruty and Paul E. Sprague, *Two American Architects in India: Walter B. Griffin and Marion M. Griffin, 1935–1937,* exh. cat. (Urbana: School of

Architecture, University of Illinois, 1997); and Mati Maldre and Paul Kruty, *Walter Burley Griffin in America* (Urbana: University of Illinois Press, 1996). For more information about Mies van der Rohe's associate, Lilly Reich, consult Matilda McQuaid, with an essay by Magdalena Droste, *Lilly Reich: Designer and Architect* (New York: Museum of Modern Art, 1996). For information about Charles and Ray Eames, see Pat Kirkham, *Charles and Ray Eames: Designers of the Twentieth Century* (Cambridge, Mass.: MIT Press, 1995). For information about Anne Griswold Tyng, consult *Louis Kahn to Anne Tyng: The Rome Letters, 1953–1954*, edited, with commentary, by Anne Griswold Tyng (New York: Rizzoli, 1997). Tyng was born in China. After 1973 she opened up an independent practice in Philadelphia, receiving her doctorate from the University of Pennsylvania in 1975. For additional information about Tyng, see Sklarek, "Women in Architecture," 349, and Adolf K. Placzek, ed., *Macmillan Encyclopedia of Architects*, vol. 4 (New York: Free Press, 1982), 232.

65. For information about the Harknesses and the Fletchers, see Louise Harpman, "Drawing the Line: Live Together/Work Together," *Practices 5/6* (1997): 61–70, esp. 62, 64.

66. Kirkham, *Charles and Ray Eames*, 81.

67. Unless noted otherwise, this and the next paragraph are based on Helland, *The Studios of Frances and Margaret Macdonald;* quotes from 130 (this paragraph), 4 (next paragraph).

68. Neat, *Part Seen, Part Imagined*, 18 (first quote), 13 (second quote).

69. P. Morton Shand to William Davidson, Mar. 1933, Hunterian Art Gallery, quoted in Helland, *The Studios of Frances and Margaret Macdonald*, 2.

70. Shand to Macdonald, Smith and Co., Mar. 20, 1933, Hunterian Art Gallery, quoted in Helland, *The Studios of Frances and Margaret Macdonald*, 2.

71. This and the next paragraph are based on Hines, "Portrait: Marion Mahony Griffin."

72. This and the next three paragraphs are based on McQuaid, *Lilly Reich;* quote from 56.

73. This and the next two paragraphs are based on Kirkham, *Charles and Ray Eames;* quotes from 2, 4, 7, 82.

74. This and the next two paragraphs are based on Tyng, *Louis Kahn to Anne Tyng;* quotes are from 59, 184, 202, 203.

75. Jill Jordan Seider, "A Building of Her Own," *US News and World Report*, Oct. 14, 1996, 67.

76. The discussion of Denise Scott Brown is based on William Braham and Louise Harpman, "Denise Scott Brown and Robert Venturi," *Practices 5/6* (1997): 5–13; quotes from 5–7.

77. See Martin Filler, "Husbands and Wives," *Architecture* 85 (June 1996): 89–124, quote from 89.

78. *Practices 5/6* (1997). See especially, articles by Braham and Harpman, "Denise Scott Brown and Robert Venturi"; Louise Harpman, "Drawing the Line: Live Together/Work Together," 61–70, and several articles in the section "Between the Sheets: Partners on Partnering," 73–129.

79. Dietsch discussed in Renee Garrison, "Architect Out to Redesign Her Profession," *Tampa Tribune*, Mar. 29, 1992, 1, 5.

80. Linda Dunyan, "Changing the Status Quo; or, Florida's Climate Is Not Sunny for Women Architects," *Florida Architect* (July–Aug. 1992).

81. Kathryn Clark Albright, "Elizabeth Plater-Zyberk and Andres Duany," *Practices 5/6* (1997): 95–103.

82. Frances Halsband, "On Partners," *Practices 5/6* (1997), 127, 128.

83. Louise Harpman, "Drawing the Line: Live Together/Work Together," *Practices 5/6* (1997): 65.

84. Data from American Institute of Architects, communicated to the author, fall 1996; see also Melissa Jo Worden, "The Critical Link: Architecture Critics, the Popular Press, and the Public" (Master's thesis, School of Architecture, University of Illinois at Urbana-Champaign, 1997).

85. E-mail from Michael Janes, "Architecture Writers" file, American Institute of Architects, to the author, Oct. 31, 2000.

86. For an insightful historical analysis of the writings of women in architecture, see Diane Favro, "Women Write: The Shaping of American Architecture by Female Authors," *Architecture California* 18, no. 2 (Winter 1996/97): 40–51.

87. Pelli quoted in Larry M. Greenberg, "Jane Jacobs Sounds Off–Again," *Wall Street Journal*, Oct. 8, 1997, B12.

88. See Wright, *Building the Dream;* Hayden, *The Grand Domestic Revolution;* idem, *The Power of Place: Urban Landscapes as Public History* (Cambridge, Mass.: MIT Press, 1995); idem, *Redesigning the American Dream: The Future of Housing, Work, and Family Life* (New York: Norton, 1984); idem, *Seven American Utopias;* Clare Cooper Marcus, *House as a Mirror of Self: Exploring the Deeper Meaning of Home* (Berkeley, Calif.: Conari Press, 1995); Galen Cranz, *The Chair: Body, Culture, and Design* (New York: Norton, 1998).

89. See, for example, K. Brock, "Piercing through the Glass Ceiling," *Business Journal* (Portland, Ore.), Nov. 24, 1995, 17, 19; R. Freligh, "Fighting for Women Architects," *Plain Dealer* (Cleveland, Ohio), Oct. 17, 1995, Sec. E, 1, 6; W. Gould, "Architecture–A 'Gentleman's Club,'" *Star Tribune* (Minneapolis, Minn.), Jan. 21, 1996, Sec. E, 11; idem, "High Profiles," *Journal Sentinel* (Milwaukee, Wisc.), Jan. 7, 1996, Sec. G, 1, 3; Linda Mack, "Designing Women," *First Sunday, Star Tribune Magazine* (Minneapolis), Apr. 5, 1992, 6–8, 20.

90. Seider, "A Building of Her Own," 66.

91. See Brown, "Room at the Top?"

92. Ibid., 240.

93. See, for example, Aaron Betsky, *Building Sex: Men, Women, Architecture, and the Construction of Sexuality* (New York: Morrow, 1995), xiv–xv; idem, *Queer Space: Architecture and Same-Sex Desire* (New York: Morrow, 1997); Joel Sanders, ed., *Stud: Architectures of Masculinity* (New York: Princeton Architectural Press, 1996).

CHAPTER 3: SEXUAL ORIENTATION, RACE, AND ETHNICITY

The epigraph that opens this chapter is from Paul Revere Williams, "I Am a Negro," *American Magazine* (July 1937): 59, 161–62.

1. See Barbara A. Weightman, "Gay Bars as Private Places," *Landscape* 24, no. 1 (1980): 9–16.

2. See Maxine Wolfe, "Invisible Women in Invisible Places: Lesbians, Lesbian Bars, and the Social Production of People/Environment Relationships," *Architecture and Comportment* 8, no. 2 (1992): 137–58; quote from 148.

3. This paragraph is based on Aaron Betsky, *Queer Space: Architecture and Same-Sex Desire* (New York: Morrow, 1997); quote from 17.

4. See Map Collective of Boston Gay and Lesbian Architects and Designers and the Boston Area Lesbian and Gay History Project, "Location: A Historical Map of Lesbian and Gay Boston" (Boston, Mass.: 1995). For a national perspective, consult Paula Martinac, *The Queerest Places: A Guide to Gay and Lesbian Historic Sites* (New York: Henry Holt, 1997).

5. San Francisco's Polk Street was a gay mecca in the late 1970s and early 1980s, but with public awareness of the AIDS crisis, the gay commercial neighborhood became concentrated in the Castro Street area.

6. Jonathan Boorstein, "Queer Style: Public Faces to Private Spaces," *Lesbian and Gay New York (LGNY)* 37 (Sept. 22, 1996): 11.

7. For a discussion of Grierson's career, see Harold P. Simonson, *Francis Grierson* (New Haven, Conn.: College and University Press and Twayne Publishers, 1966).

8. Aaron Betsky, *Building Sex: Men, Women, Architecture, and the Construction of Sexuality* (New York: Morrow, 1997), 174.

9. Jonathan Boorstein, "Staggering Tapestries," in *Building Bridges: Diversity Connections. American Institute of Architects National Diversity Conference Proceedings* (Washington, D.C.: American Institute of Architects, 1995), 27.

10. Jonathan Boorstein, "Queer Space," in *Building Bridges: Diversity Connections. American Institute of Architects National Diversity Conference Proceedings* (Washington, D.C.: American Institute of Architects, 1995), 27.

11. Jonathan Boorstein, "Toward Identifying a Gay or Lesbian Aesthetic in Interior Design," unpublished manuscript.

12. Thomas Fisher, "The Intern Trap: How the Profession Exploits Its Young," *Progressive Architecture* (July 1994): 69–73.

13. Ruthann Rudel, "On Visibility," in *Out in the Workplace: The Pleasures and Perils of Coming Out on the Job,* ed. Richard A. Rasi and Lourdes Rodriguez-Nogues (Los Angeles: Alyson Publications, 1995), 60.

14. For an interesting analysis of ethnic landscapes in American history, see Allen G. Noble, ed., *To Build a New Land: Ethnic Landscapes in North America* (Baltimore: Johns Hopkins University Press, 1992).

15. See *Walking through Old Memphis: An Historic Walking Tour of Downtown Memphis* (Memphis: Memphis Heritage Publishing Company and Memphis Landmarks Commission, 1981).

16. For a comprehensive analysis of the changing roles of urban Asian villages in the United States, see Harry L. Margulis, "Asian Villages: Downtown Sanctuaries, Immigrant Asian Reception Areas, and Festival Marketplaces," *Journal of Architectural Education* 45, no. 3 (May 1992): 150–60. For a detailed description of culturally diverse neighborhoods and how they are being preserved, see *Cultural Resources Management (CRM)* 15, no. 7 (1992). It covers ethnically diverse communities in Hawaii; Dayton, Ohio; South Carolina; Georgia; and elsewhere. For a historical analysis of ethnically diverse landscapes, see Noble, *To Build a New Land*; of special interest is a chapter by Alvar W. Carlson, "Spanish Americans in New Mexico's Rio Arriba," 345–61; and one by Philippe Oszuscik, "African-Americans in the American South," 157–76. See also *New York Affairs* 10, no. 1 (Winter 1987) on ethnic neighborhoods, which discusses Manhattan's Jewish West Side and Harlem gentrification.

17. See "Project Row Houses," <http://www.neosoft.com/prh>, accessed June 21, 1997.

18. See "Martin Luther King, Jr.: The King Center," <http://www.stanford.edu/group/King/KCenter/kcenter.htm>, accessed Feb. 11, 1998.

19. See "National Civil Rights Museum," <http://www.civilrightsmuseum.org>, accessed Oct. 4, 2000.

20. See "Birmingham Civil Rights Institute," <http://www.bcri.bham.al.us>, accessed Oct. 4, 2000.

21. Robert Garver, Director of Public Information, United States Holocaust Memorial Museum, telephone conversation with author, Nov. 8, 2000.

22. "Simon Wiesenthal Center Museum of Tolerance," museum brochure.

23. "Museum of African American History," <http://maah-detroit.org>, accessed Oct. 4, 2000.

24. Unless noted otherwise, this and the next two paragraphs are based in part on archival sources from the San Diego Chinese Historical Museum, obtained in Apr. 1997. See also *Chinese Historical Society of San Diego* newsletters; Murray K. Lee, "In Search of Gold Mountain," unpublished manuscript, San Diego Chinese Historical Museum.

25. Angela Lau, "Chinese Museum Dedicated Today," *San Diego Union-Tribune,* Jan. 13, 1996, B-1, 6; archival sources, San Diego Chinese Historical Museum, consulted in Apr. 1997.

26. Cardinal also designed the Turning Stone Casino Resort in Verona, New York, which opened in 1997. See William Kates, "Curves Swerve, Twists Turn in New Hotel," *San Diego Union-Tribune,* Nov. 16, 1997, H6.

27. For more information on the work of Jones and Jones, see Koichi Kobayashi, ed., "Jones & Jones: Ideas Migrate . . . Places Resonate," special issue of *Process Architecture* 126 (May 1995).

28. See, for example, *Cultural Resources Management;* Margaret Gaskie, "A Possible Dream: Plaza Guadalupe," *Architectural Record* 175 (Oct. 1987): 128–33; Christine Granados, "Legacy Builders: Hispanic Architects Continue a Longstanding Tradition of Beauty and Form," *Hispanic* (Apr. 1997): 49–52; Herbert L. Smith Jr., "Echoes of Plazas and Pyramids (Cigarroa High School and Middle School)," *Architectural Record* 175 (Sept. 1987): 88–91. Margulis's "Asian Villages," Gaskie's "A Possible Dream," and articles by Granados and Smith briefly describe the work of contemporary Latino architects.

29. See Bradford C. Grant, "Accommodation and Resistance: The Built Environment and the African American Experience," in *Reconstructing Architecture: Critical Discourses and Social Practices,* ed. Thomas A. Dutton and Lian Hurst Mann (Minneapolis: University of Minnesota Press, 1996), 202–33.

30. Max Bond, "Still Here: Three Architects of Afro-America: Julian Francis Abele, Hilyard Robinson, and Paul R. Williams," *Harvard Design Magazine* (Summer 1997): 48–53, quote from 53.

31. This paragraph is based on Richard K. Dozier, "The Black Architectural Experience in America," in *African American Architects in Current Practice,* ed. Jack Travis (New York: Princeton Architectural Press, 1991), 8–9. See also Carl Anthony, "The Big House and the Slave Quarters: Part I, Prelude to New World Architecture," *Landscape* 20, no. 3 (Spring 1976): 14, and idem, "The Big House and the Slave Quarters: Part II, African Contributions to the New World," *Landscape* 21, no. 1 (Autumn 1976): 13, 14.

32. This and the next two paragraphs are based on Philippe Oszuscik, "African-Americans in the American South," in Noble, *To Build a New Land*, 157–76.

33. "Chronology of African Black Architects," listed in Travis, *African American Architects in Current Practice*, 92. The chronology was compiled by Vinson McKenzie of Auburn University, Auburn, Alabama.

34. M. Adams, "A Legacy of Shadows," *Progressive Architecture* 72 (Feb. 1991): 85–87; Julie V. Iovine, "Architects: Builders of Dreams," *Emerge* 2, no. 9 (Aug. 1991): 35–38.

35. Bond, "Still Here," 52.

36. Ibid., 48.

37. Ibid.

38. See Karen Hudson, *Paul Revere Williams: A Legacy of Style* (New York: Rizzoli, 1993). See also Adams, "A Legacy of Shadows: Blacks Who Overcame the Odds," *Ebony*, Nov. 1986; K. G. Bates, "He Was (and Is) the Architect to the Stars," *New York Times*, July 26, 1990, C1–6; "Paul Revere Williams," in *The Annual Obituary, 1980*, ed. R. Turner (New York: St. Martin's Press, 1981), 51–54.

39. Michael Adams, "The Incomparable Success of Paul R. Williams," in Travis, *African American Architects*, 20–21.

40. Iovine, "Architects," 37.

41. "Black Women Architects; A Blueprint for Success," *Ebony* (June 1984): 52–53, 58, 60; "Norma Merrick Sklarek," in Travis, *African American Architects*, 66–69.

42. Iovine, "Architects," 37.

43. "J. Max Bond, Jr.," in Travis, *African American Architects*, 22.

44. Iovine, "Architects," 38.

45. "Black Women Architects: Looking Toward the Future," School of Architecture and Planning, Howard University, Feb. 1992 Symposium Program.

46. Travis, *African American Architects in Current Practice*, 7.

47. See Thomas Dutton, ed., *Voices in Architectural Education: Cultural Politics and Pedagogy* (New York: Bergin and Garvey, 1991); and Dutton and Mann, *Reconstructing Architecture*.

48. John Morris Dixon, "Editorial: Recognition for Minority Architects," *Progressive Architecture* 71 (Dec. 1990): 7; idem, "Minority Architects Meet and Honor Members," *Progressive Architecture* 73 (Dec. 1992): 15.

49. Jean Barber and Christopher Cortright, eds., *Focus Group: "Profile of the Minority Architect" and Roundtable: "Today's Minority Architect: A Major Force,"* Report Organized and Sponsored by the Minority Resources Committee of the American Institute of Architects (Washington, D.C.: American Institute of Architects, 1990).

50. Jane Holtz Kay, "Invisible Architects," *Architecture* 80, no. 4 (Apr. 1991): 106, 109.

51. See Bradford C. Grant and Dennis Alan Mann, eds., *Directory: African American Architects* (Cincinnati, Ohio: Center for the Study of Practice, School of Architecture and Interior Design, University of Cincinnati, 1991); idem, *Directory of African American Architects*, 2d ed. (Cincinnati, Ohio: Center for the Study of Practice, School of Architecture and Interior Design, University of Cincinnati, 1995), with online version at <http://blackarch.uc.edu>, accessed Nov. 1, 2000; idem, *The Professional Status of African American Architects* (Cincinnati, Ohio: Center for the Study of Practice, School of Architecture and Interior Design, University of Cincinnati, 1996).

52. Bradford C. Grant and Dennis Alan Mann, "A Question of Status: African American Architects," *Architecture California* 18, no. 2 (Winter 1996/97): 16–19.

53. Grant, "Accommodation and Resistance," 231.

54. See, for example, Darrel W. Fields, Kevin L. Fuller, and Milton S. F. Curry, *Appendx: Culture Theory Praxis* 1, 2 (1992, 1994), a journal published in Massachusetts; Sze Tsung Leong, "Readings of the Attenuated Landscape," in *Slow Space,* ed. M. Bell and Sze Tsung Leong (New York: Monacelli, 1998), 187–213; Edward W. Soja, *Postmodern Geographies: The Reassertion of Space in Critical Social Theory* (New York: Verso, 1989).

55. Bradford Grant, e-mail to the author, Feb. 7, 1999.

56. Cornel West, *Keeping Faith* (New York: Routledge Press, 1993), quote from 46. See also Cornel West, "On Architecture?" *Appendx* 2 (1994): 82–103. Another sharp criticism of the elitism of the architectural profession can be found in Garry Stevens, *The Favored Circle: The Social Foundations of Architectural Distinction* (Cambridge, Mass.: MIT Press, 1998).

57. See Ellis Cose, *The Rage of a Privileged Class* (New York: HarperPerennial, 1993). The remainder of this paragraph is based on Cose's observations.

58. Stephen L. Carter, *Reflections of an Affirmative Action Baby* (New York: Basic Books, 1991), 2.

CHAPTER 4: NETWORKS OF POWER

1. Chicks in Architecture Refuse to Yield (CARY), *More Than the Sum of Our Body Parts,* exh. cat., Randolph Street Gallery, Chicago, 1993.

2. Ann Moore, "Breaking Down the Barriers: LA's Minority and Women Architects," *L.A. Architect* (Feb. 1990): 6–7.

3. Ibid.

4. *Chicago Women in Architecture, 1991 Membership Directory;* "Organizational Objectives," *NOMA News, Newsletter of the National Organization of Minority Architects* 21, no. 2 (Fall 1993): 6.

5. CARY, *More Than the Sum of Our Body Parts.*

6. Milka Bliznakov, "Women Architects," *Structurist* 25–26 (1985–86): 121–27.

7. Paul Barkley, "Important Issues Raised at the February WIA Meeting," *Women in Architecture Newsletter* 1 (Apr. 1989): 3.

8. See discussion of the archive in Matilda McQuaid, "Educating for the Future: A Growing Archive on Women in Architecture," in *Architecture: A Place for Women,* ed. Ellen Perry Berkeley and Matilda McQuaid (Washington, D.C.: Smithsonian Institution Press, 1989), 247–60.

9. Judy L. Rowe, "From the Chair," *AIA Women in Architecture Newsletter* 6 (Spring 1991): 1.

10. Deborah Dietsch, "Presidential Precedent," *Architecture* (July 1996): 13.

11. This account of the CWA is based on Roberta Feldman, "Chicago Women in Architecture since 1974: A Brief History," *Chicago Women in Architecture Newsletter* (Jan. 1987): 2–3.

12. Feldman, "Chicago Women in Architecture since 1974," 2–3.

13. Pam Hutter, "WBE Roundtable Editorial," 2; Melissa Bogusch, "Ladies of the Corridor: A Series," 3–5; and idem, "Ladies on the Threshold: A Series: Gae Aulenti," 5–6; all in *The Muse, Chicago Women in Architecture Newsletter* (July–Aug. 1996); see also *The Muse* (Feb.–Mar.–Apr. 1999). For more about CWA see <http://www.cwarch.org>, accessed Nov. 1, 2000.

14. Stephanie Stubbs, "Breaking through a 'Thunderous Silence,'" *AIA Memo* (Dec. 1992): 4.

15. "Update on Minority Scholarships," *AIA MRC Report, Minority Resources Committee Newsletter* 3 (Fall 1990): 4; "Focus Group and Roundtable Programs Uncover Key Issues," *AIA MRC Report, Minority Resources Committee Newsletter* 2 (Feb. 1990): 1–2; Jean Barber and Christopher Cortright, eds., *Focus Group: "Profile of the Minority Architect" and Roundtable: "Today's Minority Architect: A Major Force"* (Report) (Washington, D.C.: AIA, 1990).

16. "MRC Liaison Network Provides Critical Link," *AIA MRC Report, Minority Resources Committee Newsletter* 2 (Feb. 1990): 3j. As of 1990, the goals of the MRC Committee were: "to increase minority participation and influence in the AIA; to increase awareness of minority issues within the profession; to increase knowledge within minority communities about the architectural profession and the value of quality environments and design; and to increase to proportional parity the market share for minority architects, thus promoting acceptance of minority architects as equals in the business arena." "MRC Committee Charge and Goals," *AIA MRC Report, Minority Resources Committee Newsletter* 2 (Feb. 1990): 6.

17. "Task Force Update," *AIA MRC Report, Minority Resources Committee Newsletter* 3 (Fall 1990): 4; information about AIA activities during this period provided by Jean Barber, former director, Diversity Programs, American Institute of Architects.

18. "NOMA Remembers Founder William M. Brown, 1925–1993," *NOMA News, Newsletter of the National Organization of Minority Architects* 23, no. 2 (June 1993): 3. For more information about NOMA, see <http://www.noma.net>, accessed Nov. 4, 2000.

19. "Black American Architect Archive Is Established," *AIA MRC Report, Minority Resources Committee Newsletter* 2 (Feb. 1990): 5.

20. "Upbeat Mood Marks Minority Architects," *Architectural Record* 180 (Dec. 1992): 13; "NOMA Takes a Bite out of the Big Apple," *NOMA News, Newsletter of the National Organization of Minority Architects* 24, no. 1 (Jan. 1994): 1.

21. "1991 Conference Highlights," *The Report of the National Organization of Minority Architects* (NOMA, 1991–92), 3.

22. Robert Easter, "Excerpts from an Address at the LA NOMA Achievement Dinner," *NOMA News, Newsletter of the National Organization of Minority Architects* 23, no. 2 (June 1993): 2.

23. Robert Easter, Letter to NOMA Members, *NOMA News, Newsletter of the National Organization of Minority Architects* 23, no. 2 (June 1993): 2.

24. "LA NOMA in the Forefront of Rebellion Aftermath Activities," *NOMA News, Newsletter of the National Organization of Minority Architects* 22, no. 2 (Fall 1992): 2.

25. Wiley quoted in Moore, "Breaking Down the Barriers," 6.

26. "White House Briefed on NOMA," *NOMA News, Newsletter of the National Organization of Minority Architects* 23 no. 3 (Aug. 1993): 3; "NOMA Joins NAFTA Supporters," *NOMA News, Newsletter of the National Organization of Minority Architects* 24, no. 1 (Jan. 1994): 5.

27. Stephan A. Kliment, "Preserving Affirmative Action–With a New Twist," *Architectural Record* 183 (Dec. 1995): 9.

28. William J. Stanley III, Letter to NOMA Members, in *Empowerment, Visibility, Education, "The EVE of Opportunity"* (National Organization of Minority Architects Twenty-first Annual Conference Program, 1991), 1.

29. "Big Fellows and Little Fellows," *NOMA News, Newsletter of the National Organization of Minority Architects* 21, no. 1 (First Quarter 1991): 3.

30. Information about the Organization of Black Designers, comes from the Web site at <http://www.core77.com/OBD/info.html>, accessed June 20, 1997.

31. Moore, "Breaking Down the Barriers," 6; "Asian American Architects and Engineers Mission Statement," obtained from Jeff Wong, Nov. 16, 2000; see also <http://www.aaaenc.org>, accessed Nov. 27, 2000 (information about AAAE founding and mission); Wilson Chang, "Celebrating Fifteen Years of the AAAE; History Invoked at Asian American Architects and Engineers Gala Dinner," *Small Business Exchange Construction,* Oct. 29–Nov. 4, 1992, 1, 23 (information about federal contracting, legislation, workshops).

32. Stephen Glassman, "Some Personal Views of Diversity," *AIA Memo* (Dec. 1995): 6.

33. Jonathan Boorstein, "Staggering Tapestries," in *Building Bridges: Diversity Connections. American Institute of Architects National Diversity Conference Proceedings* (Washington, D.C.: American Institute of Architects, 1995), 27.

34. Camille Victour, "Build Visibility," in *Out in the Workplace: The Pleasures and Perils of Coming Out on the Job,* ed. Richard A. Rasi and Lourdes Rodriguez-Nogues (Los Angeles: Alyson Publications, 1995), 114–19.

35. Fontaine Roberson, "CAPA Forums Focus on Homelessness," *Castro Star* 2, no. 5 (Aug. 1997): 2.

36. *Castro Area Planning + Action,* brochure, 1997.

37. Stubbs, "Breaking through a 'Thunderous Silence,'" 4.

38. "Diversity Task Force," *AIA Women in Architecture Newsletter* (Summer 1992): 5.

39. Pradeep Dalal, "'How Firm a Foundation': Fifth AIA Diversity Conference Celebrates Milestone," *AIArchitect* 5 (Sept. 1998): 1, 19; Darrell Lewis, "Roll Up for a Magical History Tour: Making Atlanta's 'Sweet' Journey to King's Tomb," *AIArchitect* 5 (Sept. 1998): 18.

40. Megan Lux, "Connecting the Dots through Diversity Workshops at D2K," *The Muse, Chicago Women in Architecture Newsletter* (Aug.–Sept.–Oct. 2000): 3, 6.

41. For more information about Walter Blackburn, see "Walter Scott Blackburn, FAIA, 1938–2000"; Marga Rose Hancock, "A Champion of Diversity"; and Robert T. Coles, "The Passing of a Prince"; all in *AIArchitect* 7 (Oct. 2000): 8.

42. Bliznakov, "Women Architects," 122.

43. "That Exceptional One," *AIA Women in Architecture Newsletter* 2 (Oct. 1989): 3; *"That Exceptional One": Women in American Architecture, 1888–1988,* exh. cat. (Washington, D.C.: American Architectural Foundation, 1988).

44. For information about the Oregon exhibit, see Randy Gragg, "Designing Women," *Sunday Oregonian,* Aug. 9, 1992, B1, B4.

45. *More Than the Sum of Our Body Parts,* exh. cat., 1.

46. For more about this exhibit, see "Facing the Issues Facing Women in Architecture," *Designer/Builder* (Nov. 1996): 18–21.

47. E-mail from Martha Thorne to the author, Mar. 4, 1999; for more about this exhibit, see *Chicago Women in Architecture: A Creative Constellation, Celebrating Twenty-five years* (Chicago: Chicago Women in Architecture, 1999).

48. Jonathan Boorstein, "Exhibits: A New York Exhibit Celebrates the Work of Talented Designers Lost in Their Prime," *Design Times* 6, no. 3 (1994): 21.

49. Victour, "Build Visibility," 116.

50. Melissa Jo Worden, "The Critical Link: Architecture Critics, the Popular Press and the Public" (Master's thesis, School of Architecture, University of Illinois at Urbana-Champaign, 1997).

CHAPTER 5: GATEWAYS AND ROADBLOCKS TO ARCHITECTURAL PRACTICE

1. Note that according to the 1996 Guide to Fair Employment Practices, *Labor Law Reports* (Jan. 24, 1996), Issue #779, Report #535, 68: "Title VII of the 1964 Civil Rights Act does not expressly prohibit preemployment inquiries concerning a job applicant's race, color, religion, sex or national origin. However, because such inquiries frequently bear no demonstrable relationship to a job applicant's ability or qualification as an employee, they can be used as evidence of discrimination in hiring. For example, an employer's unexplained inquiry as to an applicant's religion, coupled with the employer's subsequent failure to hire the applicant, provided a basis for a determination that the federal ban on religious bias had been violated."

    Fair employment practice statutes exist at both the federal and state levels. The Civil Rights Act of 1964 (Title VII) is the federal statute. It "prohibits discrimination based on sex, race, color, religion, and national origin by employers in hiring or firing; on compensation in terms, conditions, or privileges of employment; and in limiting, segregating, or classifying employees or applicants." Each state has some deviation or modification of this federal statute as their own state statute. See also Kurt H. Decker, *Privacy in the Workplace: Rights, Procedures and Policies* (Horsham, Pa.: LRP Publications), 11

2. Levine quoted in Jerilow Hemmert, "Facing the Issues Facing Women in Architecture," *Designer/Builder* (Nov. 1996): 20.

3. Ernest L. Boyer and Lee D. Mitgang, *Building Community: A New Future for Architectural Education and Practice* (Princeton, N.J.: Carnegie Foundation for the Advancement of Teaching, 1996), 120.

4. Frank E. Heitzman and Walter Lewis, "IDP Q&A," Nov. 30, 1994, unpublished document.

5. See the Web site at <http://www.ncarb.org/idp/index.html>, accessed Nov. 4, 2000.

6. *Intern Development Program Guidelines, 1996–1997* (Washington, D.C.: National Council of Architectural Registration Boards, 1996), 5. The next paragraph is drawn from this source book.

7. Category A, Design and Construction Documents, requires the most training units and addresses programming, site and environmental analysis, schematic design, engineering systems coordination, building cost analysis, code research, design development, construction documents, specifications and materials research, and document checking and coordination. Category B, Construction Administration, addresses bidding and contract negotiation, construction phase–office, and construction phase–observation. Category C, Management, requires training units in both project management and office management. Category D, Related Activities, covers professional and community service as well as other related areas.

8. Lee D. Mitgang, "Overwhelmed by Requirements, Interns Cheat on Reports to NCARB," *Architectural Record* (July 1999): 55–62. See also Beth A. Quinn and Pamela J. Hill, "Learning to Lie: Falsification in Architectural Internship," in *Proceedings*

of the Association of Collegiate Schools of Architecture (ACSA) West Regional Conference, ed. Christine Theodoropoulos and Alison Snyder (ACSA, 1999).

9. Deborah K. Dietsch, "Build a Better Internship," *Architecture* (Aug. 1996): 15.

10. See Thomas Fisher, "The Intern Trap: How the Profession Exploits Its Young," *Progressive Architecture* (July 1994): 69–73; quote from 69.

11. Ibid., 73.

12. Boyer and Mitgang, *Building Community,* 116.

13. Ibid., 121

14. Ibid., 117.

15. See Web site at <http://www.ncarb.org/are/prices/html>, accessed Nov. 6, 2000.

16. This and the next two paragraphs are based on Michael Crosbie, "The New Exam: Will It Change the Profession?" *Progressive Architecture* 76 (Apr. 1995): 49–53, 98, 100; quotes from 50. For an assessment of an earlier version of the ARE, see Theodore L. Mularz, "Architectural Education: How Well Is the Registration Exam Doing Its Job?" *Architectural Record* 173 (Aug. 1985): 53–54.

17. "Architect Registration Exam," <http://www.ncarb.org/are/prices.html>, accessed Nov. 6, 2000.

18. Information from Earl Fenwick, National Council of Architectural Registration Boards, e-mail to the author, Nov. 10, 2000.

CHAPTER 6: OBSTACLES IN THE ARCHITECTURAL WORKPLACE

1. U.S. Bureau of Labor Statistics, "Occupational Outlook Handbook: Architects," at <http://stats.bls.gov.oco/ocos038.htm>, accessed June 24, 1997.

2. Bradford C. Grant and Dennis Alan Mann, eds., *The Professional Status of African American Architects* (Cincinnati, Ohio: Center for the Study of Practice, School of Architecture and Interior Design, University of Cincinnati, 1996), 15.

3. Armendariz quoted in Ann Moore, "Breaking Down the Barriers: LA's Minority and Women Architects," *L.A. Architect* (Feb. 1990): 6.

4. See Ellis Cose, *The Rage of a Privileged Class* (New York: HarperPerennial, 1993).

5. Susan F. King, "Ladies of the Corridor–A Series," *Chicago Women in Architecture Newsletter* (Mar.–Apr. 1996): 3–5.

6. For information on Close, see Linda Mack, "Designing Women: Women Architects Make Their Way in an Old Boys' Profession," *First Sunday, Star Tribune Magazine* (Minneapolis), Apr. 5, 1992, 6–8, 20; quote from 7.

7. Grant and Mann, *Professional Status of African American Architects,* 19.

8. U.S. Bureau of Labor Statistics, "Occupational Outlook Handbook: Architects," at <http://stats.bls.gov.oco/ocos038.htm>, accessed June 24, 1997. These figures are for 1993, the same year for which I collected salary data from my survey respondents.

9. Grant and Mann, *Professional Status of African American Architects,* 18.

10. "Architects Find Underrepresented Practice Viable," *Association of Collegiate Schools of Architecture (ACSA) Newsletter* (Oct. 1993): 16, excerpted from *AIA Memo* (July–Aug. 1993).

11. Breaking down the data strictly along racial lines, again, examining only those who work full-time, the average salary for white architects was $44,930, compared to the average salary for nonwhite architects at $44,490. Specifically, the average salaries

for Asians, full-time, was $45,156; for Latinos, full-time, $44,260; and for African Americans, full-time, $43,772. None of these differences were statistically significant, however.

12. "Affirming Diversity: Building a National Community that Works," *Issues Quarterly* 1, no. 4 (1996): 4. These figures reflect 1994 data. Figures for 1997 show an even worse picture for women of color. According to research conducted by Catalyst, the research organization mentioned earlier that seeks to advance women in the business world, women of color (African Americans, Asian Americans, and Latinas) earn only 57 cents for every dollar made by their white male counterparts. They make up 10% of the work force, yet they hold only 5% of management jobs. See Maggie Jackson, "Slow Progress Seen for Minority Women," *San Diego Union-Tribune*, Oct. 23, 1997, C2.

13. "Eye Openers, The Evidence Is In: The Case for Affirmative Action," *Issues Quarterly* 1, no. 4 (1996): 6.

14. "AIA Survey," *Women and Environments* 7, no. 2 (Spring 1985): 20, quoting from *MEMO, Newsletter of the AIA* (Jan. 1984); Rochelle Martin, Wendy Chamberlin, and Sarah Haselschwardt, "Women as Architects: Have We Come a Long Way?" *Women and Environments* 7, no. 2 (Spring 1985): 18–20.

15. Sylvia Lewis, "Breaking through the Glass Ceiling," *Planning* (July 1991): 8; Peggy Layne, "The Glass Ceiling: Is It Really There?" *SWE: Magazine of the Society of Women Engineers* (Mar.–Apr. 1994): 25–27.

16. Data here and in table 7 is based on that provided in *Employment and Earnings* 43, no. 1 (Jan. 1996): 205; *Employment and Earnings* 44, no. 1 (Jan. 1997): 206; *Employment and Earnings* 45, no. 1 (Jan. 1998): 209; *Employment and Earnings* 46, no. 1 (Jan. 1999): 213; and *Employment and Earnings* 47, no. 1 (Jan. 2000): 213.

17. How do these results compare with those from the planners? Nearly one-third of all the women surveyed in the *Planning* study feel they have been denied a salary increase or promotion because of their gender. More than one-quarter of minority planners have felt victimized by racial discrimination. See Lewis, "Breaking through the Glass Ceiling."

18. *Architecture Fact Book* (Washington, D.C.: American Institute of Architects, 1994), 43.

19. "Architects Find Underrepresented Practice Viable," *Association of Collegiate Schools of Architecture (ACSA) Newsletter* (Oct. 1993): 16, excerpted from AIA *Memo* (July–Aug. 1993).

20. "Working Trends: Counting on the Nation's Women," *Issues Quarterly* 1, no. 4 (1996): 14.

21. My questions on sexual harassment drew heavily upon the Sexual Experiences Questionnaires developed by Louise Fitzgerald, an internationally recognized expert on sexual harassment in education and the workplace and a colleague of mine at the University of Illinois. See Louise F. Fitzgerald, S. Shullman, N. Bailey, M. Richards, J. Swecker, A. Gold, A. J. Ormerod, and L. Weitzman, "The Incidence and Dimensions of Sexual Harassment in Academia and the Workplace," *Journal of Vocational Behavior* 32 (1988): 152–75; and Louise F. Fitzgerald, M. Gelfand, and F. Drasgow, "Measuring Sexual Harassment: Theoretical and Psychometric Advances," *Basic and Applied Social Psychology* 17 (1995): 425–45. Fitzgerald's research on sexual harassment, the Work Experiences Project, has studied thousands of individuals in multiple organizational settings in the United States and abroad.

22. "Code of Ethics and Professional Conduct Advisory Opinion No. 4: Discrimination Against Employees Based on Gender" (Washington, D.C.: American Institute of Architects); published in *National Judicial Council* (Jan. 1992).

23. Macari quoted in Renee Garrison, "Architect Out to Redesign Her Profession," *Tampa Tribune,* Mar. 29, 1992, 1.

24. "Hottest or Coldest Career?" *Chicago Women in Architecture Newsletter* (Oct. 1986): 3; "The Twenty-five Hottest Careers of 1986," *Working Woman,* July 1986, 72–73; quote from 73.

25. "Facing the Issues Facing Women in Architecture," *Designer/Builder* (Nov. 1996): 18–21.

26. Unless noted otherwise, this and the next two paragraphs are based on Grant and Mann, *Professional Status of African American Architects;* quotes from 12–13.

27. A caveat must be added, however. Concerning the items of "racial harassment" and "racial abuse," the mean responses were relatively low (architects of color rated these 2.0 and 1.9 on a 5-point scale, respectively, where 1 = "not at all" and 5 = "very much"), indicating that the occurrence of such negative behavior is relatively rare.

28. Jane Darke, "Women, Architects, and Feminism," in Matrix, *Making Space: Women and the Man-Made Environment* (London: Pluto Press, 1984), 16, 22–23.

29. Ruth Owens, "Holding the Baby: Architects and Childcare," *Architect's Journal* 195, no. 20 (May 20, 1992): 53–55.

30. An article in a British architectural publication revealed that the three major issues affecting parents working for others are maternity/paternity leave and benefits, coping with career breaks, and flexible or part-time working hours. For more information, see Owens, "Holding the Baby: Architects and Childcare."

31. Darke, "Women, Architects, and Feminism," 23.

32. "Facing the Issues Facing Women in Architecture," 19–20.

33. Cynthia Woodward, "Issues Presented at AIA Roundtable," *AIA Women in Architecture Newsletter* 2 (Oct. 1989): 1; see also Woodward, *Human Resources Management for Design Professionals* (Washington, D.C.: AIA Press, 1990).

34. Roberta Feldman, "Research Plan for the Study of Attrition Rates of Women Architects," prepared for the Women in Architecture Committee of the American Institute of Architects. Unpublished manuscript, 1989.

CHAPTER 7: SUCCEEDING IN THE ARCHITECTURAL WORKPLACE

1. Pradeep Dalal, "Significant Growth at Larger MBEs and WBEs," *AIArchitect* 7 (Sept. 2000), 5.

2. By contrast, many women and minority architects are employed in large firms with twenty or more employees. Nationally, while these large firms constitute just 6% of all architectural firms, they employ almost half (49%) of the entire work force. *Architecture Fact Book* (Washington, D.C.: American Institute of Architects, 1994), 26, 42.

3. These and subsequent figures represent the percentages of respondents who checked either "satisfied" or "very satisfied" on a five-point scale.

4. These and subsequent figures represent the percentages of respondents who checked either "satisfied" or "very satisfied" on a five-point scale.

1.   "Architects Find Underrepresented Practice Viable," *ACSA Newsletter* (Oct. 1993): 16, excerpted from *AIA Memo* (July–Aug. 1993).

2.   For an overview of diversity in the art world, see Lynn Basa, "Focus: Complicating Any Discussion of the Significance of Fiber's Association with the Feminine Is the On-going Art vs. Crafts Debate," *Shuttle, Spindle and Dyepot* 22, no. 4, issue 88 (Fall 1991): 16–17; Maurice Berger, "Are Art Museums Racist?" *Art in America* 78, no. 9 (Sept. 1990): 69–77, and "Speaking Out: Some Distance to Go," *Art in America* 78, no. 9 (Sept. 1990): 78–85; Russell Ferguson, Martha Gever, Trinh T. Minh-ha, and Cornel West, eds., *Out There: Marginalization and Contemporary Cultures* (New York: New Museum of Contemporary Art, and Cambridge, Mass.: MIT Press, 1990); Marcia Ann Gillespie, "Guerrilla Girls: From Broadsides to Broadsheets," *Ms.*, Mar.–Apr. 1993, 69; Guerrilla Girls, *Confessions of the Guerrilla Girls* (New York: HarperPerennial, 1995); Eleanor Heartney, "How Wide Is the Gender Gap?" *Art News* 86 (Summer 1987): 139–45; Anne Higonnet, "Woman's Place," *Art in America* 76 (July 1988): 127–28, 130–31, 149; Susan Kingsley, "A Feminist Perspective," *Metalsmith* 7 (Fall 1987): 26–31; Lisa Krohn, "Against the Odds: Five Top Designers Discuss the Challenges Unique to Women in Design," *Industrial Design* 33 (Sept.–Oct. 1986): 38–43; John Loughery, "Mrs. Holladay and the Guerrilla Girls," *Arts Magazine* 62 (Oct. 1987): 61–65; Edith P. Mayo, "A New View?" *Museum News* 69 (July–Aug. 1990): 48–50; Nelken McCann, "Guerrilla Talk: A Conversation with a Member of Guerrilla Girls West," *Artweek* 22, no. 22 (June 20, 1991): 1, 15–17; Lisbet Nilson, "Coming of Age," *Art News* 87 (Oct. 1988): 104–9; Howardena Pindell, "Art World Racism: A Documentation," *New Art Examiner* 16, no. 7 (Mar. 1989): 32–36; Ginny Ruffner, "Speaking of Glass," *American Craft* 48 (Oct.–Nov. 1988): 32–35, 64; Joan Tallman, "Guerrilla Girls," *Arts Magazine* 65 (Apr. 1991): 21–22; Marcia Tucker, "Common Ground," *Museum News* 69 (July–Aug. 1990): 44–46.

3.   For an overview of diversity in science and engineering, see Mairin Brennan, "Marriage, Gender Influence Career Advancement for Chemists," *Chemical and Engineering News* 70 (May 4, 1992): 46–51; Claudia M. Caruana, "Black ChEs Cite Workplace Bias," *Chemical Engineering Progress* 89, no. 3 (Mar. 1993): 17–19; Michael F. Crowley, *Women and Minorities in Science and Engineering* (Washington, D.C.: National Science Foundation, 1977); Elizabeth Culotta, "Minorities in Science '93: Trying to Change the Face of Science," *Science* 262 (Nov. 12, 1993): 1089–1135; Anne Eisenberg, "Women and the Discourse of Science," *Scientific American* 267 (July 1992): 122; Faye Flam, "Still a 'Chilly Climate' for Women?" *Science* 252 (June 21, 1991): 1604–6; "Glass Ceiling Is Real for Women Engineers," *Engineering News Record* 229 (Sept. 14, 1992): 27–28; Ann Gibbons, "Minority Programs That Get High Marks," *Science* 258 (Nov. 13, 1992): 1190–99; Constance Holden, "Are Asian-Americans 'Underrepresented'?" *Science* 262 (Nov. 12, 1993): 1096; idem, "Minorities at the Starting Gate," *Science* 271 (Mar. 29, 1996): 1919; John Krukowski, "Does Engineering Have a 'Glass Ceiling'?" *Pollution Engineering* 24 (Nov. 15, 1992): 9–10; Peggy Layne, "The Glass Ceiling: Is It Really There?" *SWE: Magazine of the Society of Women Engineers* (Mar.–Apr. 1994): 25–27; Shirley M. Malcolm, "Science and Diversity: A Compelling National Interest," *Science* 271 (Mar. 29, 1996): 1817–19; Sharon Bertsch McGrayne, *Nobel Prize Women in Science: Their Lives, Struggles, and Momentous Discoveries* (New York:

Birch Lane Press, 1993); Calvin Sims, "Last Hired, First Fired? Minorities Retreat in Defense," *Science* 262 (Nov. 12, 1993): 1125–26; Society of Women Engineers, *A National Survey of Women and Men Engineers: A Study of the Members of 22 Engineering Societies* (New York: Society of Women Engineers, 1993); Patricia E. White, *Women and Minorities in Science and Engineering: An Update* (Washington, D.C.: National Science Foundation, 1992).

4. For an overview of diversity in planning, see Nancy Benziger Brown, "Get with It," *Planning* (Sept. 1997): 13; Ruth Knack, "Vive La Difference," *Planning* (Sept. 1997): 10; Sylvia Lewis, "Breaking Through the Glass Ceiling," *Planning* (July 1991): 7–13; *Women in Planning: A Report on Their Status in Public Planning Agencies,* PAS Report 273 (1971); Jack Wong, "Let's *Not* Stop Meeting Like This," *Planning* (Sept. 1997): 12.

5. For an overview of diversity in landscape architecture, see *1995 African American Landscape Symposium Conference Proceedings: Contemporary Contributions to American Spaces, Places and Icons. Hosted by North Carolina A & T State University, Landscape Architecture Program, College of Agriculture, Greensboro, North Carolina,* symposium program, Apr. 6–7, 1995; Charlene Browne, "The Status of Women in Landscape Architecture: Results from a National Survey of Women in American Society of Landscape Architects," *Women in Landscape Architecture, Open Committee of the Women in Landscape Architecture Newsletter* 1 (Winter–Spring 1993): 11–46; idem, "The Status of Women in Landscape Architecture: Findings, Perspectives, and Strategies for the Future," *Landscape Journal* 13, no. 2 (Fall 1994): 102–5; Joan Iverson Nassauer and Karen Arnold, *The National Survey of Career Patterns among Women in Landscape Architecture* (Washington, D.C.: American Society of Landscape Architects, 1983); Robert B. Riley, "Gender, Landscape, Culture: Sorting Out Some Questions," *Landscape Journal* 13, no. 12 (Fall 1994): 153–63.

6. For an overview of diversity in law, consult: "Did You Know . . . ," *Perspectives, A Newsletter for and about Women Lawyers* 1, no. 1 (Fall 1991): 7; Goals '95 Report: Market Research Department of the American Bar Association; Marena L. McPherson, "Sexual Harassment after Anita Hill: Resources and Action Plans for What We Can Do," *Perspectives, A Newsletter for and about Women Lawyers* 1, no. 2 (Spring 1992): 1, 6–9; Suellyn Scarnecchia, "Gender and Race Bias Against Lawyers: A Classroom Response," *Journal of Law Reform* 23, no. 2 (Winter 1990): 319–51. See also <http://www.abanet.org>, accessed Nov. 4, 2000; a check on two occasions revealed ninety-eight ABA publications on diversity.

7. For an overview of diversity in medicine, see M. Heins, "Update: Women in Medicine," *Journal of the American Medical Women's Association* (1985): 4043–50; Marianne Jacobbi, "'Just Call Me Doctor,'" *Good Housekeeping,* Aug. 1992, 64, 66, 68; "Stanford Responds to Sexism Charges," *Science* 255 (Mar. 6, 1992): 1208; *Women in Medicine in America: In the Mainstream* (Chicago, Ill.: American Medical Association, 1991).

For a more detailed comparison of the architectural, legal, and medical professions, see Robert Gutman, "Professions and Their Discontents: The Psychodynamics of Architectural Practice," *Practices 5/6* (1997): 15–23. Some of the key differences among the three fields that Gutman points out: First, open office plans are typical in architects' offices but very rare in legal or medical offices; even first-year associates in law firms have their private offices. Second, architects perform a broad range of tasks ordered according to a principle of hierarchy, whereas this is highly unusual among law and medicine. Architects often take orders from people with equivalent training and credentials; this is rarely so in the other profession. In other professions, less qualified personnel, such as paralegals and legal secretaries in law firms, or nurses, nurse practitioners and paramedics in medical practice, are likely to perform the more tedious tasks. Third, architectural schools prepare students as if each one of them will become a designer, while law and medical schools encourage specialties. Fourth, architecture has an unusually high turnover rate compared to those in other professions. Fifth, a large percentage of the work for which architects are legally responsible is carried out by people to whom they have contractual ties, but no organizational or administrative control. Not so in law and medicine. Finally, architects must move between two worlds: the office and the construction sites. No similar dichotomy is found among lawyers and doctors.

8. See, for example, Kathryn H. Anthony, *Design Juries on Trial: The Renaissance of the Design Studio* (New York: Van Nostrand Reinhold, 1991; Ernest L. Boyer and Lee D. Mitgang, *Building Community: A New Future for Architecture Education and Practice* (Princeton, N.J.: Carnegie Foundation for the Advancement of Teaching, 1996); Dana Cuff, *Architecture: The Story of Practice* (Cambridge, Mass.: MIT Press, 1991); Robert Gutman, *Architectural Practice: A Critical View* (New York: Princeton Architectural Press, 1988).

9. For information about the American Institute for Managing Diversity, consult <http://www.aimd.org>, accessed Nov. 1, 2000. For information about the Women's Bureau at the U.S. Dept. of Labor, see "Working Trends: Counting on the Nation's Women," *Issues Quarterly* 1, no. 4 (1996): 14. More information about the Equal Pay Act of 1963, which prohibits employers from discriminating on the basis of sex or race, is available from the National Committee on Pay Equity, Washington, D.C. See also U.S. Dept. of Labor, Women's Bureau, "Twenty Facts on Women Workers" (1984), cited in *Chicago Women in Architecture Newsletter* (Oct. 1986): 2.

10. See "Money Exchange: Lending More than a Helping Hand: Women Business Owners Access Capital," *Issues Quarterly* 1, no. 4 (1996): 19. Organizations aimed at helping women in the workplace include the American Association for Affirmative Action, based in Alexandria, Virginia; Business and Professional Women's Foundation, Washington, D.C.; Catalyst, New York City; Commission on Family and Medical Leave at the U.S. Department of Labor's Women's Bureau, Washington, D.C.; Conference Board's Work Family Council, New York City; National Association of Women Business Owners, Washington, D.C.; National Committee on Pay Equity, Washington, D.C.; National Education Center for Women in Business, Greensburg, Pennsylvania; Women's Legal Defense Fund, Washington, D.C.; Work/Family Directions, Boston; Online Women's Business Center, run by the U.S. Small Business Administration's Office of Women's Business Ownership, Washington, D.C., <http://www.onlinewbc.org>, accessed Nov. 27, 2000.

11. Amy Saltzman, "Life after the Lawsuit," *US News and World Report*, Aug. 19, 1996, 57–61.

12. Marilyn Loden, *Implementing Diversity* (Chicago: Irwin Professional Publishing, 1996), 74.

13. Anthony, *Design Juries on Trial*, 132–34.

14. See Sherry Ahrentzen and Kathryn H. Anthony, "Sex, Stars, and Studios: A Look at Gendered Educational Practices in Architecture," *Journal of Architectural Education* 47, no. 1 (Sept. 1993): 11–29. Tables 12–14 are excerpted from this article.

15. See Kathryn H. Anthony and Brad Grant, eds., *Gender and Multi-culturalism in Architectural Education*, subtheme issue of the *Journal of Architectural Education* 47, no. 1 (Sept. 1993).

16. See Thomas A. Dutton, ed., *Voices in Architectural Education: Cultural Politics and Pedagogy* (New York: Bergin and Garvey, 1991).

17. See, for example, R. Martin, "Sexist Designs: Women Students View Architecture School," *CRIT* (1983): 16–17; E. K. Morris, "Vignettes in Architectural Education: A Letter from the Ivory Tower," *Making Room: Women and Architecture* (Special Issue) *Heresies* 11, no. 3 (1981): 80–81; N. Aisenberg and M. Harrington, *Women of Academe: Outsiders in the Sacred Grove* (Amherst, Mass.: University of Massachusetts Press, 1988); M. J. Crosbie, "Howard University School of Architecture," *Architecture* 80, no. 4 (Apr. 1991): 52–53; Regina Davis, "Minority Environmental Design Program," *1990 Annual Report* (Berkeley, Calif.: College of Environmental Design, University of California, Feb. 1991); Linda Groat and Sherry Ahrentzen, *Status of Faculty Women in Architecture Schools: Survey Results and Recommendations*, Developed and Completed by the ACSA Task Force on the Status of Women in Architecture Schools (Washington, D.C.: Association of Collegiate Schools of Architecture Press, 1990); A. Simeone, *Academic Women: Working towards Equality* (South Hadley, Mass.: Bergin and Garvey, 1987); P. Thomas, "The Little (White, Male) Schoolhouse: Why Planning School Enrollments Aren't Very Well-Rounded–and What's Being Done About It," *Planning* 57, no. 7 (July 1991): 20–23.

18. Linda Groat and Sherry Ahrentzen, "Reconceptualizing Architectural Education for a More Diverse Future: Perceptions and Visions of Architectural Students," *Journal of Architectural Education* 49, no. 3 (Feb. 1996): 166–83.

19. Harry G. Robinson III, "We've Been Paid For . . . ," in *African American Architects in Current Practice*, ed. Jack Travis (New York: Princeton Architectural Press, 1991), 10–11.

20. Sherry Ahrentzen, "A 'Women and Environments' Course in an Architecture School," *Women and Environments* 7, no. 1 (Winter 1985): 13. Related courses are described in Sherry Ahrentzen and Janetta McCoy, eds., *"Doing Diversity": A Compendium of Architectural Courses Addressing Diversity Issues in Architecture* (Washington, D.C.: Association of Collegiate Schools of Architecture, 1996).

21. Along these lines, in an article in the *Journal of Architectural Education*, Sheila Klos, an architectural librarian at the University of Oregon, has made a passionate plea to the faculty. She argues that "students' need for instruction in successful information-seeking behaviors (what librarians call information literacy) has increased exponentially–a direct result of the ease of access to the Internet from campus and architectural offices and the wealth of information now available through the Internet. . . . The nature of library research is changing at a rapid pace, and architectural faculty cannot be expected to keep up with every aspect of that change. Rather, they should be expected to refer their students to the professional most involved in coping with the information explosion we are experiencing and therefore the professional best qualified to instruct students in bibliographic tools and research methods: the architec-

ture librarian." See Sheila Klos, "Information Literacy for the Next Generation," *Journal of Architectural Education* 49, no. 3 (Feb. 1996): 204–6; quote from 206.

22. Unless noted otherwise, this and the next three paragraphs are based on the work by Janice R. Long, "Issues Surrounding Discrimination and Harassment in Workplace Explored," *Chemical Engineering and News* 69 (May 6, 1991): 27–29. Speaking at a symposium for chemical engineers, four Georgia attorneys offered practical advice about ways employers can ensure that their workplaces are not discriminatory.

23. Long, "Issues Surrounding Discrimination and Harassment in Workplace Explored," 29.

24. See R. Roosevelt Thomas Jr., *Beyond Race and Gender: Unleashing the Power of Your Total Work Force by Managing Diversity* (New York: AMACOM, a division of American Management Association, 1991), 133–43.

25. "Code of Ethics and Professional Conduct Advisory Opinion No. 4: Discrimination Against Employees Based on Gender" (Washington, D.C.: American Institute of Architects), published in *National Judicial Council* (Jan. 1992).

26. Ibid.

27. See "Diversity Resources," unpublished document available from the American Institute of Architects National Diversity Committee.

28. Loden, *Implementing Diversity*, 118.

29. Programs and announcements sent to author by Jean Barber, former director, Diversity Programs, American Institute of Architects.

30. See *Lawyers and Balanced Lives: A Guide to Drafting and Implementing Workplace Policies for Lawyers* (Chicago: American Bar Association, 1990).

31. "Family and Gender-Based Policies," *AIA Women in Architecture Newsletter* (Spring 1992): 6.

32. See American Council on Education/National Network for Women Leaders in Higher Education brochure and the Web site at <http://www.acenet.edu/programs/owhe/home.cfn>, accessed Nov. 4, 2000.

33. Michael A. Tomlan, "Who Will Care in the 1990s?" *Preservation Forum* 3, no. 4 (Winter 1990): 21.

34. Unless noted otherwise, this and the next four paragraphs are based on Karen Easter, "Cultural Diversity in Georgia: For the People or By the People?" *Cultural Resources Management (CRM)* 15, no. 7 (1992): 23–24; quote from 24.

35. See Boyer and Mitgang, *Building Community*.

36. See Map Collective of Boston Gay and Lesbian Architects and Designers and The Boston Area Lesbian and Gay History Project, "Location: A Historical Map of Lesbian and Gay Boston" (Boston, Mass.: 1995).

Index

Harlem Hospital, 87
Harold Washington Library, 101
Harvard University, 40, 48 72; admission of women to, 48; graduate school of design at, 9; graduate school of landscape architecture at, 48; Widener Library, 84
Hastings, L. Jane, 54, 98
Hayden, Dolores, 66
Hayden, Sophia, 48, 137
Hearst, George, 38
Hearst, Phoebe Apperson, 38, 49
Hearst, William Randolph, 38, 49
Hearst Castle, 49
Hearst Hall, 38, 39
Hearst Mining Building, 39
Heathrow Airport Terminal 4, 55
Helland, Janice, 58–59
Hellenic Cultural Center, 75
Henderson, Cornelius, 85
Hermit's Rest, 49
heterosexism, 5
Hicks, Margaret, 48
hierarchy, 22; of arts, 57–58
Higher Art and Technical Studios (Moscow), 52
high house, 82
Highway Beautification Act of 1965, 44
Hill, Anita, 142, 182
Hill, Octavia, 37
Hispanic, 11, 134
historic preservation, 21; of racial and ethnic districts, 75
HIV-positive status, 74, 156
Ho, Mui, 3
Hoekstra, Tracey Jo, 9
Holocaust, 16, 77
homelessness, 104
homogenism, 148
homophobia, 5, 70, 93
Hopi House, 49
Hotel Del Coronado, 78
Howard University, 82, 87, 89, 101, 190; fine arts complex at, 83
Howe, Lois, 50
Hudson, Karen, 84
husband-wife architectural partnerships, 56–65
Huxtable, Ada Louise, 65

Illinois Institute of Technology, 205
immigrants: Chinese, 78; Cuban, 14; Mexican, 14; Puerto Rican, 14
Institute of American Indian Art, 80

Institute of Fine Arts (New York University), 84
interior design, 21, 164
Internal Revenue Service, 194
internal trainer pairs, 33
International Committee Against Racism, 185
International Archive of Women in Architecture (IAWA), 97, 108, 112
International Frankfurt Fair of 1926, 59
International Lesbian and Gay Design Conference, 110
International Union of Architects, 103
International Union of Women Architects and Town Planners, 96
Intern Development Program (IDP), 119–21; Coordinating Committee, 119; guidelines of, 119; objectives of, 119; periods of training, 120
internet, 89, 112, 187, 194
interns: exploitation of, 197, 121–22; salaries for, 137
internship, 10, 118–25, 197; family-friendly environment lacking in, 123; glass-ceiling barriers in, 124; men's perceptions of, 124; minorities' experiences of, 124–25; mirror-imaging in, 201; women's experiences of, 124–25
interviews, 8, 114–18; exit, 196; experiences of, 116–18; gender in, 115–16; inappropriate questions, 116–17
intolerance, costs of, 30
isolation, 133
Israel, Frank, 73, 106
Ivy League schools, 48

Jackson, Jesse, 112
Jackson Square, 45
Jacobs, Jane, 44, 66
Jacobsen, Robin, 110
Jamaican urban house, 82
Jamestown Exhibition, 83
Janis, Kay, 108
Japan Architectural Association, 55
Japanese-Americans, in relocation camps, 15
Jerde Partnership, Inc., 86
Jim Crow laws, 15
job satisfaction, 10; for architects, 174; as personal challenge, 174; regarding salary compensation, 174; of white men and men of color, 174, 175; of white women and women of color, 174, 175

KATHRYN H. ANTHONY is a professor in the School of Architecture and an adjunct faculty member in the Department of Landscape Architecture and the Women's Studies Program at the University of Illinois at Urbana-Champaign. She is the author of *Design Juries on Trial: The Renaissance of the Design Studio* and numerous articles in scholarly, professional, and popular journals. She is the recipient of the 1992 Creative Achievement Award from the Association of Collegiate Schools of Architecture.

Typeset in 9/15 Berthold Walbaum

with Helvetica Neue display

Designed by Copenhaver Cumpston

Composed by Jim Proefrock

at the University of Illinois Press

Manufactured by Thomson-Shore, Inc.

UNIVERSITY OF ILLINOIS PRESS

1325 South Oak Street   Champaign, IL 61820-6903

www.press.uillinois.edu